The Modern Elegiac Temper

The

Modern

Elegiac

Temper

JOHN B. VICKERY

LOUISIANA STATE UNIVERSITY PRESS ⚜ BATON ROUGE

Published by Louisiana State University Press
Copyright © 2006 by Louisiana State University Press
All rights reserved
Manufactured in the United States of America
First Printing

Designer: Michelle A. Garrod
Typeface: Baskerville
Typesetter: The Composing Room of Michigan, Inc.
Printer and binder: Edwards Brothers, Inc.

Library of Congress Cataloging-in-Publication Data
Vickery, John B.
   The modern elegiac temper / John B. Vickery.
      p. cm.
   Includes bibliographical references and index.
   ISBN 0-8071-3142-3 (alk. paper)
   1. Elegiac poetry, English—History and criticism.   2. Elegiac poetry, American—
History and criticism.   3. English poetry—20th century—History and criticism.
4. American poetry—20th century—History and criticism.   I. Title.
PR509.E4V53 2006
821′.0409091—dc22

                                     2005026793

Pages 249–251 constitute a continuation of the copyright page.

Contents

Preface

In what follows I explore a number of issues broadly connected with the elegy and the elegiac temper in modern British and American literature. My basic approach is through a relatively close examination of a number of poems by a wide range of authors, from Siegfried Sassoon to Geoffrey Hill. The representative nature of these works underscores the fact that they are all simply *examples* of prevailing attitudes. On this point, I agree with G. B. Conte when in his *Genres and Readers* he remarks that "For those of us who are looking for texts and want to read them and distinguish between them, it is the flesh that makes the difference. . . ." Hopefully, then, the individual texts that I examine adequately flesh out the general argument being advanced, thereby making unnecessary any kind of concluding statement.

My interpretations endeavor to keep the issue of examples in the foreground by subjecting them to close scrutiny and treating them not in the currently fashionable manner as inherently self-contradictory but as basically saying what they mean even when that, to mix a metaphor, is bifocal. That is, if forced to, I side with Lewis Carroll rather than Derrida. As a result, my individual readings are content to stay quite close to what the texts themselves assert. In a sense, my intent is loosely philosophical rather than rhetorical. It concentrates more on the authors' themes than on their techniques for presenting their views. At the same time, my assertions about individual authors should be taken as applying only to the texts being discussed. In doing so, I take heart from Wallace Stevens's remark that "the final authority is the poem itself." At no point is it my intent to formulate, much less quarrel with, generalizations of the order of critics assessing individual canons, such as Edward Mendelson on Auden, Hugh Kenner on Pound, or Harold Bloom on Stevens.

In choosing texts for consideration, I have been guided, again, by a series of factors less theoretical and ideological than practical. Thus, I have sought to provide a sufficiently broad spectrum of works so that some proximate critical and historical judgments or inferences may emerge at least inferentially and provisionally. This spectrum is also designed to reveal the extremely wide variety of actual attitudes making up the elegiac temper in much of modern literature. To that end, it endeavors to set out some introductory and perhaps familiar taxonomic delineations that may prove helpful in charting the full scope of the modern elegy. This has often entailed attending to writers infrequently a part of current discussions, such as Edith Sitwell and George Barker. As justification, I can only say that my concern is with understanding a historical phenomenon rather than contributing to the shaping or endorsing of literary fashion.

A further refinement in choices of individual texts consists in the exploration of those patently identified by their authors as elegiac in intent, whether innovative, conventional, ironic, or satiric. In effect, I am concerned to assess the nature of the modern elegy by considering what its creators take and make it to be. Perforce this has required an inclination to concentrate on works authorially identified as elegies per se.

Hopefully, such an approach will enable the reader to sense the ways in which today the elegy as a genre is subsumed by the elegiac temper pervasive in modern literature. As I see it, the modern elegy has enormously diversified in form, theme, and attitude compared to its predecessors. This diversification leads to at least two things. First, the multiplying of traits to be associated with a genre that consequently, like many others today, appears to be veering toward fragmentation if not actual dissolution. And second, the developing of a culturally generic attitude or temper marked by the effects of consciousness of loss, of regret for the fact and infinitude of losses suffered, and of the generation of a reflective spirit largely devoid of final or, often, even satisfactory answers.

And finally, the writers selected have been chosen with an eye to supplementing rather than repeating choices made by other critics of the modern elegy. The reason for this is my conviction that in this way the scholarly community is most likely to inch toward a full history of the modern elegy.

Thus, I deliberately slight Yeats in deference to his extended treatment by Jahan Ramazani and Peter Sacks. I do, it is true, touch on some of the poets—principally Stevens, Auden, and Heaney—dealt with by Ramazani in his *Poetry of Mourning*, but not with the same concern. In a sense, his concentration is largely author-driven while mine is text-centered. My attending to but a few, mostly non-war-oriented poems by Sassoon and Owen also silently acknowledges the many critics who have mined the canons of these and related World War I poets. Similarly, I remain largely silent on the feminist, gender, and sexual preoccupations of Melissa Zeiger's *Beyond Consolation*. A similar silence operates in connection with Celeste Schenk's *Mourning and Panegyric*, though dictated rather by our different foci. Her central concern is with the pastoral elegy and its premodern examples, while mine is restricted to works from World War I to the present. The same is true of Eric Smith, whose concentration on six major pre-twentieth-century British elegies in *By Mourning Tongues* served to keep me aware of the continuities inherent in the tradition. In a similar fashion, scholars such as O. B. Hardison Jr., Ruth Wallerstein, Dennis Kay, G. W. Pigman III, Ellen Lambert, and others who carefully delineate the elegiac traits of earlier periods underscored the need for caution in claiming undue uniqueness for the modern era. I have also benefited from David Shaw's densely argued and historically informed *Elegy and Paradox*, perhaps significantly more than my notes may reveal. Unfortunately, R. Clifton Spargo's *The Ethics of Mourning* appeared after my manuscript was completed. Consequently, I was unable to draw on his insights about the elegies of Randall Jarrell and Sylvia Plath.

Nor do I pretend to engage in theoretical questions (whether philosophical, psychological, or critical) bearing on the notion of genre in general and the elegy in particular. Only when the details of the modern elegy have been carefully explored is it critically and logically appropriate, it seems to me, to consider what sort of theory is likely best to underwrite it in relation to other genres. All of these factors when taken together provide, I hope, a perspective both empirical and interrogative. First, the empirical stance demonstrates, admittedly only by selective examples, the enormous diversity of elegiac responses to be found in modern literature. Further, the interrogative note probes, and implicitly questions, the implications for the genre of such a diversity. And finally, such an approach underlines the likelihood that the elegiac temper itself constitutes perhaps the major trait of twentieth-century culture, extending as it does measurably beyond the boundaries of elegiac modernism.

The Modern Elegiac Temper

Introduction
The Elegiac Matrix

As I see it, the modern elegy has enormously diversified in form, theme, and attitude compared to its predecessors. Whereas Renaissance, Romantic, and Victorian elegists hewed pretty sedulously to death as their prime subject, one finds a distinct tendency in the modern period to broaden the focus to include loss of all kinds as the basic stimulus and concern.

Loss of life, of course, continues to play a central role in the elegiac imagination. But to it have been added losses in cultures and civilizations (as with T. S. Eliot and Ezra Pound); dissolutions of the family and families (as with James Joyce, F. Scott Fitzgerald, and William Faulkner); changes and concomitant losses in personal relations such as romantic love and marriage (as with Edna St. Vincent Millay, Edith Sitwell, Henry James, John Updike, and Ernest Hemingway); intellectual excisions and reconfigurations of philosophical notions such as time (as with Virginia Woolf), and self (as with John Berryman, George Barker, Malcolm Lowry, and Joan Didion); and efforts to assess the contemporary nature and value of war (from Stephen Crane and the World War I poets to Hemingway and Mailer). Each of these has occasioned profound elegiac attitudes ranging from regret, sorrow, confusion, and alienation to outright despair. All of these attitudes stem largely from an increasingly perceived need for a form of authority that does not invoke the eternal as solace and support in living life and enduring losses of which mortality is only one. As a result, even texts focusing on the conventional elegiac triad of lamentation-confrontation-consolation reveal a hesitancy of attitude, a probing of intellectual boundaries, and an exploration of themes and conclusions hitherto considered only marginally related to the elegy.

This diversification of emotions and attitudes follows from the modern elegy's propensity to incorporate or absorb dimensions from other related poetic forms and traditions such as the lament, the meditation, the philosophical reflection, the complaint, the ode, the epitaph, as well as the dirge, threnody, obsequy, idyll, eulogy, planh, and eclogue, and traditions like that of the ruins and the *ubi sunt*. And out of this absorptive activity there has developed a culturally generic attitude or temper marked by the effects of consciousness of loss, of regret for the fact and infinitude of losses suffered, and of the generation of a reflective spirit largely devoid of final or, often, even satisfactory answers.

Both of these—the diversifying of elegiac traits and the emergence of a distinct elegiac temper—underline the likelihood that the elegiac temper itself constitutes perhaps the major trait of twentieth-century culture, extending as it does measurably beyond the boundaries of elegiac modernism. My thesis about this temper, put most succinctly, is that the twentieth century expands the elegy as a result of the decline in a rhetoric that provided a series of clearly defined subkinds of poetry together with the occurrence of large-scale historical events that created a distinctive cultural attitude affecting the modern Western world. Essentially, it consisted of a diminution of large-scale and public lamentation, a sobering recognition of the irreversibility of such losses, a sometimes frenzied effort to explore any and all avenues to nullify the particular loss suffered, and a desperate and sustained search for grounds on which to find solace and explanatory answers for the inevitability of mankind's exposure to so many and so diverse losses.

Seminal events of the modern period—most notably World War I, the Great Depression of the 1930s, and the advent of the Holocaust—generated responses that broadened and diffused the function of the elegy. As a result, greater preeminence was given not only to the varieties of confrontation with death but with all the forms of personal, intellectual, and cultural loss suffered by mankind. In effect, the concept of death was extended from living creatures to include institutions, cultures, forms of authority, and ways of thinking. The result was the development of a pervasive elegiac temper in the age. Consequently, its literature reveals a steady accrual of objects of loss, lamentation, reflective regret, and disquieted foreboding. From such an accrual the movement toward an elegiac temper reflects a growing awareness that loss, ruptures in expectancies and responses, and existential discontinuities may be engendered not only by individual persons but by families, romantic relationships, cultures, and historical ages, as well as by philosophical *topoi* such as time, self, war, and spiritual consolation.

From the poets of World War I such as Siegfried Sassoon and Wilfred Owen through the high modernism of Eliot and Pound to historically postmodern chroniclers—such as Geoffrey Hill and Thom Gunn—of a pervasive stoicism in the face of their sense that loss lies all around them, one can discern a measure of common ground. All in their distinctive ways—anger, anxiety or apprehension, irony, regret, doubt, and helplessness—share in shaping an elegiac temper with which to capture the precariousness of the lives they were living in a world whose signature testified increasingly to loss as the basic human condition.

Distinguishing traits of the elegiac temper are multiple. Yet it is possible to single out several major ones—anger, anxiety, and doubt are preeminent—that came over the course of the twentieth century to shape its historical character. World War I poets injected the traditional elegiac lament with anger and anguish, which shaped it into active fury. Similarly, the Great Depression caused entire societies to experience an anxiety and apprehension that grew into a pervasive and deep-seated fear that haunted their every waking moment. The acute familial and communal strains suffered led to the rupture, severing, or radical limiting of trust of, confidence in, and the very durability of any form of authority capable of resolving, or consoling them for, the experience of elegiac loss.

The subsequent rise of a series of polar political ideologies—principally fascism and communism—and their intensely dogmatic attitudes led to a concomitant weakening of past ground bases of societal authority. Whether moral, religious, or broadly philosophical, these bases were called in question by most people seeking grounds for consolation and hope in the face of the losses confronting them. Thus, the elegy incorporated a basic skepticism about personal, social, and historical values and futures.

As a response to such skepticism, the classical modernists, principally Eliot and Pound in particular but also David Jones and Charles Olson, instituted a comparative search of past cultures coupled with an extended critique of a dubious present. This venture was part of a larger, and perhaps simpler, tendency of the elegiac temper to look backward to a national past of preferred security and achievement and in doing so formed an implicit political dimension of the elegiac temper. Such looking back was carried out from diverse but related vantage points, as Sherwood Anderson, William Faulkner, Allen Tate, and Robert Lowell severally demonstrate. Their backward glances occasioned both irony and nostalgia and ran the gamut from apprehensive concerns over threats (real or imagined) to regional homes (as with Sherwood Anderson and William Faulkner) to a growing awareness of exile in all its varieties (as with T. S. Eliot, Ezra Pound, James Joyce, Ernest Hemingway, F. Scott Fitzgerald, and James Baldwin).

The shift in societal focus from humanistic to scientific methodologies insidiously weakened in the minds of themselves as well as the culture as a whole the status and authority of poets and novelists. This shift produced in them what amounted to a kind of psychological exile brought on by the haunting prospect of irrelevance to the world at large. With it, there developed a relatively sustained effort to analyze and interrogate the nature and contemporary role, if any, of the poet. This interrogative activity clearly emerges in poets as divergent as Charles Olson, W. H. Auden, Edith Sitwell, and George Barker. As a counter to their anticipated loss of a social role—one that had been steadily growing since Alexander Pope's time—poets such as Dylan Thomas, Robert Duncan, and John Berryman pursued even more sedulously than in past ages the inner realm of mind, soul, and personal emotions the threats to which they could elegize. Such a concentrated exploration of the self almost inevitably led to a sustained interrogation of the nature, boundaries, and rationale of their impulse to lament, mourn, confront, and resolve the losses they faced with increasing frequency and intensity. This interrogation produced a range of speculations and answers, almost all of which recognized the precariousness and the changing nature of the genre and the uncertainties of its practitioners.

Hence, this broad social and cultural loss came to invest the modern elegy with a deep-seated ironic and even satiric cast as revealed by, among other things, a resurgence of elegies on animals by poets as dissimilar as Yvor Winters, Richard Wilbur, Louis MacNeice, Galway Kinnell, Richard Eberhart, and J. V. Cunningham. The society's apparent growing propensity to judge quickly, superficially, and on largely irrational grounds begot, ironically enough, a counter-attitude consisting of a deep-seated hesitation in making final judgments on events, persons, and ideas. As a result, the panegyrical lamentation, long a staple of the traditional elegy, diminished to a more intimate, personal, and judicious assessment of the loss being recorded, such as can be found in James Wright or Edwin Muir.

For the artist as well as his audience, both attitudes—the easy willingness and the cautious reluctance to judge and assess—conspired to weaken the elegist's powers of resolution or consolation while intensifying his or her concern with confronting the challenge inherent in such losses. Consolation in the eternal and life after death advocated by traditional Christianity or in a rationally inspired absolutistic ethic or in a socially sanctioned *civitas* no longer seemed readily possible or even viable either to artist or audience, though notable exceptions such as Father Thomas Merton, the later W. H. Auden and Edith Sitwell, and Yvor Winters continued to so ground their elegiac perspectives. The overall result was the development of an elegiac indecisiveness concerning satisfactory justifications of loss coupled with an almost frenzied interrogation of self and world for solace. Losses of friends and relatives produced in poets like Dylan Thomas, Theodore Roethke, Jon Silkin, and Patrick Kavanagh realistic recollections and

fond memories rather than formal panegyrics. Also, horror and recoil at the bru-
tal physical and moral indignities revealed in the death camps of Belsen and
Buchenwald and in the witnessing of the slow and minute disintegrative power
of cancer and AIDS led elegiac poets to chronicle these sedulously. Similarly, a
covert nostalgia for cultural losses informed the works of many modernists, from
Ezra Pound to William Faulkner, which endeavored to analyze and monitor
scrupulously the details, causes, and consequences of those losses.

Two later twentieth-century historical events gave rise to additional facets of
the modern elegiac temper. Both the Holocaust and the creation of the atomic
bomb dramatically exposed the idealizing tendencies generated on behalf of the
authority of science as well as of the individual self. Both instilled in the elegiac
temper a sense of apocalypse not only as mythological but also as historical and
immediate. Apocalyptic disaster, it was felt by many, could happen both actually
as well as hypothetically, in the existential present as well as in some religiously
ordained remote future. Coupled with this was the inclusion of cataclysmic sur-
prise as yet another factor brought on by events as divergent as assassination for
political purposes and quite unexpected political acts, such as the fall of the Berlin
Wall and the dissolution of the USSR. Such events enveloped the age in a
quandary based on their unpredictability and inexplicability. Earlier anxieties
and apprehensions were intensified into a protracted fear of the imminence of
the end of the world as we have known it.

And with this fear there came for the elegiac temper the additional quality of
intrinsic doubt as to whether there would be time to or point in constructing ele-
gies on behalf of anything or anyone. Deepening this insecurity yet further was
the perceived worldwide tendency to fragment into widely different and com-
peting shared-interest groups. At root, what this spelled out for the elegist was the
likely impossibility of meaningful communication itself and hence of the con-
tinued existence of his craft, a note caught most economically and powerfully in
W. S. Merwin's one line "Elegy."

Works of the elegiac temper continue, of course, to register the impact of the
death of individuals. But in the main, their attention is focused less on the oc-
currence of such a loss and more on its inevitability. The penumbral shadow of
mortality that hangs over or surrounds the conventional elegy now moves more
into the limelight of the poetic consciousness. Such a shift begets impulses vary-
ing from shocked recoil, as in, say, Dylan Thomas; a sense of personal victim-
ization as with Jon Silkin; an overarching feeling of pathos for man's fate such as
can be found in Seamus Heaney, to a sober conviction of the sort inherent in

William Carlos Williams on D. H Lawrence or Wallace Stevens on George Santayana that death is less an implacable adversary and more an inevitable part of life.

Works dealing with losses other than those of human life and marked by the elegiac temper differ from earlier elegies in several ways. For one thing, they tend to minimize or constrain the amount of attention devoted to mourning and lamentation per se. Their expressions of grief are inclined to be brief and intense, anecdotal vignettes rather than sorrowful and panegyrical assessments of entire lives and careers. Where they focus on losses other than that resulting from death, they are oblique, not direct, notations of the loss suffered and often invested with irony calculated to repress or suppress the older effort to gauge and proclaim explicitly the impact of the loss on its audience.

Now, the confrontation with the fact and nature of the loss suffered, which forms a critical stage in the older elegiac form, is extended, deepened to a greater and more intimately individualized level of the psyche. It becomes radically diversified in the character, immediacy, and growing recognition of the likely hopelessness of the effort to face all of the manifestations entailed by any effort to confront the loss sustained. The personal and psychological loss felt by the poet and, he hopes, his audience is probed persistently for its broader ramifications—national, social, cultural, historical, and philosophical. This effort is dedicated to developing a broader or longer context within which to set the loss he is celebrating. The elegy's past focus on the individual's death centered either on the poet's claim that his grief is reflected in the widespread mourning of nature itself (as in the pastoral elegy) or in the poet's formal, almost ritualistic, effort to review and celebrate the achievements and life of the one being mourned (as in the funereal elegy). Now it increasingly concentrates on recalling detailed specifics of the loss, as, say, in Donald Hall's recalling of his wife's protracted struggle with cancer. The same is true at a macro-cultural level of T. S. Eliot's, Ezra Pound's and Charles Olson's scrupulous meditating on the welter of precise losses wrought by a comparative perspective taken on a variety of cultures and historical eras.

As the kinds of loss celebrated in works of an elegiac temper grow to include not only death but loss of love, family, ways of life, cultures, and even spiritual and philosophical answers to existence, the confrontation comes increasingly to be haunted by the unnerving prospect that the individual's encountering the particular loss is doomed never to produce a satisfactory explanation for its occurrence. Out of this emerges an anxiety and apprehension about the entirety of human life that was felt if not first then certainly most oppressively by the stifling effects of the Great Depression on the bulk of the population. The prevailing response to such uncertainty is the settling into a basic stoicism ranging from grim to philosophical acceptance. Basically, it accepts what it sees as unchangeable in life and couples it with a stubborn determination to capture and celebrate human existence and its institutions as they are perceived actually to be.

I

The Personal Elegy

1

Friends and Relatives

The friend—whether simply an acquaintance or a relative and whether identi-fied by name, blood relationship, or left anonymous—occupies a central position in the history of the elegy. It is at once the focal point for the poet's acknowledg-ment of a self other than his own whose loss is a surrogate and anticipation of his own mortality. Classical, Renaissance, and Romantic poets have all celebrated in richly complex and sustained ways the implications of the death of a friend, acquaintance, or family member. Modern poets have, naturally enough, contin-ued this practice but with the difference that their focus is more centered on elab-orating variants of personal loss rather than on the fact of death itself. This shift follows from or is occasioned by the transition from the elegiac genre to the ele-giac mode and the transition from the "tame" death of earlier times to the more recent "invisible" death.[1]

At the risk of appearing overly precise or paradigmatic, one can single out several facets of the specific nature of the loss of friends celebrated elegiacally by modern poets. Ones that I will deal with in this chapter include what I call con-cealed, personal, and impersonal forms of loss. Basically, these move from inti-mate recollections and expressions of loss to philosophical puzzling and interro-gating of the mystery and significance of death.

Concealed Losses

The first of these is the concealed loss, in which the writer, for intimately personal or socially constrained reasons, announces his response to the loss at the same time as he suppresses or represses the grounds for his emotions. A case in point is Siegfried Sassoon's "Elegy" dedicated to Robert Ross, who died suddenly and unexpectedly of heart failure just before leaving England for a trip to Australia.[2] The title as well as the poem itself clearly indicates that the poem is one of mourn-ing, yet it is equally clear that the poem lacks much of the consolatory note so fre-quently found in earlier instances of the genre.[3]

Nevertheless, it does have other traits drawn from the elegiac tradition, such as the reliance on a series of topical polarities.[4] This suggests that Sassoon is trying simultaneously both to use and to depart from his predecessors. Thus, he begins with multiple abbreviated dichotomies (wit versus grief, past versus present, laughter versus death, transience versus permanence, charm versus love, day versus night, and honor versus shame), all of which suggest the initial disruption occasioned by the sudden loss of a dear friend.[5] Quickly, they are resolved by several brief rhetorical figures that rely on their smooth verbal conventionality characteristic of late nineteenth-century elegies to counter the sorrow expressed at the trauma of personal loss.

It is only in the last stanza that the formal expression of sadness falls apart under the burden of the inexpressibility of the speaker's deepest personal feelings:

> So, in the days to come, your name
> Shall be as music that ascends
> When honour turns a heart from shame . . .
> O heart of hearts! . . . O friend of friends! (107)

The last line, though rhetorical enough, represents Sassoon's injection of the personal into the impersonal celebratory tradition of the conventional elegy. The preceding lines tacitly acknowledge Ross's right to be praised, for they allude to Ross's support of Oscar Wilde both in prison and afterward by identifying him as a signal instance of honorable behavior and personal loyalty. And in predicting that Ross will receive greater public recognition and admiration for his conduct in the future, Sassoon evinces another trait of the elegiac tradition, that in which memory undergirds and sustains public recognition. But for him and others of his generation, the public future and the individual virtue replace the afterlife as the place where true rewards and just deserts are apportioned. The dominant loss, then, felt by Sassoon is that of a socio-moral yardstick, a complex of wit, laughter, charm, kindness, love, and honor that emblemizes the values most appreciated by his immediate circle.[6] It is a loss that focuses not at all on Ross as a physical presence nor on his actions or public achievements.[7] Nor is there anything to mark it either as a funeral or a pastoral elegy; neither nature nor the grave figure in the poem.

At the same time, the honor-shame dichotomy may carry a more personal, if more guarded, implication bearing on Sassoon's own relationship with Ross.[8] The latter's frequent hospital visits during Sassoon's recuperation from his wounds could easily be seen as acts of honor, especially since Sassoon was inclined to feel

a soldier's misplaced but understandable shame at no longer being able to partic-
ipate in the war. Thus, Wilde's public shame and Sassoon's more private and per-
sonal humiliation fuse at Ross's death from heart failure. He is the friend of both
whose personal honorableness and public courage are tacitly taken to elevate him
above his two artist-friends. The expostulatory last line, then, captures both the
personal and hidden or secret possibility as well as that of the more public and
overt sense of shame perhaps at still being alive while his friend is not. It achieves
this by conjoining so fervently the personal commitment implicit in "heart of
hearts" with the strong social or public note carried by "friend of friends."

Given the social and legal climate of opinion in England around World War
I and taking into account Sassoon's own sexual predilections, one may well view
the grief at the loss of Ross as involving an additional and somewhat subter-
ranean dimension.[9] The poem can also be seen as a covert declaration of sorrow
and anguish at the loss of a fellow homosexual, one who made clear his sexual
identity more courageously and openly than the poet was prepared to do.[10] If so,
the poem stands as a testimonial to the need for public suppression of a personal
sexual nature. As such, it gains added poignancy and pathos through the very
inarticulateness of the exclamatory utterances of the last line. Indeed, the issue
of inarticulateness balances the poem's conclusion evenly between elegiac con-
vention and innovation. It partakes of what has been called the Renaissance el-
egy's inexpressibility *topos* even as it reaches hesitantly out in the direction of the
contemporary confessionals such as Lowell and Sexton.[11]

In any case, the poem exists on its surface primarily as the expression of the
loss of a particularly admired close friend. As such, through its final line, it takes
on a note of encomiastic inflation that moves it away from the personal lament.[12]
So seen, Sassoon strives to maintain the English elegiac tradition at the same time
as he gropes toward a more direct and personal expression of grief. His elegiac
shift thus documents the difference between past and present historical ages and
the concomitant assessment of the nature and role of the poet.

In Sassoon's case, the deep ambivalence he felt about his sexual identity was
in conflict with his late Victorian commitment to the ideal of same-sex friendship
so sedulously cultivated in the English private schools and universities of the pe-
riod.[13] This, together with other factors, resulted in a profound tension between
his impetus to write in the elegiac tradition and his striving for a less conven-
tional—more open and honest—mode of grieving. For him, the former invoked
the strategies of concealment and evasion of personal feelings at odds with the
social and legal codes of the times.[14] The latter called up the strong desire for

freedom from cultural constraints and imposed sanctions. In this, of course, he was enacting in verse the struggle that dominated his character and career: between traditional fox-hunting gentleman and "Mad Jack," the rebel against war, needless death, and those conventions that gave rise to them.[15]

Ironically enough, he finds in Ross precisely those virtues associated with the prewar gentleman that the war, to Sassoon's mind, had largely destroyed as a societal ideal, much less a reality, leaving only rage, disgust, and contempt. For survivors of the war, like himself, Ross stands as an emblem of human behavior and conduct respected only by a small subset of human society, his immediate friends, and so doubly precious because clearly diminished in public estimation. Thus, Sassoon counters such a central change in his world by doggedly insisting Ross's values and nature will in the future again be recognized universally. The earnest exaltation of Ross's virtues he predicts so unequivocally, nevertheless, has an undertone of desperation that suggests the poet is driven more by desperate hope than firm conviction. This is supported, too, by the final expostulatory line of the poem, which by implication extends the bitterness of Sassoon's personal loss into an understanding that the Edwardian prewar world of his youth also is lost permanently.

Personal Losses

Other variants of the loss of a friend are found in two poems by Edwin Muir, the Orkney visionary. Both "For Ann Scott-Moncrief (1914–1943)" and "To J. F. H. (1897–1914)" are more detailed and personal laments for the death of a friend than that provided by Sassoon. The latter essentially concentrates on the loss he himself is experiencing, on the deprivation of Ross's social talents, and its immediately felt impact on the surviving self. Muir, on the other hand, focuses on the person lost, on an assessment of her traits and on an exploration of the possible interrelationships of death and living. In doing so, he exercises one of his major poetic gifts, namely, the ability to root his archetypal quest for personal insight in the ordinary daily events of his life.

Thus, "For Ann Scott-Moncrief" is both a memorial and an elegy of vision.[16] It opens with a low-keyed statement of regret quickly broadening out into a denial of death's effect:

> Dear Ann, wherever you are
> Since you lately learnt to die,
> You are this unsetting star
> That shines unchanged in my eye. (156)

The plaintive note of the first line is balanced by the confident assertion that death has changed nothing. Yet as the balance of the stanza makes clear, it is only the speaker's memory that retains her changelessness. In fact, she has—in an image rich in Muir's thought—fallen out of the sensory world. Consequently, he is driven to admit the deprivation of her physical presence despite the protestation of his memory.

To this point, the poet-speaker can only flatly record the loss of attributes and talents ripe with promise: "These are no longer now. / Death has a princely prize" (156). The magnitude of this loss is suggested in the term "princely," which carries some of the tradition-laden solemnity of a phrase like "princely ransom" to convey the value of her presence to those who knew her. At the same time, the adjective non-grammatically spills back over "Death" so as to invest his personified presence with the majestic status of a royal figure summoning a subject. Both Death and Ann are thereby exalted. The paradoxical nature of this is clear from the fact that death is the cause of her loss as well as the bestower of her exaltation.[17] Death, it would seem, is and is not princely.

Because of this enigma in which he finds human life and mortality to be wrapped, Muir turns in the second stanza from death as a personification to Ann as a person. She becomes the focus not of the disruption of time and the loss of a friend but of a ruminative contemplation of the continuity of time and personality as the individual moves from youth and life to death. First, he singles her out for her greater sense of self and speculates that her response to death is the same now that she herself is dead as it was when she was alive. This persistence of being and continuity of character, however, is not, he claims, unique to her but is a function of her very continuity as a human being:

> For though of your heritage
> The minority here began,
> Now you have come of age
> And are entirely Ann. (156)

Here Muir attempts to counter the loss occasioned by Ann's death by dramatically inverting the customary sense of life's being ended by death. Through asserting that her maturation as a person is concomitant with her loss of life, he suggests that a person's existence extends through or beyond death. In so doing, he sharply parts with the elegy's traditional sorrow for an untimely death and a life prematurely cut short, as in Shelley's *Adonais*. Instead, he gives the person per se a priority over both life and death; the individual who dies early comes to her maturity despite or because of death. Yet this stance is not wholly removed from the elegiac tradition, for its skepticism partakes of the third kind of elegiac vision sketched by one critic, that of "the imaginative thinker whose intellectual eye ranges rebelliously through universal darkness toward some new scintilla of light from a world of yet undiscovered meaning and value."[18]

And yet the muting of grief is not an elimination of regret or sorrow, as the final two lines of the stanza indicate. The phrase "entirely Ann" indicates the stasis of death deprives her of the opportunity for change, for development, and for new opportunities in living. To be "entirely Ann" means she is a fully completed entity, a totality beyond which there is no embryonic, putative, or emergent identity to anticipate or contemplate. And this is a loss for the poet-speaker, who as a living participant has had his memory so constrained and limited by death. The very memory and its projective powers on which he relies to refuse the physical loss entailed by death is, he suddenly but quietly sees, itself subject to the loss of future changes in the person and the delight and surprise they occasion. All that his memory can summon up are past images of the person who was.

In the face of such stark and sobering reflections, Muir is restricted in the consolatory sentiments he can summon up. All he can do is balance the impersonal and mythic fact of the Fall which brought death into the world against the recollected personal assessment by Ann that "Yet 'the world is a pleasant place'" (157). And in remembering that Ann was one of those who, although beset by "ills of body and soul" (157), nevertheless endeavored to recover the pre-lapsarian state of perfection or integrated being, he is able to counter the reality of the loss with the final memory of her quietly heroic stance toward life:

> Yet 'the world is a pleasant place'
> I can hear your voice repeat,
> While the sun shone in your face
> Last summer in Princes Street. (157)

This combination of auditory and visual memory, Ann's quiet, casual statement, and the image of the sun and summer, all work together to render Muir's dogged yet understated conviction that the trials of living are both worth it and a profound counter to the fact of death.

Ann's voice symbolizes the ordinariness and the accepting qualities of the mature human being faced with the almost insurmountable challenge of living in a fallen, imperfect world. It also captures the poet's own sentiments with which he seeks to counter her loss from that physical, empirical world. For him, the elegiac consolation is limited to acceptance of her death and the memory of her life. Similarly, the elegiac effort to transcend death is thoroughly naturalized. A sense of soaring triumph over the inescapable limitations of life and the world is caught in the hesitantly sacred image of nature as creation: the sun shining on the face of a beloved human being facing her final and ultimate challenge quietly and almost diffidently.

Where Sassoon capitulates to shocked, inarticulate grief at the loss of his friend, Muir elaborates a view of the continuity of life and death dependent upon the capacity of memory to sustain a naturalized transcendency of the ordinary world. The simplicity of the poem's diction, its laconic statements, and its almost phlegmatic manner toward its subject conspire to make its utilization of the elegy tradition a virtual denial of it. In doing so, Muir counters both the dominance of the Romantic form of elegiac conventions and the modern world's reluctance either to accept the legitimacy of a supernatural realm or to see it as one with the ordinary secular daily life of men and women. Like Sassoon, though in a quite different way, he betrays that "hesitancy of attitude" toward the traditional elegiac form noted earlier.[19] Sassoon hesitates over its conventional linguistic and rhetorical resources, declaring implicitly that he cannot trust in them to convey the grief he feels for Ross's death. Muir, on the other hand, is concerned with that "probing of intellectual boundaries" identified as characteristic of the modern elegist.[20] This probing explores his reflective sorrow at Ann's loss, the power and limits of personal memory, and the need for a new and less encompassing concept of spiritual transcendency, one that depends on a more complex notion of belief. In this, he is undogmatically following his nineteenth-century intellectual inheritance, when belief as centered in religious faith started to yield its authority. For Muir, belief is centered instead in what he experiences personally as psycho-empirical fact. In aligning himself with the authority of analytical psychology (especially Jung) rather than the Protestant faith of his fathers, he moves part of the way from a religious to a secular belief-structure. By so doing, he reflects a dominant shift in twentieth-century thought. Thus, he is concerned to interrogate as well as to accept reality as it is given to him.

The closeness of the supernatural world to that of the living is more full registered in Muir's memorial poem "To J. F. H. (1897–1934)" even as it departs even further from Romantic paradigms of the elegiac. Standing, as it does, midway between the narrative and philosophic modes, the poem largely eschews personal sorrow for a puzzled probing of the nature of reality.[21] It begins with a déjà vu experience of seeing someone who at first glimpse looks like a dead friend.

Surprise, shock, and memory conspire to create a genuine existential paradox. The speaker almost simultaneously registers an awareness of having just seen a friend coupled with the sharp and undebatable memory that the friend has been dead for seven years. These contradictory impressions immediately project the poet into puzzled speculation as to "what world I walked in, since it held us two, / A dead and a living man" (91).

Here, one sees sharply the difference between Muir's tentative, uncertain sense of the relation between the dead and the living and the conventional one historically preceding it. For him, dead and living are co-terminous rather than successive or sequential; they exist simultaneously and possess limited interaction. The social convention, in contrast, regarded them as eternally committed to exclusive realms in a linear time. It is his sense of the strangeness of this contrast that leads him to feel powerfully but uncertainly that the gap between the two worlds is but a "low dike / So easy to leap" (91) rather than the momentous crossing of the broad and dangerous Styx. The transition from life to death is physically casual, not cataclysmic except for the speaker's persisting and conventional apprehension of the event itself: "And yet the fear?" (91).

Thus, the real focus of Muir's quasi-philosophic memorial is not so much J.F.H. as a friend and person.[22] Rather it is the relationship of the two worlds, and, in particular, the moment of complex realization of the nature of the transition between them. His friend, he believes, has "felt the terror of the trysting place, / The crowning test, the treachery and the glory" (92). Each of these four strands relates to separate facets or modes of being that confront the individual moving from life to death. Terror obviously is an attribute of the physical, sensory, empirical realm. It implicitly stands over against the test, which embodies the spiritual assessing of the individual's ability to bear the renunciation of the physical, bodily existence. In the same way, "the treachery and the glory" (92) counterpoise the human self against the presence of the deity or supreme being. The self at the moment of death, Muir appears to argue, must face the question of its own responsibility for now being transformed into another order of existence. Its culpability in the person's loss of life is balanced by its also coming into the presence of its creator, the goal of life itself. By calling the person to face the earlier suggestions of impetuosity, headstrong recklessness, and a driven compulsion "to be elsewhere" (91), Muir suggests, starkly put, the dead man in some measure is not only responsible for his death by his actions but also by his attitude toward life in general.

In effect, Muir counters categorically the existentialist or Gidean conviction of the possibility of the gratuitous act devoid of a causative factor. However sobering the charge of one's responsibility for one's own death, Muir judiciously seeks to balance this treachery of the self by the self, a motif novelists such as Malcolm Lowry and Joan Didion plumb in greater and starker detail. He does so by a deeply felt declaration of the inescapable presence of a glory that is more than human by virtue of its being infinite and eternal. By weaving together these four strands—terror, test, treachery, and glory—as he does, Muir develops an abbreviated version of the traditional elegy's consolatory powers. It accomplishes its purpose through de-emphasizing the personal or the individual and with it the need for lamentation. In their place is a focus on the narrative occasion and philosophical ground of death itself. The result is a substantially less inflected and more generalized solace found to reside ultimately in the inescapability and the spiritual reality of death.

Another variant to the personal loss of a friend or relative occurs in Dylan Thomas's "After the Funeral." It provides a stylistically and thematically quite different approach to the interaction of self and death.[23] Here the focus is unrelievedly on the personal and individual rather than on the philosophical and general.[24] Muir, as we have seen, uses the deaths of his two friends to probe reflectively the relation of death as a universal phenomenon to life and the living rather than to mount a full-scale lament for their passing. Thus, his memories of Ann are controlled and muted in the measure of specificity they possess, while those of his friend Holms largely focus on the accident in which he died. Both trigger the poet's efforts to understand their deaths in general terms applicable to the phenomenon itself rather than to create full-bodied portraits of the individuals in their immediate actuality. Thomas, as we shall see, takes a quite different tack, one which differs radically from Muir.[25]

The challenge to Thomas, the poet-speaker, is to summon the worlds of man and nature to an appropriate appreciation of his aged relative's true worth. At the same time, he is concerned to create an adequate expression of the intensity of the felt grief of the speaker. Paradoxically, this intensity lies beyond expression even as the poet deploys the full resources of his rhetoric to convey his almost inarticulate but extremely powerful feelings of loss, sorrow, and pity.[26] In doing so, he implicitly contrasts his personal and profoundly genuine responses to those of the communal world. The latter partake of the conventional and societal so as to verge on a distorted falsification of the deceased's true nature.

As the subtitle—"*In memory of Ann Jones*"—makes clear, the poet's principal concern is with the memory, the true memory of the deceased relative rather than with the idea of public memorializing of her.[27] For him, the genuine grieving begins after the funeral and concentrates on recalling and voicing the old woman's concrete actuality as an individual human being rather than on merely a ceremonial observance of her passing.[28] In so doing, Thomas moves toward his customary dialectical organizational structure for the poem.[29] Thus, its imagery polarizes the poet or individual against his community or society, nature against mankind, and the genuinely spiritual against institutional religion. Where Muir tacitly stands midway between religious and secular grounds of authority for facing death, Thomas categorically contrasts them and opts for the latter insofar as it reflects his own intransigent contempt for his society's religion.[30] The intent is to establish a linkage between the younger poet as author and his older relative whose nature and life might be thought to be the antithesis of the poet and the poetic.

His first act is to "stand, for this memorial's sake alone / In the snivelling hours with dead, humped Ann" (87). This description implicitly sets the voice of the *poèt maudit* over against the distorted and crippled body of the deceased. The "I" is valorized over the "funeral" with its "mule praises" and the post-funeral reception with its "stuffed fox and a stale fern" (87). The heroic individuality of honest grief commits itself to remembering Ann as she was in actuality. The poet's voice stands in contradistinction to the public civilities and clichés that warp the person into the stereotypical figure of the dead of whom no ill is to be spoken.

Thomas casts himself as "Ann's bard" (87) in order to counter her own impulse to silent acceptance of her mortality.[31] He calls at least nature, if not human society, to celebrate her as an integral aspect of the natural world itself. She functioned as a life-preserving warning, one likely not heard by "the hymning heads" (87) of her community. In effect, she attests to the primordiality and inescapability of nature's worship or acknowledgment of itself. Such a worship takes no account of status or hierarchy, that is, of power however envisaged or construed. Instead, it is content with the humbleness of a love beyond ego-worship as embodied in the casual, natural motion of "four, crossing birds" (87). They are invoked by the poet-bard to bless her spirit both in its passing and for its past presence.[32]

In this way, the poet articulates his own acceptance of her reality. This admission entails his acceptance of her linkage with religion, dutifulness, and the dehumanization wrought by intense physical pain. The physical exhaustion of a fatal illness is itself an image for life as lived by Anne. These are part of her reality even as the poet's lauding of her natural being is an idealization of her essence. His recognition of this constitutes the poem's final dialectical reversal. Just as at its outset, the conventional praises of the funeral are idealizations that the poet struggles to dismiss, so finally he admits them and the "skyward statue" as legitimate and real. It is in this fusion of realities, his and the community's, the individual and the collective, that the poet finally comes to an ultimate memory of her.[33] This memory is not of her as she was but as she now is, a statue with "marble hands" and a "hewn voice" (88).[34] They are capable of shaking him powerfully until the artifice of dead, natural things like the fox and the fern effect a similarly magical or incredible transformation of themselves. In so celebrating finally by word and action the love and fecundity of life itself, they make death and the constructions or inventions it entails surmountable and endurable until, at least, we ourselves confront it.[35]

Impersonal Losses

In addition to those variants of loss that are either concealed (as with Sassoon) or personal (as with Muir and Thomas), there is another, which can perhaps be called the impersonal. This form is best exemplified by Geoffrey Hill's "In Memory of Jane Fraser." Where Thomas involves the authorial "I" almost as much as he does the deceased Ann Jones, a far different poet, the contemporary Geoffrey Hill, resolutely eschews the personal. In terse stanzas, he exercises a relentless control on his metrics as well as his subjectivity in an ostensible remembrance of a woman identified solely by her name of Jane Fraser. So specifically realized is his descriptive portrait of her that we are startled, even shocked, to learn that she is apocryphal and wholly a creature of his imagination.[36] From this, it is clear that Hill is concerned to explore the elegiac convention with a resolute quizzicality rather than to articulate either public or personal grief for a close acquaintance or friend.

Though a brief elegiac exercise, "In Memory of Jane Fraser" clearly shows its congruence with the tradition in its careful identification of and progression through a threefold sequence: the apocryphal individual's facing of death, the death itself, and the aftermath or response of the natural world to the death. Where Hill departs from the elegiac convention is in his refusal to mourn explicitly and in his declination to exalt his subject extravagantly. His carefully structured approach to the whole history of the elegy is established at the very outset.

The heroic note so frequently associated with the confrontation with death is both deliberately muted in tone and pointed up through the images in the poem's opening:

> When snow like sheep lay in the fold
> And winds went begging at each door,
> And the far hills were blue with cold,
> And a cold shroud lay on the moor,
> She kept the siege. (11)

These flat, declarative statements remind us of the eighteenth-century pathos of the isolate rural setting so powerfully mined by Wordsworth for sympathetic purposes. At the same time, the setting is saved from the charge of sentimentality by the apt concluding military image of strongly resisting an implacable adversary.[37] Immediately following, Hill, like Thomas, proceeds to underscore the character's strength and stoical courage. However, unlike Thomas, her audience is carefully kept neutral about her circling awareness of death as a foreboding presence:

> . . . And every day
> We watched her brooding over death
> Like a strong bird above its prey
> The room filled with the kettle's breath. (11)

The spectatorial "we" includes by implication the authorial "I," and in this pronominal shift Hill segues around the conflict between individual and society lurking in Thomas's poem. Both are content simply to watch the impending struggle that is the polar antithesis of the pathos of the opening rural scene of isolation and physical hardship. The living person (though apocryphal) is undeniably in danger. But by foregoing punctuation until the end of the stanza, Hill suggests that she is a truly formidable adversary even for death itself. The absence of punctuation also links the bird image with the kettle's steam circling upward in the room.[38] The effect of this is to soften or call into question the possibility that Jane is capable of making death her prey. It also heightens the scene's waiting and watching qualities by extending them to nonhuman elements, such as the kettle's steam. In so doing, the poet subtly restores the awful imminence of her demise while controlling and almost suppressing it by the homely domestication of the scene.

The maintaining of suspense as to the outcome of her struggle with death slows the poem's pace even below that of the initial winter scene. This culminates in the next stanza with the confluence of the ordinary and the extraordinary found in its opening statement: "Damp curtains glued against the pane / Sealed time away" (11). Time and motion both are caught in a stasis that presages the cessation of life itself that spreads from Jane to her audience to the world:

> Her body froze
> As if to freeze us all, and chain
> Creation to a stunned repose. (11)

The momentousness of the consequences of her death is tightly controlled by the low-keyed nature of its rendering. It effectively captures the impact of the emotional shock of her cessation of life in its interplay of suspended animation and stasis with a consciousness of the impossibility of any kind of reaction. In effect, Hill here captures vividly the immediacy of the effect of an actual personal death through the exercise of a totally imaginative or inventive effort. The result is that he brings into the elegiac tradition the actual emotions and responses elicited by the death of an individual even though that individual is nonexistent. What he achieves in actuality is the introduction of personal emotions qua emotions into the rhetorical conspectus of the elegy or if not the elegy per se at least of its near relative and frequent companion, the memorial.

Such a startling achievement, in its own quiet, understated way, almost threatens to pull the poem free from the elegiac context. The poet verges on making it an exercise in the rhetoric and practice of writing as art rather than as personal expression. But even here, Hill balances his and the poem's response by firmly cementing the last stanza to the elegiac convention and the annual natural cycle:

> She died before the world could stir.
> In March the ice unloosed the brook
> And water ruffled the sun's hair,
> Dead cones upon the alder shook. (11)

The natural world of water, tree, and sun comes to life in an image of freedom, loving playfulness, and kindly motion that counters the stasis, imprisonment, and limitation dominating the third stanza.[39] The quiet resonance of this image echoes at least some of the dying and reviving god pattern held by some to be so endemic to the English elegiac tradition.[40] It does so, however, without intruding anything that could be dignified as allusion. Instead the poem ends where it began, as an artful indirect exposition of the power inherent in the rhetoric of description and understatement. It extends both by inventing the subject and scene, by investing them with a mimesis of actuality, and by linking them with a purely literary and rhetorical effort or exercise. In so doing, Hill calls attention to the individuality of a poem even as he celebrates its participation in the tradition of a literary form.

The final variant of loss to be considered here follows directly from the impersonal form represented by Hill. Two other poets equally dedicated to self-control, powerful emotion, and craftsmanship carry his neutral manner and declarative phrasing into actual interrogative argument. Elder Olson's "Elegy (In mem. Dr. P. F. S.)" and Yvor Winters's "The Cremation" are dominated by the interrogative, the philosophical, and the dramatic as they endeavor to plumb the mystery of the death of another human being. For them, the central concern is not with the individual self, its ability to assess the true worth of the deceased, and its impulse to shape a critique of the conventional communal response. Nor is it with the poet's active alienation from his community and society, nor with the differing relations to and adaptation of elegiac conventions. Instead, they see the impact of death on the speaker to be the generation of a philosophical puzzle, the formulation of a philosophical argument that entails or leads to the consideration of an elegy for the possibility of writing an elegy.

Olson's speaker is dramatically personal and intensely nervous, almost distressed in manner. Quickly he moves to probe the reality and meaning both of the present absence and his memory of the past presence:

> Here, amid landscape
> Austere as the cold profile of the dead,
> No mark. O, but remembrance is a mark.
> . . . .
> Vanished; the flesh
> Snatched like a cloth; . . .
> Was the live man, then, only
> Illusion of the wizard's cabinet? (65)

For Olson, death's introductory fact is that of the person's disappearance, which immediately generalizes into an interrogation of the nature of reality. Is that which occasions life and death an ironic dispenser of illusion and reality capable of blurring the human mind's determination of which is which: "Is the skull, then, the real? The vivid face, its mask? / Death the one mummer, masking in all forms?" (65). For this poet, these questions are by no means rhetorical gestures that tacitly call up the speaker's sorrow. Rather, they are questions for which answers are sought and presented: "the Sphinx of death, maw crammed, and ravenous still, / Reads me her riddle: now answer true, or die" (65).

The initial response of the bewildered speaker is to view himself as a "Fool of vanity" (66) who has not grasped the nature of reality and its dependence upon death. Nor standing as he does by the grave of his friend does he recognize that this renders him immediately vulnerable to the same fate. For the speaker, compassion for the deceased is replaced by a philosophical puzzle—the nature of reality—and a philosophical quest—the nature of death—both of which endanger the speaker with extinction.[41]

Stylistically, this produces a structure of repeated almost simultaneous interrogation of the empirical and intellectual worlds. Thus, the speaker confronts the Sphinx, Plato, the Arctic North, and churches of the Christian faith, each of which in its individual fashion leads him to death and its various aspects. In turn, he sees death as a ravening, devouring monster; a cypher-like absence—"That One is none" (66)—; a mechanical cycle incapable of advancement beyond moving back to where it has already been; and an Abyss of ending rather than the River of life. These differing aspects of death coalesce enough into one of the entirety of existence. Ironically enough, it is not the image of Christ the Savior that the speaker summons up but rather "The Angel of Pestilence" which is "All death, death" (67). The religious cycle culminating in salvation and eternal life is philosophically found to be no different or better than the human mechanical cycle of repetition: both end with death as a totality of the human fate.

This mood of nihilistic despair is faced when the speaker tells himself to submit to his destruction at the hands of death the conqueror. Its image is first inflated to that of Tamburlaine and then deflated to that of "a starving dog" (67) prepared to chew on his bones. With this, he envisages at least an end to the puzzle and the quest both, a cessation of the question-and-answer of the philosophical enterprise. Neither the puzzle nor the quest is answered or concluded satisfactorily; only the stark silence and emptiness of the undiscoverable and the unanswerable remain. Only at this point is Olson able to respond directly to his friend and his death. His philosophical quest is an epistemological equivalent to the empirical journey of his friend through life and into death. Consequently, the speaker identifies his intellectual progress with the physical experience of his friend so that "into your grave I fall, am dead with you" (68).

With this identification, the speaker's tone and attitude to death changes. The metaphor of entering the grave changes to a set of ironic, almost comic, specifics through which the speaker plumbs the nature of death. He concludes finally that death is not simply physical discomfort or bodily erosion or nothingness, but rather "sown seed" (68). The grave after all is part of the earth and there the speaker becomes aware "how furiously life rages till it lives," transforming the inanimate elements into "bird, beast, flower, and tree" (68). This insight is finally assessed as not a matter of knowledge but one of belief endemic to his nature. Because this belief is integral to him, and implicitly to mankind at large, he sees the phenomenon as being a "miracle of this puppet on three strings" (68). Man's belief in the eternal persistence of life is the closest the twentieth-century philosophical mind can come to the concept of immortality. It makes him, however, a puppet rather than a creator, one controlled by the three strings of motion, speech, and thought. Together, they shape his existence. The recognition of this as the human reality of death is achieved by the elision of physical and intellectual sight: "As I see / Because my being is seeing" (68). Now he abandons both memory and prediction. The former is linked with the deceased, the past, and his sorrow. The latter involves the future and is associated with the philosophical puzzle and quest with which he started his elegy. In abandoning both, however, he does not surrender the human concern with pity, regret, and sympathy. Instead he internalizes and universalizes the traditional elegiac expression of grief for its specific subject into a Shakespearian echo of the heartbreak central in Lear's "prithee, undo this button" and the compassion for the dead Hamlet:

> Break, memory, break:
> Who recalls the future?
> Peace, poor ghost. (68)

Yvor Winters's "The Cremation," though stylistically different, is like Olson's "Elegy" in its philosophic grounding and in its articulating an attitude at odds with generally received opinion. The major differences are: Winters does not dramatize the discovery of a different outlook than that with which he began his poem; he engages in no sustained exploration of alternative historical or intellectual attitudes to death; and he adopts a stance of quietly persistent irony toward contemporary burial practices. Instead he articulates a reflective observation developed through selective illustrations forming an integral part of a sustained argument or point of view.

"The Cremation" betrays few traces of the traditional elegy despite its dedication's suggesting its impetus was the death of a specific individual. It expresses no grief over death, invokes no traditional features of the genre, and culminates with no particular consolation for either the deceased or the poetic speaker. In so doing, it moves toward some of the principal traits of the truly modern elegy: a refusal to shrink from the fact of human mortality, a reticence about public lamentation, an internalization of whatever solace may be available, and a concern for acting within the bounds of reality as presently conceived. If the implications of its argument are followed out, it can be seen as pointing to what might be called an elegy for the possibility of future elegies. Essentially what Winters argues is that ancient Egyptian cremation is antithetical to its modern form. For one thing, it preserves rather than destroys the body. For another, with the obliteration of the latter also destroyed forever are memory, history, and human records. Hence, Winters simultaneously indicts the modern or Western world for its practices and presages a time when not only "there is no footprint where you tread" (167) but no possibility of a consciousness of a past.

The sustained polarization of "Egypt" and "we," of Eastern and Western global regions, of ancient past and modern present runs through the entire poem. His argument steadily develops toward its conclusion that ultimately there will be no ocular record of the present. The first stanza establishes Egypt as a region whose burial practices maintain the unity and integrity of the human being. In contrast, the regions to which Winters belongs "sever the body from its ash" (167). The second stanza, then, develops or draws out the consequences of this severance. It finds a hierarchy of value in the body's components ranging from the ash to the body to the spirit. Of these, only ash and body are in any way identifiable after death and still present. "The ash is but a little dust" begins what "the powdered lime sinks back alone" (167) concludes. Thereby it creates as an object of contemplation a silent vista of the loss and pathos attendant upon death. Gone will be human ethics and law, individual perception, and personal speech, all stemming from the disappearance or obliteration of the spirit. To this contemplation, as with Olson, no answer is available to the questions to which it gives rise.

At the midpoint of the poem, then, Winters suggests that his world, by its burial practices, loses both contact with the reality of the world of the spirit and the ability to plumb its existence. What it is left with is a sense of a personal isolation surrounded by all that is unknowable. Consequently, the sense of man's facing his own extinction is extended in the third and final stanza. Here it becomes an inference explicitly drawn from the preceding stages of his reasoning. It follows from the contrast between the two sets of burial customs as well as from the preceding establishment of the primacy of the spirit. This last generalization is established via the instance of the individual whose death is the subject of his poetic commentary or reflection:

> Thus you have left a fainter trace
> Of what the spirit bore for hire
> . . . .
> Than ages of the drying dead. (167)

The final two lines of the poem powerfully and compactly tease out the final ground for regret by Winters:

> Once and for all you went through fire:
> There is no footprint where you tread. (167)

The opening phrase here is central to the meaning. It sets this action over against the whole long religio-historical record of fire as an image of the ultimate purifying ritual available to man from which he emerges transformed and transfigured. In contrast, the cremation fire is not revivifying but completely and irreversibly destructive of man as an object of history and human record. Like Olson, Winters seems to suggest that the act of seeing is a dual phenomenon, both physical and mental or imaginative. This act is also essential to the creation and perpetuation of human memory. In turn, memory is history and provides evidence of as well as from the past. And part of that past is the human record of the elegy as an art form focused on remembering and celebrating both the fact and the significance of those who have preceded us in time.

Forms of Affection

This section extends the analysis of modern poets' treatment of the death of friends and relatives in two ways. First, it considers the forms or kinds of affection operative in their elegiac tributes: that for a friend who was also a lover; for a student who was also a friend; for several friends' burial arrangements; and for a fellow poet who was essentially an acquaintance. Then, it turns to the variety of ways in which relatives—brothers, aunts, mothers, fathers, and children—are remembered. In so doing, an effort is made to outline how quite different poets adapt their very personal recollections to some of the traditional elegiac conventions and thus articulate both transformations and innovations in that extended historical tradition. These modifications reflect such historical changes as those imposed by two quite different world wars, the alienation of the elegist from his

society and its official sentiments, the continued effort to maintain a place for re-
ligious faith and views amid an increasingly secular world, and the growing in-
clination to opt for a broadly elegiac temper toward life as a whole.

In contradistinction to the philosophical impersonality we have just seen in Ol-
son and Winters stand a number of other poets. They invest their remembrances
of personal friends with fond specificities and the direst of predictions concern- .
ing the consequences to follow from the loved one's death. In this, they approxi-
mate at least one major aspect of the elegiac tradition: the impulse to panegyric
and extreme grief for the friend who has died, such as is found in Shelley's *Ado-
nais*. One can view, for instance, George Barker's "In Memory of a Friend,"
Theodore Roethke's "Elegy for Jane," James Wright's "Arrangements with Earth
for Three Dead Friends," and Charles Olson's "The Death of Europe" as a con-
spectus of personal responses to the death of a friend.[42] One can easily see a pro-
gression from Barker's intensely, sexually personal, and intimate grief to Olson's
comparative cultural concerns founded on casual, informal allusions and en-
veloped in the deceased individual regarded as a symbol of larger socio-cultural
problems that seem virtually beyond solution. In the process, it becomes clear that
the mourning of a friend gradually comes to include a rich variety of losses be-
yond that of the death of an individual.

Perhaps the most striking thing about George Barker's "In Memory of a
Friend" is the way in which it yokes traditional and innovative poetic elements.
Structurally, it hews closely to the conventional elegiac pattern of grief-denial-
reconciliation. At the same time, stylistically, it deploys the neo-Romantic rhetoric
developed first by Dylan Thomas and the New Apocalypse writers. To a degree,
the latter serves to conceal or overlay the poem's traditional elegiac structure in
such a way and to such a degree as to blur or obscure its presence. Taken together,
however, they capture one initial way in which the modern poet sought to write
a friend's personal elegy that could be thought appropriate to a new era while still
observing the dignity and solemnity of earlier times. And if the heightened
rhetoric applied to the anonymous warrior-lover occasionally sounds excessive
and exaggerated, it also reflects the poet's awareness that his is a personal, not a
communal, mourning.[43] In effect, he has no poetic basis for comparison with
which to assess the appropriateness of the language to be employed. To this can
be added his own lifelong struggle against the conventions of decorum, appro-
priateness, and manners of whatever society in which he was temporarily resid-
ing at the moment. Contributing further to the sense of fissure between structure

and style, theme and form, is Barker's allegiance to the Romantic elegy and its concentration on the individual ego standing isolated against an incipiently alien world. Such an allegiance almost necessarily entails a high style, a panegyric mode, and an attitude verging on desperation.

"In Memory of a Friend" carefully observes the traditional elegiac pattern in that its first half (five stanzas) is devoted largely to lamenting the friend's death before turning in the next three stanzas to critically examining the viability of several of the customary forms of consolation and then in the final stanza to an understanding of love's power to shape an acceptance of the death. At the same time, his hardheaded probing of the interrelated roles of time, faith, and transfiguration lead not to acquiescence in their emotional relevance but to a reformulation of the nature of his loss. He recognizes the enduring nature of love as capable of transforming death into merely a long sleep. Here Barker confronts both the liabilities of the elegiac tradition for the twentieth-century mind and the limitations of his own rhetoric to transcend the fact of death. In doing so, he shapes, even as he is shaped by, the priority given by classical modernism to the work of art as a sustaining counter to the innumerable losses likely to be visited on the individual during his life. How he also shapes an innovative adaptation to the tradition is to be found both in his strong, intellectual assessment of the adequacies of the conventional consolations, his Romantic persistence in finding solace in the endurance of love, and his extension of the modern elegiac form to include the love lyric. Skepticism about past reality, commitment to the present state of existence, and trust in the efficacy of language constitute the major aspects of the elegiac temper on which he relies.

One of his departures from the elegiac tradition can be found in his response to the role of historical context. The poem sets its lament in the context of World War II and the Battle of Britain, but not in order to provide any sort of historical perspective on the era. Sedulously, he avoids making his friend and lover an epitome of military gallantry or a symbol of that crisis-laden period of European history. For him, a very close friend's death in a fighter plane crash arouses none of the anger at society and its civilian and military authorities that, say, Sassoon, Owen, and Graves expressed for World War I fatalities. Instead of anger at the fate of others, Barker pities and sympathizes with the survivors like himself. As one of them, he has only an "empty and insignificant world" in which, as "the disremembered," he is left with his memories and past "unforgettable allegiances" (252). Thus, the poem's context is scarcely broadly historical at all. Rather, it is intensely personal, consisting simply of the day itself and the mourner's individual anguish at the suddenness and swiftness with which he is thrust into the bitterest of anguish for the death of a friend and lover.[44] Unlike Dylan Thomas's mourning for Ann Jones's death, Barker neither attends to nor sets himself over against any communal mourning. Instead he concentrates on the Romantic intensity of feeling aroused by the death. He fiercely praises and exalts the casual insouciance of the fallen pilot as the "tall Jack with the sun on his wrist / And a sky stuffed up his sleeve" (252). In doing so, he makes his friend into the almost archetypal Romantic hero whose predilection for risk-taking and living on the edge makes him both awesomely admirable and foolhardy. By so seeing his lover, he makes the grief virtually a necessary consequence of the love. Both the grief and the love are thus made unconditional.

At the same time, the second stanza following the introductory couplet suddenly widens the focus by implicitly invoking a welter of such deaths. The effect of such an increase in fatality is to intensify the changes wrought by death, memory, and past prewar relationships. The tone, however, is reflective rather than angry and the attitude that of pathos instead of outrage:

> They walk in silence over the same spaces
> Where they once talked, and now do not,
> The dumb friends with the whitewashed faces
> Who lifted a hand and died. They forget us
> In the merciful amnesia of their death,
> But by us, the disremembered, they cannot
> Ever be forgotten. For always, in all places,
> They will rise eloquently up to remind us
> Of the unforgettable allegiances behind us. (252)

Crucial here is the role of memory in the elegiac experience; the dead cannot ever be forgotten because they and the past persist in the memories of the living. Each of the dead had a veritable web of personal and social associations and relationships, the memory of which, it is asserted, will persist permanently for the survivors. Over against the lover's death and his permanent absence, the poet appeals to his memories of the whole spectrum of lived and encountered history experienced by himself and the dead pilot as well as all the others like themselves.

Nevertheless, though generally mindful of this broader context and historical experience, the poet is primarily intent on his own grief and the loss occasioning it. Thus, in the next stanza he underlines his sense of personal isolation, bereavement of love, and futile questioning of the pilot's present whereabouts. All of these indelibly underline the separation brought about by death. The poet's anguish is set over against the pilot's love of flying. For the pilot, flying was a kind of natural playing with danger and death that the poet recalls with a tacit envy overlain with desperate regret:

> Knowing that you . . .
> . . . will never again
> Kiss the teeth of the morning at a vivid four hundred,
> Uncurling, at nine angels, the gold and splendid
> Wake on which you walk across the sky. (252)

After celebrating the almost divine actions of his sky-god lover in elaborately metaphoric images, the poet turns in the next stanza to underlining the loss occasioned by the forces of memory. Everywhere he experiences the presence of the dead man, which serves to underscore his absence and the permanence of his loss. The beloved, in effect, is magnified in the first half of the stanza by his virtual identification with the natural world. But in the latter part of the stanza he is again the uniquely and personally beloved, and the poet promises to "hold him in my dreams / Until every moment seems / To reclaim part of him" (253). These memory-inspired visions rhetorically swell the degree and scope of the poet's sense of loss while tacitly making suspect his protestations of devoted recall and the likelihood of their permanence.

This oscillation between the immediately personal and individual grief on the one hand and the long-term declarations of the permanency of memory continues. Its aim here is to intensify the poet's sense of love and loss. Thus, in the next stanza the salt of the sea is fused with the poet's tears, and in doing so it "engenders the more of love" (253). With this intensification, the poet, as in *Lycidas,* visualizes the dead body in its full physical transformation by drowning: "his wreck is like a rock in my mouth / With his body on my tongue" (253). The starkness of this image and its unendurable weight brings the lamentation phase of the poem to its conclusion.

What follows in the second half of the poem is Barker's effort to explore the emotional and intellectual or spiritual counters to the finality of death. It is time that he identifies as remorselessly discountenancing any surviving lover and proving conclusively that "the heart needs more than faith / To help it to recover" (253). Like Thomas, Barker implicitly sets religious or spiritual faith over against human truth and finds the former lacking and the latter ineluctable: "under Northern Seas, his face / Fades as the seas wash over" (253).

Here he formulates a strikingly modern response to the dilemma of how to survive meaningfully. He invokes the dead lover himself to assume the responsibility to "dismiss the dividing / Grief. Bring, bring again the kiss and the guiding glory" (254). Viewed realistically or naturalistically, this invocation can have little force or power or effect; it is but the desperation of desire devoid of hope. This is perhaps why Barker, in the succeeding lines, calls upon another force or image to assist in this reversal of death, an image that is both natural and spiritual in its associations:

> . . . From his hiding
> Place in the cleft of the cloud, O dove of evening,
> Lead him back over the dark intervening
> Day when he died. (254)

This return of the dead, however, is not simply for the pilot's sake; it entails "a loving return to that room where I / Look out and see his death glittering in the sky" (254). Thus, it is an assuagement of the speaker's shock and grief as well through the invoking of the dove—a both natural and divine creature—to intercede in reversing the irreversible.

In ever so subtly shifting the poem's concern from the victim to the living sufferer, Barker makes more credible his invocation to the deceased. He modulates from the present into the future and invests the dove with more than natural powers. For with the raising of the dead, which ultimately is what Barker is asking of the dove, all killers are to be reconciled, their natural equivalents—storms—subdued, and mankind possessed of universal accord. Save for the pilot and the other dead, the entire world, Barker proclaims, will feel itself warming in a life-enhancing activity. This qualification, however, arouses fresh and challenging questions, questions which reorient the direction and the function of the poem itself. For if it is the return of the pilot from death that restores the speaker and the world of the living, how can the pilot still be dead? And if he is still dead, then the transfiguration has not really occurred and the spiritual power of the dove in all it associative force is subject to question and doubt.

At this point, the poem's elegiac focus gets fully absorbed into that of a love lyric as subject.[45] Its counter to death is seen to be the very poem itself and its highly inflected rhetoric. In the poem's final stanza, Barker tacitly reverses his invocation to his beloved. No longer does he request his "loving return" to their past togetherness. Now he enjoins the deceased to "sleep, long and beautiful," so that the poet may never again be tempted nor cheated "with the mirage / Of sensual satisfaction" (254). Instead his solace is found in a denial of death and a celebration of it as but an extended sleep: "To those that love there are no dead, / Only the long sleepers" (254).

The tacit abandonment of the lovers' togetherness is an implicit admission of the impossibility of transfiguration's occurring. It is also an acceptance of the harder fact that the beloved's loss need in no way constrain nor end the love of the living speaker. This last gives the central ground of the elegy to memory of love shared rather than to transcendence of grief explored. Indeed, so strongly is this felt that the speaker prefaces his concluding rejection of "sensual satisfaction" (254) with an anticipatory warning. As the deceased's resurrection is contemplated, the poet warns against it:

> Look, look, the grave shakes over his head
> And the red dirt stands up, as
> Across existence I beg him heed. (254)

The repudiation of transfiguration and resurrection is Barker's way of dramatizing that his central concern is the permanence of his (their) love rather than the persistence of the beloved's presence. It also is his way of establishing that his central act of remembrance is the creation of the poem itself and its enactment of his range of emotional responses, from the news of the death to his sublimation of it in his poetic rhetoric.

Barker's elegiac memorialization and celebration of the dead pilot is highly rhetorical, verging on the mythic, and resolutely general to the point of concealment of identity. The exact opposite is the case with Theodore Roethke's "Elegy for Jane."[46] Here the poem is immediately detailed and specific about the remembered reality of the dead girl, clear as to the poet's relation with her both through the subtitle and the text itself, and simple, almost conversational in language.[47] Unlike Barker, Roethke makes no effort to reflect the elegiac tradition other than in his commitment to memory as the medium for his largely tacit lament.[48] It is to the fullest realization of the once living person that the bulk of the poem is addressed. Only with the last two stanzas does Roethke inject his own feelings. These are expressed with the same simplicity and directness as the descriptive earlier stanzas. He focuses on three sentiments: the absence of the girl from the natural settings in which Roethke is accustomed to seeing her; the sense of helplessness he feels in the face of the fact of her death; and the lack of any socially sanctioned relationship with the deceased. In so doing, he attains a singularly poignant and immediate expression of sorrow and loss felt by a teacher for a student and one human being for another. For him, the avoidance of the traditional elegiac structure and the explicit rhetorical figures of grief enables him to break through the superstructure of convention that threatens to block the immediacy of his feelings.

Another chief difference between Barker's and Roethke's elegies is that the former dwells primarily on the speaker-poet's suffering and anguish to which the deceased is almost a cipher filled out only by his love of flying. Barker begins with the Romantic "I" as his center of concern. In contrast, Roethke focuses on his specific memories of the girl alive in all her individuality and personal uniqueness. He concentrates on the girl as object to be described and thus characterized rather than on himself as suffering subject. It is the thought of that liveliness, intensity, and vulnerability set in the context of an immediate natural setting and of their now irrevocable absence that dominates Roethke's vision. This recalled bevy of concrete traits of appearance and behavior fuses her as a person with other living creatures. The fish and birds are specifically identified with her for the purpose of intensifying her bodily slightness, her visual distinctiveness, her elusive intensity of moods, and, above all, her fragility and vulnerability in the face of the world. Roethke sees her as having lived always subject to overwhelmingly powerful and threatening forces wrought with implicit dangers.

Apart from the deep concern for her essential condition as a living creature and the absence of any consolation for her death, he can only testify to his helplessness and his outsider status in her life:

> If only I could nudge you from this sleep,
> My maimed darling, my skittery pigeon.
> Over this damp grave I speak the words of my love:
> I, with no rights in this matter,
> Neither father nor lover. (98)

In a very real sense, Roethke makes of his "no rights in this matter" an implicit plea for the elegiac note to be sounded for the death of anyone known casually and fleetingly. It is to be sounded by any empathic individual capable of words of love for the loss of life. Thus, a poem that appears at the outset to be resolutely personal becomes part of that extension of the self to the bounds of the attainable, which was one of Roethke's main poetic themes as well as one of his central activities.

A poem that purports to be personal in character and, like Roethke's, to employ a simple, direct style grounded in the natural world is James Wright's "Arrangements with Earth for Three Dead Friends." That the subject matter is the death of more than one friend suggests that the poem, unlike Roethke's, is bound to be more reflective than dramatic, more philosophical than directly elegiac. The anticipated poetic distance implied by the title with its almost technical term of "Arrangements" is reflected in the poem's structure and organization. The titular "Arrangements" conveys the intercessor role of the speaker/voice/poet and suggests the formal nature of funerals. This quality is extended by several structural facets. These include: the speaker poet's identifying a different aspect or characterization of the earth—"sweet," "bright," and "dark"—in each stanza; his shifting or changing the nature of the request or directive provided to earth in each stanza; and his modifying the major emotion or attitude—pity/pathos, celebration/joyful vitality, and sympathy/respect—dominating each stanza.[49]

All of these testify to the poet's conscious control of his material and to his using the elegiac occasion as an opportunity to think through what the death of friends truly entails. They also give a different focus to the poem than that of the shock and recoil from the immediate fact of death. They concentrate rather on the thought process and reflective summation instigated by the several deaths. In so doing, they prevent the elegiac form from collapsing into an almost comic maudlinity which the effort to attend simultaneously to three different deaths of three sharply different individuals would seem inevitably to produce.

By formalizing his responses to the deaths of a male child, a male singer, and a stoical woman "who knew / The change of tone, the human hope gone gray" (18), Wright subtly shifts the poem from being an outright elegy to an expression of the elegiac temper.[50] Such a shift is occasioned by the elimination, at least explicitly, of any expression of the poet's responses to or feelings about the deaths, that is, by the element of lament. What is left is a series of descriptive and metaphoric assertions about the dead individuals, the earth in which they are interred, and the natural worlds that they inhabited. Taken collectively, the three stanzas read almost like a series of epitaphs or monodies that, though heartfelt, dispassionately render summary judgments and assessments of the deceased individuals.[51] The effects of these low-keyed observations are multiple. They remind us of the frequency and the variety of death-forms in human affairs. They stifle or choke off the voice about to be upraised in lamentation. And finally, they acknowledge the specific sorts of loss suffered not by the poet alone but by the human world of sentient, articulate, and sensitive persons. All of these effects testify to the gradual emerging of an elegiac temper generated by the age's growing sense of the multiplicity of losses, the diversity of deaths, and the futility of giving vent to grief and sorrow over any of them.

This avoidance of the full elegy form and tone is also demonstrated by another of Wright's poems, namely, "Lament for My Brother on a Hayrake." The title points up the ominousness of the scene, but the poem itself both encourages and thwarts it by an internal clash of metaphor and literal statement. The death of a younger relative in a farming accident is anticipated by the haying season's being cast as a sacrificial one. Thus, the lethal nature of the farm equipment is rendered directly and laconically: "That bright machine / Strips the revolving earth of more than grass" (18). That the brother is an actual victim of the season and the harvesting activity is suggested most explicitly by the line "And so my broken brother may lie mown / Out of the wasted fallows" (18).

The all but mute implications that the brother functions as a simulacrum of the dying god of ancient harvest rituals shadow the metaphoric thrust of the poem. In so doing, they seemingly afford the poet / speaker a significant measure of emotional control. By making the brutal reality of death part of a time-honored ritual in which the individuality of the person is absorbed into the archetypal victim, the poet is able to move the death from accident to sacrifice. And yet this is but part of the suggestiveness of the poem's images and statements.

Other images and statements pull in an opposite direction, one in which lines carefully avoid direct or complete commitment to the poem's being a lament for an accidental death. Of these, perhaps the most compelling are: "He need not pass / Under the blade to waste his life and break" and the concluding lines "Corn-yellow tassels of his hair blow down, / The summer bear him sideways in a bale / Of darkness to October's mow of cloud" (18). In particular, the first of these suggests that the brother's fate is not that of death via accident so much as it is a life wasted. Implicit perhaps is the poet's critical view of his brother's commitment to the life of the body and farming. This life, as the poem stresses, is one of hard labor and inevitable and recurrent death. The fusion of the laborer and the task performed, of the "broken brother" and the "burlap shroud" indicates that farm life is not essentially a persistent physical struggle in which nature and man meet as "a bale / Of darkness to October's mow of cloud" (18). In effect, then, this lament appears to be less a lament for a death suffered by one known personally by the poet than a regretful, but deeply felt, lament for a wasted life.

As such, it implicitly raises many of the issues and attitudes in the age-old debate over the role of the artist versus that of the practical man, of language versus action, of contemplation versus performance. And whatever the merits of such a theme, and they are many, they create a focus and an effect that is not so much that of an elegy as a contemplative and incipiently celebratorial judgment of the poet's role in relation to that of his brother. In other words, while regret and sorrow for the death-in-life of a close relative permeates the language of the poem, there is also a logical implication of the preferable existence of the poet, and with that of an unspoken defense of poetry.

A more fully developed version of this perspective essays a broader vision of the place of the poet in the modern world. This is found in Charles Olson's "The Death of Europe." It contemplates Olson's own future as a poet through a lament for the death of a fellow poet, Rainer Gerhardt, whom he knew only through letters and manuscript exchanges.[52] Olson's response to Gerhardt's death is one of stunned disconcertment. This leads him into iterating casual and almost irrelevant events in his life that accompanied learning of his acquaintance's passing.

Yet Olson struggles to maintain his mind's focus on major issues of importance to both poets. Among these is the essentiality of articulating the full cultural significance of Rainer's death. Another is William Carlos Williams's cultural and poetic importance to both poets as they struggle to change the nature and role of poetry in the contemporary world. A third bears directly on his immediate elegiac concern: how to mourn properly Rainer's death so that even mankind's earliest past becomes a memorializing part of that death. And finally, there is Olson's own determination, only partially and fleetingly articulated, to persist in opening up poetry to new forms, rhythms, and perceptions emanating from life itself even as the ordinary man's life is opened to poetry. It is through this last aspiration that the poem generates its title and identifies its subject as the death of a continent and a culture with that of a single avant-garde poet. The enormity of this equation becomes a testimonial both to Olson's aspirations and to the centrality that poetry occupies for him.

This opening of poetry to life's ordinary experiences is dramatized at the outset by Olson recounting his mishearing of Rainer's fellow countryman remarking about Dionysus. The accident of mishearing is seen later to be a part of Rainer's symbolic value for Olson as the fertility god who no longer carries the thyrsus. In the same way, the classic elegiac poet's involved assessment of the difficulties inherent in appropriately mourning the subject's loss is transformed into Olson's flat, rhetorically uninflected statement:

> for my sense, still, is that,
> despite your sophistication
> and your immense labors . . .
> It will take some telling. (309)

Coupled with such beginnings, ostensibly consisting of randomness and casualness of utterance, is the sense of his diversified mental focus. Thus, Olson suddenly veers off into comments about Williams and the similar cultural positioning of Americans and Germans. All of these efforts at communicating significance appear at first sight to be acts either of accident or irrelevancy. To Olson and Gerhardt, however, they are authentic and meaningful utterances expressed in the staccato, abbreviated telegraphese first heard in poetry with Pound and Williams. Casual sounds, personal associations, and large encompassing themes are all part of the poetic Olson feels he and Gerhardt are destined to bring into being.

The intellectual and poetic struggle between equals sketched here has been transformed by death into a consolatory celebration of loss. With this, Olson recognizes his personal loss as entailing the loss of Rainer as an ally. Henceforth, he must face his poetic and cultural battles alone:

> Now I can only console you,
> sing of willows,
> and dead branches,
> worry the meanness'
> that you do not live,
> wear the ashes
> of loss
>   Neither of us
> carrying a stick
> any more (310)

The classical echoes of these lines capture Olson's characteristic conviction of the presentness of the past. They also underscore how far he is from that past through living in the twentieth century. Teddy Roosevelt's maxim about walking softly while carrying a big stick fuses with the ostensible abandonment of defensive postures by both America and Germany with the end of World War II. This fusion, of course, tacitly reflects the prevailing polar American political views at the time of the poem's composition in 1954. In addition, the lines reach forward by an anticipatory allusion to primitive and classical practices of marking out territory and asserting stability and permanence of being. In an extraordinarily complex range of associations, the stick image captures the full range of the loss Olson is feeling, which, he is convinced, factors into the whole scope of modern culture.

And yet one finds a curious kind of dissatisfaction with the lack of explicitness as to the *qualia* of the loss. Olson mantically invokes the past as a residuum of significance beyond words. As a result, he both arouses expectations, partially satisfies them symbolically, and then, in a subsequent section of the poem, thwarts their fulfillment by announcing the living poet's inability or incapacity to help the "last poet / of a civilization" (313):

> I can no longer
> put anything
> into your hands
>
> It does no good
> for me to wish
> to arm you. (312)

In a sense, Olson here begins by calling up the mantic origins of the poet in order to acquire the power of poetry's original role. Then, he tacitly admits the inefficacy of its ancient symbols and images to draw the specifics of Rainer's loss into the full range of his consciousness and the whole spectrum of contemporary cultural reality.

The reason for this tacit admission of personal and historical incapability lies in the inescapable fact that the present world is conditioned by several crucial factors. One is that historically mankind has not been correctly informed or informally taught: "our grandmothers / . . . / did not tell us / the proper tales" (312). Another is that only belatedly does he realize the limitations of physical mortality: "the body / does bring us / down" (314). And finally, the recognition of the things of the world as metaphysically constrained is reached reluctantly: "The stick, / and the ear / are to be no more than, they are" (314). Taken together, they result in the grim admission that human existence consists, at least at the present time and perhaps since its beginning, of an "impossible / life" (314).

Such a conclusion is only partially a pessimistic denial of the resources and promises inherent in language, poetry, aspiration, and personal effort. It is also, and more centrally, a drawing back from the eternality of promise resident in the Romantic view of the world and existence. It is a scaling down of human effort by setting it in the full context of reality and history as comprehended by a single consciousness facing without mediation the conditions of living. All that the modern poet, unlike his predecessors, can do is more restricted philosophically. He can recognize his limitations: "I give you no visit / to your mother" (314). He can perform those tasks of which he is capable, however simple they may be: "I open my hand / to throw dirt / into your grave" (315). He can recognize the value of aspiration no matter how apparently pointless in view of the conclusions drawn earlier in the poem: "It was your glory to know / that we must mount" (315). And finally, he can persist in affirming the duty of poets and others who still live to make the effort to effect change: "Let us who live / try" (316). Together, all of these amount to taking clear-eyed stock of the possibilities inherent in actual life.

What, then, "The Death of Europe" does is affirm the elegiac temper as endemic to human affairs. It does so through an intricate process of calling up the conventions of the elegiac dating from classical and preclassical times. These all have to do with death, revival, transformation, and celebration. Yet this process of recall shows that "The images / have to be / contradicted / The metamorphoses / are to be / undone" (314). All that is left and all that matters is the ongoingness of the complex human effort. Contemporary mankind can persist in bringing change into the world, in getting man's relation to the universe right, and, in Pound's phrase, making it new. For Olson, the death of Europe fundamentally involves two things. One is the disappearance of a civilization enshrined in the physical loss of one human being. At the same time, it is coupled with the persistent effort to create something radically new and different for the living to inhabit. As such, the poem stands poised as an unsentimental but not unfeeling farewell to the modernism of Pound, densely and intrinsically historically tendriled as it was, and an uncertain, tentative reaching out of creative welcome to postmodernism.

Perhaps the most striking feature of these four poets' elegies for individual friends is the diversity of their concerns. At one pole stands Barker with his structurally conventional lament for an individual who was also his lover. At the other extreme, Olson, summoning up many of the innovative technical strategies of twentieth-century verse, transforms a casual acquaintance known only at a remove as it were into a symbol of the contemporary poet. By seeing him in relation to his society and culture, he makes the lament for his passing into a desperately concerned probing of its broadest implications. Among these are the possible cultural loss of the poet as a figure and role and the resultant crisis of understanding that loss entails through man's gradual loss of history and the knowledge of the past.

The difference between a friend who is a lover and one who is a cultural icon obviously is enormous. Sexual passion and cultural change represent the extremes of personal individuality and general differentiation. To group them both under the term "friend" is to chart both a change in definition and a transformation in the kind of lament and sorrow the loss of each occasions. Between them stand two other forms of affection as well as distinct modulations in the elegiac temper they generate. For Roethke, a friend who is a student arouses compassion rather than passion. The loss he registers is that for someone he has carefully observed and cared about intensely but dispassionately. The untimeliness of her demise points up the pathos of her loss. Sorrow for the loss of someone known solely but closely through the externals of demeanor is significantly different in intensity and focus from grief over the loss of a person with whom one has known physical intimacy. The intensity of the latter reflects the loss by the survivor of his dominant role in life, while the sorrow for another human being's death generates in the survivor only a desperate uncertainty as to his justification in shaping an elegiac remembrance at all. In effect, the one clings to a past relationship while the other questions the existence and nature of any relationship other than that provided by the artificially generated one of social custom.

As for Wright, the affection whose loss is celebrated issues not so much in specifically individual recollection as in assessment of the changes wrought for the survivor by the deaths of the three he only tacitly elegizes. Both he and Roethke represent forms of uncertainty about the very act of elegizing. The latter captures the century's shift away from public mourning by an entire community and echoes its concentration on the select individuals entitled by society to articulate their feelings. Wright, on the other hand, tentatively and therefor somewhat obliquely records in summation the lives of the dead. He is concerned to characterize, as is Roethke, but his effort is to arrive at generalizations that concretely summarize the individual's life and what the survivor can do to provide them with succor and sustenance. Wright's uncertainty about the appropriate form for elegizing is shrouded in his distancing himself from the full identities of his friends. He compensates for this by substituting epitaphs that celebrate the diversity of death and of friends and that encapsulate brief directives for remembering them as they lived:

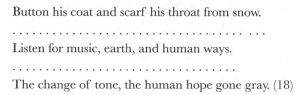

> Button his coat and scarf his throat from snow.
>
> . . . .
>
> Listen for music, earth, and human ways.
>
> . . . .
>
> The change of tone, the human hope gone gray. (18)

Wright, like Olson, sees starkly the grave uncertainty of the past, but his concern is personal rather than cultural. At the same time, his tone is not that of Barker's rhetorical exclamatory reliance on the power of language to achieve a fresh understanding of death. Instead it is the almost mute recognition that the response of the survivor is limited almost exclusively to acknowledging the fact of mortality.

A final group of poems continues, in part, this struggle to reconcile the poet's concerns with the specific and the general, the individual and the universal, while also endeavoring to capture the almost inarticulate moan of pain and grief at the death of a relative.[53] It begins with Archibald MacLeish's "Memorial Rain" and Thomas Merton's elegy for his brother killed in World War II. Each deals with the death of a family member set in a broader historical context of death and cultural destruction. And it ends with Jon Silkin's fiercely controlled description of the death of his infant son. Here, by way of contrast, the poet's attention is relentlessly focused on the child to the exclusion of virtually any context whatsoever. Mediating between these two extremes are three poems that focus on the action of memory and the emotions it arouses: Theodore Roethke's "Elegy," Patrick Kavanagh's "In Memory of My Mother," and Dylan Thomas's "Do not go gentle into that good night." Each deals with a parent or quasi-parental figure who occupies a position of prime personal and emotional significance for the poet.[54]

What this group of poems also raises is a series of questions that challenge the elegiac tradition in a variety of ways. For one, they probe the effectiveness of the praise-lamentation duo in dealing with the full range of losses that bear on the contemporary poet. Thus, MacLeish and Merton suppress any form of praise of the deceased, while Roethke and Kavanagh evade direct expressions of sorrow by focusing on remembered everyday acts of the dead and seeing them as somehow still alive. The thrust of all these poems is toward a realistic recollection rather than an encomiastic celebration.

They display, too, the developing uncertainties in the modern world for the traditional grounds of authority underlying the elegy. MacLeish, sensing the loss of cultural and psychological authority, tacitly deploys nature as authenticating his feeling of loss while stressing a satiric response to its cause. Both deny prevailing modes of remembrance; neither praise nor lamentation are voiced directly, largely because neither appears effective or defensible. Merton, it is true, finds a rhetorical confidence in his Roman Catholic tradition as centered on the figure of Christ. But in so doing, he points up the special nature of his case and its role as an exception to the prevailing temper of the age. His personal history and his stress on Christ, too, as a slain figure call in question the viability of religious authority for the modern elegist. Or to put it another way, the authority in which he trusts operates for him personally, and in so doing, it characterizes him as a member of a subclass, as a religious or Catholic poet, whose supporting authority is unable to command the assent of the bulk of other modern poets and their audience.

A kind of corroboration of this assessment is found in Patrick Kavanagh's poem in which a poet who shared Merton's spiritual faith sedulously avoids relying on religious authority. Instead Kavanagh focuses on memorializing his mother without elegiacally mourning her. By achieving a resolution to her death through recalling her in images and metaphors drawn from their everyday life, he essentially elects to find his ground of authority in the elegiac temper that sees death as controllable or endurable by avoidance of its contemplation and mourning as substitutable by past memories. His thoughts of his mother and Silkin's of his infant son both center their search for less traditional forms of authority in specific personal memories whose secular cast constitutes not so much a rejection as an avoidance of religion as such a ground. The latter in particular sidesteps his subject's temptation to sentimentality by electing the position of a largely detached observer who almost clinically chronicles the infant's slow movement from birth defect to death. Their aim is not so much the venting of sorrow and grief in explicit and sustained lamentation as the exercising of rigorous control over powerful emotions that are felt to be inexpressible.

Dylan Thomas's "Do not go gentle into that good night" confronts the issues of elegiac authority and the adaptation or modification of the elegiac tradition both more directly and innovatively than the other poems in this group. Between himself and his dying father he admits of no intermediary voice: not nature as with MacLeish, not secular and personal memories as with Roethke and Kavanagh, not religion as with Merton, and not clinical observation as with Silkin. There is only his own voice speaking directly and forcefully, enjoining his father to a concentrated and ferocious anger against his own mortality. The authority on which his novel handling of the elegiac form rests is purely personal, powerfully emotional, and calculated to support his creation of a new addition to the tradition. He declines the various forms of consolation inherent in the elegiac convention in part because he is concerned to articulate not an elegy so much as a pre-elegy for a still living subject. The present and life, not the past and death, are his chief focus. Neither memories nor mourning, neither acceptance of death nor enduring of loss are his immediate concern. Stoicism, faith, and acceptance, variously invoked by the other poets, are alien both to his personal feelings and to his poetic challenge. Only anger, not at others, as with MacLeish, but at mortality itself, can provide the impetus to his pre-elegiac shaping of what cannot be a lamentation of death but rather an enjoining of life to resist mortality endlessly, and if not endlessly, then as long as possible.

With the completion of this conspectus of concerns, it is time to turn back to these poets's efforts to mesh the general and individual concerns raised by the loss of a friend or relative. MacLeish's poem, in particular, stands in relation to Olson's in an illuminating way. Both focus the death of someone close to them through the prism of history. In doing so, they underscore two phenomena: the survivor's view of and response to a recently past war, and the nature of the deceased as a victim of society and culture, both of which ironically still live. Thus, both poems embody a characteristic attitude of their age toward its war and those who officially sanctioned it.

MacLeish, writing some seventy years before Olson, sharply polarizes the poet's remembrance of his brother against the official, ambassadorial response. His aim is to undercut the essential trivializing role of the latter in the face of the personal sense of physical loss. In doing so, he implicitly establishes a sharp distinction between the corrupt, valueless world of officialdom and the memory-haunted world of the individual and the personal; the latter is held to be guiltless and free of any responsibility for the death or deaths being memorialized. The poem's basic attitude—a co-mingling of the satiric and elegiac—recalls the caustic anger and outrage of Sassoon, though muted or restrained by a more dispassionate irony. Such a view emblemizes a common attitude of the 1920s toward World War I: a bitter sense of betrayal, public indifference, and heartbreak at young lives wasted wantonly.

In contrast, Olson merges or fuses the public and the personal. In so doing, his poem testifies both to the greater complexity of awareness and to the increased uncertainty of belief and conviction of those surviving World War II. Olson's own poetic habit of moving abruptly and without connectives from cultural to individual perceptions and concerns, like Pound's, is a testimonial surely enough to the aesthetics of high modernism. But it also reflects its age's uncertainty as to there being a viable intellectual or cultural framework capable of ordering consciousness and thinking per se. And yet Olson is aware, too, that this uncertainty testifies also to there being a closer, more fundamental—more organic if you will—relationship between public/cultural matters and personal/individual concerns than MacLeish and his era were willing to admit. In effect, it is precisely here that Olson's primitivism plays a crucial role. His allusions to classical and preclassical objects, symbols, and ways of thinking capture the sense of mankind's struggles to comprehend things unclear and imprecise by their very nature. In effect, the primitive references identify for Olson that contemporary man's efforts at comprehension are of essentially the same order as those of his earliest counterparts.

For MacLeish the loss of his brother is memorialized not by a traditional elegy. Such a formal public address using the language of polite discourse and invoking the sentiments of convention is left to his satiric target, Ambassador Pusey. Instead he draws on personal awareness and reflection. These employ memory and immediate sensations to somehow energize the dead into, if not life, then at least its imminence. In effect, MacLeish suggests language, his own very medium, is suspect, corrupted by officialdom. Consequently, his elegiac temper can express itself only through his own private acts of memory and sensory awareness of nature. Both generate an empathetic response to the fact of the dead soldiers and to the psychological need for regeneration:

> *This earth their bones have hallowed, this last gift*
> *A grateful country . . .*
> . . . .
> Under the dry grass stem
> The words are blurred, are thickened, the words sift
> Confused by the rasp of the wind, by the thin grating
> Of ants under the grass, the minute shift
> And tumble of dusty sand separating
> From dusty sand. The roots of the grass strain,
> Tighten, the earth is rigid, waits—he is waiting—
> And suddenly, and all at once, the rain! (103)[55]

Paradoxically enough, MacLeish makes a poem out of what amounts to a diary of sensations, memories, reflections, and feelings, that is, out of nonlinguistic elements. The poem is, in effect, a transcript of these personal awarenesses and as such implicitly denies or rejects culture and language in favor of nature and the natural. The rationale for this lies, ironically enough, in the ambassador's words, which suggest that the dead soldiers are better off because they are beyond pain and hurt and so can be called *"these happy, happy dead"* (103). A society and government whose gratitude consists of such sentiments delivered in a distant, foreign country betray their loss of cultural and psychological authority. They are incapable of recognizing—much less saluting—the fact that the dead brother's being "a stranger in that land" intensifies "a tightening of roots" (102) for home in both him and his surviving brother. Mere words declaring that the dead buried in Flanders make it part of America persuade neither the dead nor the living. The society's de facto denial of the elegy as a cultural monument drives the poet toward the elegiac temper as a surrogate form of mourning and release. Solace and reconciliation (if that is possible in this case) must come, then, not from rhetoric and conscious mental manipulation. For MacLeish, they are found in the actuality of the natural world: from "the wind's flowing"; from the sensation of "his bones in the sand / Listening" (102); from "the thin grating / Of ants under the grass"; and "the roots of the grass" (103).

This sensory minimalism, reminiscent of Hemingway's response to World War I, is the antithesis of Olson's elegiac temper. Olson opts for William Carlos Williams's focus on the physical object. Yet unlike Williams, his objects are enshrined in an unstructured welter of cultural phenomena resurrected from a plurality of cultures. The object—Rainer's suicidal body—is seen through and with the aid of an overlay of competing cultures rendered by the poet. In effect, Olson, the postmodernist, functions more like a modernist poet such as Eliot or Pound than does MacLeish, the sedulous imitator of modernism who was a compatriot of Eliot and Pound rather than a member of another generation. Here, at any rate, MacLeish functions more in the manner of the imagist poet, though, to be sure, without the full austerity of limitation practiced by Pound or H.D.

A quite different approach to lamenting the wartime death of a relative is taken in Thomas Merton's "For My Brother: Reported Missing in Action, 1943." Unlike MacLeish, Merton directs no attention, sardonic or otherwise, to society's part in occasioning or perpetuating the conflict, much less in celebrating its memory. In doing so, he not only contrasts with a poet like Sassoon but reflects the attitudinal shift from World War I to its successor. Generally speaking, the latter avoids the sharp attack on military decisions and actions and the equally sharp differentiation between civilian and military personnel. Merton's focus is exclusively on his brother and himself, the dead and the living, and their existence in the image of Christ. The central figure of the Christian religion is the only reference to the poet's cultural nexus allowed to enter the poem, and it does so exclusively for its religious symbolism, not for its cultural implications. Christ's tears are shed not only for His own death but for Merton's brother's death as well as for Merton's own life-threatening sorrow. Yet in being so shed, they are seen by the poet in the closing lines as the instrument for the homecoming of the missing one:

> The silence of Whose tears shall fall
> . Like bells upon your alien tomb.
> Hear them and come: they call you home. (13)

This desire to effect a homecoming rather than recoil from the fact of the death or desire for easing of the sorrow at the loss is what dominates the poet's consciousness. The reason for this essentially is to document the secular sacrifices wrought by war as having been subsumed in the greater sacrifice of Christ's death:

> When all the men of war are shot
> And flags have fallen into dust,
> Your cross and mine shall tell men still
> Christ died on each, for both of us. (12)

Indeed, the poem as a whole functions almost as a kind of imitation of Christ, with the poet obliquely striving to emulate in subdued and homely fashion the actions of Christ. The first stanza reiterantly stresses the poet's abnegate view of himself in relation to his dead brother. A series of conditional statements concludes with the brother imaged as a "poor traveller" rescued by the paradoxical transformations of the poet's physical sufferings (sleeplessness, inability to eat, fasting, and thirst) into "springs for you" (12).

The second stanza moves from the conditional mode to the interrogative and, in so doing, the poet assumes a Christ-like attitude of commiserative pity and selfless concern: "And in what landscape of disaster / Has your unhappy spirit lost its road?" (12). The sacrificial attitude of the living for the dead reaches its most overt expression in the third stanza:

> Come, in my labor find a resting place
> And in my sorrows lay your head,
> Or rather take my life and blood
> And buy yourself a better bed—
> Or take my breath and take my death
> And buy yourself a better rest. (12)

The poet's effort to bring his brother home is clearly symbolic or psychological, but to him it is also a profoundly religious, Christian act that emulates those of Christ Himself.

As such, this effort must perforce risk ridicule and suspicion if there is to be a true and full sacrifice of self. Merton consciously faces this, such as when he allows his commiseration to spill over into what can be taken for condescension toward his brother. The references to the brother's travels during war and death, to having lost his way, to being offered the opportunity to buy a better bed, all suggest an almost smug superiority of attitude by the priest-poet toward the secular life of the soldier. In so doing, they recall Wright's similar covert feeling for his farmer brother. Merton accepts such a challenge secure in the religious conviction that Christ's sacrifice of his own life is for all men and not simply for those who have chosen wisely. In effect, this conviction fuses the brothers into a unity of being that redeems the elegiac object, the dead brother. He moves from a stranger's existence in a "landscape of disaster" (12) and a residency in an "alien tomb" (13) to the ultimate home, shared with all men, in the salvation of Christ where no one is ultimately lost or dead in a "desolate and smokey country" (12).

Essentially, Merton begins by lamenting the loss of his brother in a foreign land, then moves to a growing sacrificial identification with his sibling, and concludes by finding both his life and his brother's death subsumed in the paradoxical image of Christ, who both "lies slain" and also continues to weep for both the dead and the living. This image fuses the figure of the elegiac object (the dead brother) and the elegist (the living poet) in a manner that both deepens the lament for the dead and includes the lamenter as spiritually warranting inclusion in the lament.

Theodore Roethke's "Elegy" for his Aunt Tilly is more completely a memorial of its subject, a strong, caring, independent woman on whom change is wrought less by death than by illness. For the poet, his memories are of a woman whose life brims with compassionate acts for both the living and the dead. Yet she is not afraid to "laugh at herself" nor to chase children from her fruit tree in order to pursue her acts of kindness to "the infirm, the mad, the epileptic" (215). In zeroing in on the specific acts of concern that characterize his aunt, the poet both creates a full-bodied character and a moral question that implicitly impinges on Merton's religious view.

After recounting her embodying of true charity in small, neighborly gestures, he condenses her demise into a single image and statement whose irony is neither blunted by outrage nor carried beyond its utterance: "And yet she died in agony, / Her tongue at the last, thick, black as an ox's" (215). Why such kindliness and charitable behavior should be so served at her final reckoning is seen by the poet exactly as Aunt Tilly would have regarded it. Death simply is a part of life in which neither justice, moral reward, nor public recognition are to be expected. His limiting his focus to the physicality of her dying is, in effect, his acknowledgment of her own attitude to her life: "And, with a harsh rasp of a laugh at herself, / Faced up to the worst" (215).

In doing so, he also catches up his initial perception as to her outlook and why it has moved him to elegize her: "Between the spirit and the flesh—what war? / she never knew; / For she asked no quarter and gave none" (215). The unity of body and spirit, the natural and the transcendent or divine, allows no room for sighs or expressions of mourning.

Roethke's enunciation of this viewpoint clearly is at odds with his determination to elegize her reality as a person of substance and worth. The conventions of the elegy are ostensibly denied to him and so he is compelled neither to acknowledge her death nor to find consolation in or through it. Instead, he daringly celebrates her as having triumphed over death in the same characteristically homely and strong fashion as she lived:

> Terror of cops, bill collectors, betrayers of the poor,—
> I see you in some celestial supermarket,
> Moving serenely among the leeks and cabbages,
> Probing the squash,
> Bearing down, with two steady eyes,
> On the quaking butcher. (215)

Such a scene has more than a touch of the comic, as does the poem's subject herself. Yet this does not lower the emotional gravity of the poem's essential morality. Actually, the comic setting and cast of characters are Roethke's ways of moving past the moral indignation at a universe and its creator which compel the genuinely good person to suffer indescribable agony. By seeing his Aunt Tilly not with her tongue as "black as an ox's" dying in agony but as roaming still alert through "some celestial supermarket" (215), the poet sees her not as dead but as alive in some other place. The moral and religious question of how a divine being can countenance suffering for the individual undeserving of it is set aside or bracketed. Instead, he makes a concentrated imaginative effort to create a world in which she still lives as she always had, namely, as a strong, courageous, independent defender of those incapable of their own defense.

Through Roethke's transformation of elegiac conventions, he achieves a secular equivalent of Merton's religious effort to achieve solace. Both, in effect, surrender their being to the image of a person greater than themselves capable of "moving serenely" (215), relentlessly, and eternally through the world in pursuit of a timeless goal. Roethke's poem, then, functions as an elegy, a celebration of the absence of a vital presence, without direct or explicit mourning. As the poet/ speaker's attitude, it substitutes admiration and humorous recollection for sorrow and grief. Merton's poem, on the other hand, follows a more conventional approach to the elegiac subject by invoking a religious rather than a secular perspective. He distances the speaker from the one he has lost and then reconciles them in an image of transcendency in which the principal power is not that of memory or recollection but belief or faith.

Patrick Kavanagh's "In Memory of My Mother" is in many ways closer to Roethke than to Merton even though religious faith is part of the setting in which the mother exists. Kavanagh, too, begins with an act of conscious memory, but he deliberately contrasts the memory of present actuality with that of past recollection. In doing so, he, like Roethke, opts for the past as a way of memorializing without explicitly mourning:

> I do not think of you lying in the wet clay
> Of a Monaghan graveyard; I see
> You walking down a lane among the poplars
> On your way to the station. (163)

The poem as a whole is an extended effort at recollection of four past incidents and scenes through which the mother moves "happily" and thoughtfully "so full of repose, so rich with life" (163). Each incident, as in Roethke, recalls a characteristic daily action that occasions no public attention yet movingly captures the nature of the mother and her close and easy relation to her son. These are surrounded by opening and closing stanzas that create a frame for these memories. This frame focuses on the poet's deliberate act of choice with regard to the memories available to him. The poem's conclusion asserts this even as it indicates his resolution of the problem occasioned by the actuality of his mother's death:

> O you are not lying in the wet clay,
> For it is a harvest evening now and we
> Are piling up the ricks against the moonlight
> And you smile up at us—eternally. (163)

His choice is, in fact, tantamount to a rejection of the elegy as a form in favor of an elective series of happy memories. And yet the elegiac temper of these lines indicates that Kavanagh is aware that he is avoiding the realities forced on the elegist—acceptance of death and mourning of loss. In their place is a metaphor that hangs tantalizingly between the secular and the sacred. Thus, like Roethke, he makes of metaphor and image a resolution to a situation that he either wishes not to or cannot face directly. The literal fact of the death of one who is not only deeply loved but whose life occasions admiration akin to awe is a basic topic of the elegiac tradition. And in avoiding or deflecting it, the poet celebrates its replacement by the modern elegiac temper. Kavanagh here calls up an earlier memory that functions as a substitute-formation analogous to Eliot's Shakespearian allusion to the drowned father's eyes of pearl.

Unlike the other poems just examined here, Dylan Thomas's "Do not go gentle into that good night" functions as a pre-elegy. It was his almost convulsive desire to avoid having to face his father's death that gave rise to this justly celebrated poem. Out of the fact that he is not yet in a position to write an elegy, his subject still being alive, Thomas launches a furious appeal to his father to choose the manner and mode of his death. It is important to recognize that the poet does not try to have his father avoid or escape death; the inescapability of the elder Thomas's passing is not questioned.[56] Thus, it is possible for his son to write a poem whose injunctive mode nevertheless allows it to assume much of the form and manner of the elegy save for the actuality of the death on which the poem depends. In essence, Thomas here achieves a kind of pre-elegy.[57] The poet's feelings of frustration, rage, anguish, helplessness merge into a plea for a final effort of resistance. To struggle against "the dying of the light" and the onset of "that good night" (116), which signals the ultimate separation of the dead from the living, is, in effect, to avoid having to write an elegy per se by composing instead such a pre-elegy.[58]

In enjoining such an effort, Thomas rigorously structures the poem so as to make his plea more than a heartfelt plea of a son bereft of all but despair and language. By focusing on the attitudes and reactions of other men to their deaths, the poet implicitly shapes a tradition and convention into which the subject of his pre-elegy can and should fit if he will but elect to do so. The poet's choice of those who are wise, good, wild, and grave to constitute this tradition allows him to reconcile his father's and his own quite different foci for living. The wise and the good correspond to the taciturn propriety and good sense of his father. The wild and grave "who see with blinding sight" (116), on the other hand, more nearly capture the outlook of the socially unconventional and visionary poet.[59] In making the pre-elegy encompass both his father's and his own values, Thomas implicitly directs the injunctions at himself as well. And since he saw the poet as a symbol of man as articulate, language-using being, he moves this most personal of poems on to a level of universality as a cry of resistance to mankind as a whole to "rage against the dying of the light" (116).

Nor is Thomas's convention of the dead a recollection of triumph on the part of the departed. Quite the reverse. Precisely "because their words has forked no lightning" (116) the wise refuse to go gently to their death. The same "might-have-been" recoil against death is true of the good. At the end, they apprehend that their deeds could have commanded greater public recognition had they manifested the power to rage against the darkness of living. Similarly, the wild ones, the poets who "sang the sun in flight" (116), come to see too late that their actions were also part of the passage of time and the movement toward night.[60] The convention is, in short, a monument to human mortality and fallibility and a tacit admission of the necessary incompleteness of human life. For Thomas, the only appropriate final response to this is furious anger either at the waste of life ever to achieve its ultimate goals or at human misconceptions about the nature of life. What the convention testifies to above all else is the essential human need not to acquiesce in the limitations of existence but to shout furiously, energetically, and unconventionally. To "rage against the dying of the light" (116) is the elegiac temper's response to the futility of such efforts.

For Thomas, death as occurred fact is less the adversary than is death as oncoming inevitability signaling the end of human effort, aspiration, and struggle. Death is not something to be overcome or to be reconciled with through elegiac conventions nor to be transcended by religious invocations of image and icon. It is something whose advent is the occasion for instinctual, violent resistance.[61] Because the advent is the moment of poetic as well as physical action, Thomas writes a pre-elegy rather than an elegy proper. In it, new and different conventions are invoked to channel and release the anticipatory responses to the loss of a father. These include: the irretrievability of the absence; the unexercised opportunities for personal contact, whether of cursing or blessing; and the implicit sense that all the responses felt are for the mourner-to-be as well as for the mourned one.

The final poem in this series—Jon Silkin's "Death of a Son"—differs dramatically from Thomas's angry plea to his father by creating a figure of unrelieved pathos through an extended metaphor linking an old house and silence. A heart-wrenching pathos founded on an almost inarticulate acceptance of death stands in the place of Thomas's furious insistence on resisting its approach.[62] It captures the perceived nature of the child even while chronicling his brief, sad life. The emotional focus for the poem is presented by the subtitle—"(who died in a mental hospital aged one)"—which embodies the subject's condition and dictates the sentiments aroused by the poem. In a very real sense, the subtitle is crucial in conditioning the significance and resonance of the images. It also justifies the slow remorselessness of the narrative's progress. By its steady implacability, it becomes a mediating conveyor of the welter of inexpressible emotions aroused by the events it records.

What keeps the poem under control is precisely Silkin's avoidance of directly sentimentalizing the subject. Thus, he steadfastly refuses to link his son to the ordinary appearance and reactions of human beings:

> Something has ceased to come along with me.
> Something like a person: something very like one.
> And there was no nobility in it
> Or anything like that.
>
> Something was there like a one year
> Old house, dumb as stone. (8)

The child's constant silence contrasts with the only intermittent quietness of other children. He exhibits no response nor betrays any function. The child neither blessed nor forsook silence, "but rather, like a house in mourning / Kept the eye turned in to watch the silence" (8).

In effect, the child's being linked to such a house makes of him a kind of mourner of his own condition. Consequently, the father/poet who is mourning through the very language of the poem is made to stand at a distance from the event. He becomes, as it were, a kind of secondary mourner to the primary one. This self-reflexivity of suffering is so intense and watchful for its end that it compels the secondary mourner to liken it to "something religious in his silence . . . something to do with death" (9). Though speechless, the child's demeanor conveys to his father that his son is awaiting his death in the contemplative quietistic manner of a religious attitude. In short, the primary mourner's manner compels the rigorous control of the narrative presented by the secondary mourner, the poet. Only in that way can the poet fully honor the event of his child's short life and the death which ends it.

The variable line length, the absence of rhyme, the slow repetitive rhythm, the recurring images all yield a sense of agonizing solemnity to a situation that easily could veer into sentimentality of an egregious order. And yet these tactics themselves carry their own risk of emotional bankruptcy. By tempting the poem to continue unduly, they could easily reduce its genuine pathos to the bathos of many late nineteenth-century elegies. Silkin avoids this temptation in his two culminating stanzas, where he records the child's direct confrontation with his death while appearing to mourn it silently:

> And then slowly the eye stopped looking
> Inward. The silence rose and became still.
> The look turned to the outer place and stopped
> With the birds still shrilling around him.
> And as if he could speak
>
> He turned over on his side with his one year
> Red as a wound
> He turned over as if he could be sorry for this
> And out of his eyes two great tears rolled, like stones,
> and he died. (9)

The swiftness of the death, the mute confrontation of it, and the explicitness of the self-reflexive mourning conspire to make of the narrative an almost unspoken elegy of an elegiac death. In doing so, the final stanzas maintain the poem's integrity and control while enabling the secondary mourner ultimately to supplant the primary one. This dual achievement fuses the traditional elegiac form with this strikingly dramatic innovation.

The supplanting of the child as mourner by the father is achieved by the latter's deft turning to the repeated simile "as if." It establishes unequivocally that the child's reactions and demeanor are attributions made by the father and so are subject to his feelings and perceptions. And yet the simile comes to rest against the observed fact that "out of his eyes two great tears rolled" (9). This observation is definite and unqualified, but it is the simile's role to render it a fully human rather than a merely physical reaction. This is done by attributing to it the human possibilities of speech and sorrow. With this, the grief of the parent is unspokenly intensified into an apex of feeling. This is achieved through the linguistic projection unto the child of those human feelings which in life it had never been able to exhibit. In such a manner, the bond between parent and child is finally established. By reiterantly relying on the image of child and house, the rest of the poem has declined to do this, and in so doing, has allowed the parental feelings to remain under control. At the same time, the last lines suggest the psychic resolution of the father's sorrow.

Historical Presences

*G*etting a fix on the nature of historicity for the elegiac poet and temper is a complex undertaking. One obvious way is to consider who and how they respond to persons that warrant memorialization of their loss. This entails treating such persons as cultural and personal presences. Representative poems by a diverse number of poets can be ordered into three main groups. First, there are historical figures carrying some compelling justification, at least in the poet's eyes, for their recognition. These constitute the focus of the first section of the present chapter. Then, there is a range of writers of varying degrees of reputation, from the world-famous to those of regional appreciation and finally to those enjoying simply individual regard by the poet. These are dealt with in the next section. The third and last group consists of a variety of elegiac poems on a single poet, namely, Dylan Thomas. They are considered in the last section of the chapter. From such an examination, one may well be able to tease out some implications for the modern age's sense of the diverse functions of the elegiac form, for the historical nature of memory in general, and for the collective assessment of the role of the poet in the modern world.

The first and largest of these subgroups has to do with those historical personages singled out for formal remembrance by poets ranging from Ezra Pound to Frank O'Hara. They memorialize figures as historically distant as Prince Henry Plantagenet and as central to popular culture as Billie Holiday. In so doing, they are testifying both to the scope of meaningful memory and to its increasing centrality for an age whose history is growing incrementally. They are also documenting two things of historical significance. The first, albeit largely unconsciously, is the deformalization of history as a factor in human life. And the second is its increasing identification with the past viewed as a totality rather than as a collection of segments.

Prominent Figures

A pivotal poem here is Ezra Pound's "Planh for the Young English King," which introduces the problematic nature of the historical at the outset. It does so by itself being based on another poem from an earlier age, a poem written in a foreign language (Provençal) by Bertrans de Born (1140–1215).[1] In doing so, it raises the question of its own poetic nature and its relation to de Born's earlier poem. The issue of whether it is an original, autonomous poem or a translation or an imitation or a modal recognition raises a series of problems having to do with its historical reality and perspective.[2]

The title, epigraph, and language of the poem all testify to its deliberate involvement with a distinct and specific historical period and culture. And yet the implications of this earlier age for Pound's own are deliberately suppressed by the dramatic monologue form used by the poet.[3] Such a tack, however, serves only to raise the identity of the poet to problematic status. Is the poet the troubadour de Born rendered through Pound's "translation" or is he, Pound, assuming the voice and mask of a predecessor? In the former case, the "translation" has to be regarded as a transparent medium that seeks simply to make de Born's sentiments accessible to a later, foreign culture. But in the latter, which from historical and documentary evidence available is the more likely,[4] the language and the speaker's attitude both bring Pound's age and personality into the interpretive equation. In effect, what is Pound's purpose in using de Born as an embodiment of the Provençal troubadour culture?[5] And how does he see that culture as well as that of its subject, twelfth-century England, in relation to his own Anglo-American modern world?

The poem's speaker laments Prince Henry's death essentially as a witness to the uniqueness and cultural centrality that he occupies in the speaker's own world. It is not as a Romantic sorrower for his own personal and private loss of a deeply beloved individual that he declares:

> If all the grief and woe and bitterness,
> All dolour, ill and every evil chance
> That ever came upon this grieving world
> Were set together they would seem but light
> Against the death of the young English King. (36)

The enormity of this loss is virtually beyond the mind's capacity to encompass fully since, implicitly at any rate, it postulates a universe that is eternal and infinite.[6] And yet over against all the other forms of loss possible in the world stands the single historical moment of the prince's death, which renders all other loss as "light" (36). The logical structure of this encomiastic lament is akin to that propounded by Christ's passion. Its uniqueness, its scope, its imperative value, its incommensurability, its centrality to the world and culture, its devastating impact on the good of the world, all are mourned. They are lamented, however, in a bifocal fashion that fuses the poet and his culture. The former ultimately is identified with the spokesperson for and of that culture. And yet to modern eyes, like Pound's, Prince Henry is not a religious symbol; he is a personal embodiment of the secular dimensions of his culture. He stands apart from and profoundly different from any Christ figure. In his own time, the closest he came to Christ was in being considered a Christian knight and warrior.[7] As such, he surreptitiously aligns de Born's world with the contemporary one Pound inhabits. Both are essentially secular in that religion is a secondary factor in the daily life of its denizens.

Only with the last stanza does the religious perspective enter. It does so in response to Love's inability to counter the anguish that befalls all things in "this faint world" (37). The passage of time chronicles the gradual but inescapable diminution of the power and value of this world's life. The encapsulation of the bitterness that follows love is found in the death of the "young English King" (36). It totally changes the world by the loss of his physical presence: "Gone is his body fine and amorous, / Whence have we grief, discord and deepest sadness" (37). The finality and completeness of this transformation can be countered only by an appeal to Christ. Yet this appeal is cast more in the tone of formal politeness appropriate to a socio-political request of a powerful noble than a heart-rending call for mercy addressed to a supreme being.[8] In short, Christ is seen as a secular figure capable of pardoning an erring subject and so of admitting him to the festive celebration "with honoured companions / There where there is no grief, nor shall be sadness" (37).

Pound's (and/or de Born's) strategy here of invoking a Christian motif to overlay a basically secular knightly code of values coupled with his taciturnity as to his own point of view poses an interpretive problem for the existence of the poem itself and its elegiac temper. Is the "Planh" an exercise in scholarly reclamation of the attitudes of an earlier and foreign age, and if so, to what end or purpose? It does indeed capture—to the extent that it is an accurate rendering of de Born's words—something of the values of a courtly romance society. But Pound as a poet is concerned with more than verbal archaeology, with mining shards of another culture to demonstrate his skill, dedication, and disciplined commitment as a preserver of a limited portion of the historical past. He is at pains to bring his knowledge to bear on an implicit cross-cultural critical perspective on his own age and its values.[9]

For instance, we note that Prince Henry's most distinctive trait is that of generosity. In this, we find that Pound is implicitly distancing the cultural values of de Born's age from those of his own. It indeed is remote from the London he, like

Mauberley, was to abandon with contempt and loathing for precisely, among other things, its lack of generosity. For Pound, the values expressed by de Born convey a simpler, more ideal realm than his own, one in which public and social values are more important than personal and individual ones.[10] Thus, in relation to the values Pound identified as dominant in his early twentieth-century world, the cultural impact of de Born's words reads as a judgment of the later values. These are viewed as either morally irresponsible or socially destructive or both.

In a different fashion, the handling of the religious-secular polarities suggests that Pound also relates the two ages as having essentially the same attitude. Both accept the religious perspective as something to be tolerated or drawn on for imagery as part of a last effort to find a resolution for the anger, sadness, and grief that inaugurates and establishes the elegiac temper. Yet both do so poetically rather than theologically. This is evidenced by Pound's rendering of de Born's appeal to Christ in the form of a simile: "Him do we pray as to a Lord most righteous" (37). This appeal is also a statement about social practices made ostensibly by a member of the society. As such, it firmly establishes the prayer as social request rather than religious beseechment. In doing so, it makes clear that religious invocation is fundamentally poetic rhetoric in this society. And that the same essential phenomenon is operative in the twentieth century, only in a more perfunctory, cynical, and skeptical fashion is essentially Pound's view. Thus, he, like Eliot, invokes other historical periods to dramatize both their differences and their similarities to our own. Both, however, aim not to identify all ages as fundamentally one. Instead, they seek to differentiate each by individual assessments of the complex of differences and similarities operating in each age.

If such a critical perspective is fundamental to modernist writers, it clearly is not for all modern writers. This can be seen, for instance, from Sir Herbert Read's "The Death of Kropotkin." Its poetic mode is essentially that of premodernist narrative verse. Yet it was written after the modernist poetic option was readily available to Read.[11] Unlike Pound, Read chooses a figure from recent history who bisects the literary and political realms. The only point of resemblance is that Read, too, reaches out to a distant and unfamiliar land for his setting. Even so, the chronological proximity of 1917 and the public curiosity and concern over the Russian Revolution had made its notables topics of polite and not-so-polite conversation in English circles from at least the early 1930s. Read's own interest in and affinity for anarchism, of course, gave him an increased personal interest in Kropotkin as a public figure.[12] Indeed, just beneath the surface of Read's simple concrete narrative of Kropotkin's passing lies a heartfelt identification with the man who throughout his life struggled with the apparent contradiction of royalty and anarchism and the moral decisions related thereto. Kropotkin is the silent symbol of the writer as public embodiment of the moral gesture. It is in this role that he underlies Read's careful tracing out of the anarchist prince's funeral.

Pound conveys the nobility and preeminence of Prince Henry dramatically through the direct speech of a contemporary. Read, on the other hand, captures the essential nature of Kropotkin by narratively tracing the gestures and behavior of his widespread mourners. Pound's speaker commands assent to the central importance of Henry's death for the society. In contrast, Read makes the recalled details of Kropotkin's funeral process generate a sense of the profundity of their impact on the poet himself. His logic operates by persuasion. Someone so beloved and tenderly regarded by "poor humble people" as well as by "old revolutionaries, young students / and children" (226) clearly should command the quiet respect of a foreign poet not present at the scene itself.

Indeed, it is the disjunction between the narrator as spectator and as imaginative function that points up the implicit forward-looking thrust of the poem. Read admits repeatedly during the first three stanzas that he himself was not a witness to Kropotkin's death in 1921 in Russia. Yet he provides such a welter of specific details drawn from eye-witness reports that he virtually obliterates the distance between the poet-narrator and the historical observer, Emma Goldman. By so doing, the cultural and political gulf between the two countries (England and Russia) and regions (West and East, Europe and Asia) is bridged. In effect, Read is testifying by this strategy to the Romantic conviction of the power of the imagination and its ability to conceive of that which has not been directly witnessed.

But not only is the scene itself an amalgam of report and imaginative extrapolation; it also preserves an awareness of the difference between the historical realities of the two countries and cultures. Read vividly summons up the actualities of the physical and philosophical loss of Kropotkin: the silent mourning throngs, the funeral procession with its banners and wreaths, the tacit participation of the natural world as seen in "the feathery snow . . . falling / gently" and "the winter sun / sinking red / and stain[ing] the level glittering plain" (227). But in doing so, he looks back at the scene with an almost unconscious nostalgia for an older, simpler, more directly heartfelt time, which, he seems to suggest, is beyond his own post–World War II culture to produce. Thus, he reinstates the "foreignness" and the historicity of Kropotkin's death in his poetic context.

What he is testifying to is the loss of a prophet by a people, the loss of a people's future capability to mourn and to recognize such a loss, and the incipient or anticipated loss of the opportunity to pursue the anarchist goal of completely unlimited human freedom. Running throughout the poem as a subtext is the historical fate of the Russian Revolution. It is subtly captured by the observation concerning Kropotkin's mourners, namely, that "Lenin had let them come" (226), by the potentially grim political portentousness of the image of "the winter sun / sinking red / stained the level glittering plain" (227), and the implicit futility as a reaction to political revolution of "the Tolstoyans [who] had gathered / to play mournful music / as the cortège passed" (227). All suggest the gradual shutting down of the opportunities for viable human responses to seminal losses. In particular, they convey the Russian Revolution's descent into authoritarian control, repressive violence, and the abandonment of hope for political freedom.

The major difference between Kropotkin's prophetic manner and that of the poet is in their sense of the future. The former foresaw the emergence of a new life full of freedom and self-realization. The latter's view is rooted in the history of his own time from, say, Kropotkin's death, which could offer little but the frustration of hope, the deprivation of freedom, the loss of enlightenment, and the absence of challenge. The gravitas of the poet's prophecy is intensified through its contrast with that of Kropotkin, which focuses on the idealization of human thought, the future, and the symbolic.

And yet Read's sensitivity to the dangers of polarizing views prevents his rejecting of Kropotkin as a figure of value and his position as one of merit. This is captured most fully in the closing of the poem. There Read brings Kropotkin's own words into direct congruence with his own declaration. It moves the prince's role into the poet's context without denying its significance, and at the same time giving it a radically different inflection:

> . . . "The waters before us
> flow now to the Amur.
> No mountains more to cross!"
>
> No mountains more to cross
> dear comrade and pioneer.
> You have crossed the Great Khinghán
> travelling eastward into rich lands
> where many will follow you. (227)

The Prince's words have an Old Testament ring of someone emerging from a country of threats and dangers into an Edenic world of relief and release. In contrast, the poet's final stanza acknowledges the culmination of the dangerous journey of life. It transmutes death into an ongoing passage into a mysterious world accessible to those who continue to hope for freedom, illumination or insight, and a rich reward for having faced the challenge of crossing many mountains. In this way, Read transforms an essentially political event—the Russian Revolution—into a mythopoeic vision of thwarted desire, bitter acceptance, and historical reality that anticipates the future of the late twentieth-century.

Where Read's poem generates an irony of acceptance grounded in the continuing growth of historical reality, Allen Tate's "Elegy" for Jefferson Davis provides a more sardonic modern assessment of its subject.[13] Tate's poem is founded on a backward look which ironically penetrates the romanticized legend that emerged from the American South with the cessation of the Civil War. More immediately apparent is the degree to which Tate's poem focuses on a deeply familiar subject rooted in the essential history of the United States. In so doing, it counters Read's concentration on the "foreignness" and unfamiliarity of his excursus into modern Russian history. What Tate does, however, is to confer his own kind of foreignness or strangeness or unfamiliarity on Davis through his ironic perspective on both the man and the land.[14]

Nevertheless, the first two stanzas present a basically conventional and nonironic approach to Davis. It stresses his "fine courtesy" (176) of manner, the discredit he incurred by his leadership role in a devastating war, and the uselessness and helplessness of a current or modern love for him and his memory. It is only with the third stanza that there is heard a stark cry of and for assessment: "What did we gain? What did we lose?" (177). It is followed by a less than grandiloquent description of those who provide "grief for the pious dead" (177). With this, the transition from the traditional lament of the South for one of its greatest heroes to Tate's more personal, independent, and private expression of the nature of the elegiac begins to occur.[15] His declaration that "grief for the pious dead / Suspires from bosoms of kind souls / Lavender-wise, propped up in bed" (177) distances his elegy from those of past southern tributes to Davis in several ways. The "pious dead" phrase makes Davis but one of a number of deceased so that his individuality as a person and leader is diminished. It also suggests that the invocation of piety is a conventional gesture that reduces its subject to an idealized image. The same diminution of the mourner is caught in the phrase "kind souls" and in their being relegated to a helpless gentility marked by old age and impending death. In effect, Tate here is disclaiming the traditional southern attitude toward Davis as a classical tragic hero.[16] He does so because its romanticizing and legendary propensities distort Davis's actual role and historical significance. Also, as the figure of genteel aging suggests, such an attitude is now no longer appropriate, accurate, or relevant to the occasion, if ever it was.

The sharp contrast of Tate's view of Davis and what he signifies to the South of the twentieth century is presented bluntly and uncompromisingly in the fourth stanza:

> Our loss put six feet under ground
> Is measured by the magnolia's root;
> Our gain's the intellectual sound
> Of death's feet round a weedy tomb. (177)

To equate the death of Jefferson Davis with the size and length of the roots of the tree that symbolizes the glory, beauty, and romance of the Old South is both to diminish the significance of that death and to chart the demise of a historical region as a dwindling to a mere natural emblem. In effect, to equate Davis's death with "the magnolia's root" per se is to suggest that his original symbolic power and elegiac force requires a clinging to the romantic legend of the South. Both Davis and the legend inherently require the imagination to turn backward.[17] This is further underscored by Tate's ironic assessment of the actual benefit for southerners and the South in seeing Davis's death as an elegiac celebration. Thus, to hear the sensory awareness of death only in one's intellect as compared to one's imagination or emotions is to diminish its significance. And to envisage his tomb as one no longer maintained physically is to foreshorten the historical significance of the leader's death into a bitterly realistic version of Shelley's Ozymandian vision of human achievement.

Despite the traditional southern insistence on seeing Davis as a hero in the War Between the States, he is, nevertheless, Tate insists, a failed hero.[18] For he is the one who presided over the losing of a war critical to the stature and self-esteem of the region. This fact dominates the private awareness of southerners of Tate's generation as well as subsequent ones. It also haunts the public consciousness of those engaged in making its political and economic institutions function despite the continuing setbacks instituted by the loss of the Civil War.

Yet, as Tate's allusions make clear, Davis is not simply a figure from southern history; his historical role has consequences that link him with both Belial and Orestes. This broadening, deepening, and complicating of Tate's view of Davis is attained in the poem's final two stanzas:

In the back chambers of the State
(just preterition for his crimes)
We curse him to our busy sky
Who's busy in a hell a hundred times

A day, though profitless his task,
Heedless what Belial may say—
He who wore out the perfect mask
Orestes fled in night and day. (177)

To be cursed by his society's descendants and associated with Satan, the con-
summate liar and rebel inmate of hell, is to render Davis as still a hero only in
minds addicted to romanticizing of the sort that created the Legend of the South.
Similarly, to be linked with Orestes, the quasi-renegade avenger of his father and
murderer of his mother, is to see him as the antithesis of the traditionally elegiac
figure of the southern legend of the Confederacy.

And yet Tate builds into his counter-legend a final intellectual irony that fuses
the Christian and classical involvement with guilt and crime and extends it to en-
compass his own poetic vision of the fate of the Confederacy.[19] For to curse the
current state of the South and to place the blame exclusively on Davis—a blame
which entails a residency in a hell of perpetual and pointless activity—is to turn
the hero into the scapegoat of history. In short, to blame the efforts at secession,
the resultant Civil War, and the destruction and despoliation of an entire region
on one man is to warp historical reality fully as much as did the romantic myth
of a defeated but unbeaten South. Thus, Tate ultimately creates an inverted cel-
ebratory tribute to Davis and his South through suggesting that his own sardonic,
modernist South is not so much the victim of the Confederacy and the Civil War
as the perpetrator of a false indictment of it. And it does so precisely because it
lacks the single-minded formulation of values compounded of honor, nobility of
character, and acceptance of responsibility possessed by Davis and his kind.

In perhaps an overly compressed fashion, the poet begins with a simulacrum
of a traditional elegy on Davis. He then ironically and savagely reverses it by in-
dicating that the hero is truly a cultural scapegoat whose death has historically
confined his region to a stereotypical warping of reality. Finally, he concludes with
an even deeper revelation: this reversal is itself a rendering of the contemporary
age's refusal to accept involvement in or responsibility for history's long legacy of
crime and guilt. To accuse is, for Tate, to self-convict. This sentiment implicitly

drives the traditional pattern of the elegy back on itself by endorsing its conviction that cultural loss is the poem's dominant sentiment. Tate, in effect, recognizes with ultimate irony that what has been lost in the South is a way of living that, though flawed, was nevertheless far better morally than that of the elegist's own. What he deploys is a complex historical imagination to uncover the elegiac dimension of a lost culture.[20] His elegiac attitude is one that deploys contempt or criticism of one's predecessors rather than simply resting in scorn based on a simplistic sense of the losses occasioned by cultural change.

Tate concentrates his historical attention on a major public figure from his own geographical region. In doing so, he strips him of his traditional image as part of an effort to penetrate to the historical reality he possesses for the modern mind. He indicts both the conventions of the past and the limitations of the present in order to present the relentless irony of history itself. This consists of its inability or refusal to reveal a single, changeless image consonant with what the observer is impelled to regard as the full reality of the person, scene, or setting under examination. For Tate, history is dependent upon an appropriate and defined moral vision, and it is this which he criticizes his own age and country for not possessing.

A quite different tack is taken by Wallace Stevens in his philosophically reflective "To an Old Philosopher in Rome." Stevens implicitly questions not only the functions of the conventional elegy but also the dominant impetuses to the contemporary elegiac temper. Ultimately, what he does is to recast both through his sophisticated interrogation of the abstractions generated by the human mind. Rather than focusing, as Tate does, on a specific geographical region, its culture, and a crucial historical period, Stevens pursues a dispassionate philosophical course worthy of his subject.[21] He contemplates George Santayana's life with a reflective inclusiveness that implicitly relates it to the whole scope of human existence. In paying tribute to Santayana as an old man waiting for death in the Holy City, Stevens, unlike Tate, is acknowledging the presence not of a public figure but of a prominent mind. Santayana is not a politically significant individual but a principled man who has led his life by his own lights.

It is this *sub specie aeternitatis* note coupled with the sense that Stevens is acutely aware of operating at the periphery of human experience and awareness that confers an elegiac note to the poem. Man as an empirical, biological entity standing "on the threshold of heaven" can ultimately conclude that human life faces only "unintelligible absolution and an end" (508). Yet even the limitations of this all-too-human creature are not absolute, for he can recognize that there is a "more merciful Rome / Beyond" (508) the physical, geographical city in which the aged Santayana presently abides. And yet the two cities are conceived by the same structure of the mind, which operates for Stevens as the ground of existence as consciousness.[22] Thus, the relationship between the two Romes and the realms of matter and spirit is explicitly established in the third stanza and part of the fourth.[23] Mind and body are not separate and distinct regions but rather ones in which contact and continuity are seen to be possible if but barely so:

> How easily the blown banners change to wings . . .
> Things dark on the horizons of perception,
> Become accompaniments of fortune, but
> Of the fortune of the spirit, beyond the eye,
> Not of its sphere, and yet not far beyond,
>
> The human end in the spirit's greatest reach,
> The extreme of the known in the presence of the extreme
> Of the unknown. (508)

By being the embodiment of this perception, Santayana becomes the focus for Stevens's unique elegiac temper. The old philosopher captures by his very presence the inevitability of his physical absence from the empirical world. Yet there is to be no absolute, inconsolable loss of the sort central to the traditional elegy as a poetic form.[24] Essentially, then, Stevens is concerned to contextualize the elegiac loss by reflective anticipation. In so doing, he mutes its impact through transmutation of its significance.

And yet there is still a felt impact, however quiet and subdued it may be, even though it reverses the customary speaker-subject relationship in the traditional elegy. Santayana himself is requested to speak accurately and "without eloquence" of his own symbolic role as the embodiment "of the pity that is the memorial of this room" (509). Now, the elegist is to be the subject of the elegy rather than an observer or commentator on the subject. He, in effect, becomes the elegy. In so doing, he becomes a representative of mankind by which each man identifies with the old philosopher and hears his own elegy in Santayana's observations.[25]

The philosopher's room conveys to the poet "the celestial possible" (509), the more than merely logical possibility that a world exists other than the one we call

real and that it is not only attainable but unavoidable. The great difference be-
tween Stevens's sense of the implications of such a worldview and that of other
religious and philosophical dualisms lies in two things.[26] One is his steadfast in-
sistence on the value of the ordinary, physical world even as the individual stands
on the threshold of the "celestial" (508) and "more merciful Rome" (509). The
second is the seemingly contradictory insistence that the "grandeur" of another
world can be found "only in misery, the afflatus of ruin / Profound poetry of the
poor and of the dead" (509). Stevens seeks to acknowledge the value of both
worlds because for him both are real because both are possible since, as we see at
the end of the poem, thinkable.[27] It is the imperfection of this world which makes
"the celestial possible" (509) both celestial and possible.

And central to this imperfection is the nature of language, of human speech,
for "it is poverty's speech that seeks us out the most. / It is older than the oldest
speech of Rome. / This is the tragic accent of the scene" (510). Again, however,
Stevens approaches his subject far differently from the bulk of contemporary
thinking. The limitations of language are not seen as shabby or pretentious dis-
guises or evasions to be exposed ad nauseam. Instead, they are part of the "given-
ness" of life and history whose "tragic accent" (510) is both ineluctable and com-
pelling. They form the veritable core of "poverty's speech" that Santayana
himself speaks "without speech" and that nevertheless consists of "the loftiest syl-
lables among loftiest things" (510).

In short, Stevens celebrates Santayana's language as consisting not of words
but of living actions (or declinations to act). His is a language that refines itself of
rhetoric to the point at which it becomes a voiceless communication of and from
the dead to the living, who too will join the dead. And in using such a "language,"
Santayana becomes "the one invulnerable man" (510) rather than the "commis-
erable man" (509) he was identified with in stanza eight. As the latter, he was
linked with mankind; as the former, he is singular. He is essentially separate from
the "crude captains" (510). In using language, they inherently abuse it by expos-
ing its inadequacies rather than rendering them as actualities beyond blame or
change like "bird-nest arches and . . . rain-stained vaults" (510).

The initial pity for Santayana is that felt for a mortal man destined to die and
fully conscious of that fact. It is not the conventional elegy's pity for its particu-
lar subject's untimely or sudden or surprising demise but rather is a broadened
and universalized lament for the fate of all human beings. Balancing the initial
pity is the prospect of the death itself as achieving "a kind of total grandeur at
the end" (510) in which culmination rather than loss is the result. The old philoso-

pher becomes the epitome of a life and career created by himself through a cease-less process of mental interrogation and examination:

> Total grandeur of a total edifice,
> Chosen by an inquisitor of structures
> For himself. He stops upon this threshold,
> As if the design of all his words takes form
> And frame from thinking and is realized (510–511).

The philosopher realizes he and his goal are one through the poet's words. Con-sequently, the poet, too, in a sense, shares in the exaltation and relief of another's transcendence of the limitations inherent in existence. In this, Stevens captures for himself the traditional elegy's surcease from mourning and regret and its fi-nal acceptance of loss as integral to the human condition.

Stevens's selection of Santayana as an elegiac subject is in many ways charac-teristic of his approach to knowledge and experience. His choice of an aged, no longer fashionable philosopher, who absented himself from the academy as part of a decision concerning how he wished to live his life, is driven by his calm, dispassionate scrutiny of the boundaries of what man actually can know and how it is that he knows it. Equally driven by an overall attitude is W. H. Auden's choosing of Freud as the subject for one of his major elegiac explo-rations of loss as a cultural phenomenon.[28] Where Auden differs is in his en-gagement with the historical and cultural attitudes informing the contempo-rary world and his passionate responses to them. Equally characteristic are his tone and attitude, both of which are dramatically different from those of Stevens. Auden begins by affecting a manner of sad, tired, or reflective uncer-tainty in the face of the apparent end of an epoch, an uncertainty as to whom to mourn:

> When there are so many we shall have to mourn,
> when grief has been made so public, and exposed
> to the critique of a whole epoch
> the frailty of our conscience and anguish,
>
> of whom shall we speak? For every day they die
> among us, those who were doing us some good,
> who knew it was never enough but
> hoped to improve a little by living. (*CSP,* 166)

Auden presciently anticipates the tidal wave of death about to be unleashed by World War II and with it the combination of criticism, admission of responsibility, and guilt.[29] By so doing, he defines the poet's role of semidetached observer and yet necessarily historical participant in his times. Thus, there is the traditional Auden invocation of the first person plural pronoun whereby he simultaneously addresses the societal norm and the individual. In effect, his strategy and point of view is the reverse of that taken by Stevens. Auden makes Freud a representative of "those who were doing us some good" by their presence and "hoped to improve a little by living" (*CSP,* 166).[30] Stevens, on the other hand, finds Santayana essentially unique in his asocial, single-minded exploration of the barely perceived boundary between life and death. The one is essentially historical, the other philosophical.

Auden's depiction of Freud is sympathetic to a "gradualistic" approach to human and social problems. It, thus, favors an approach that proceeds by piecemeal social engineering (to use Popper's phrase) rather than more grandiose and overarching strategies.[31] As such, Freud as sympathetic expediter is less successful than Santayana as symbolic exemplar for mankind. Freud's desire to advance the cause of humanity but a bit more "was denied him" (*CSP,* 167), unlike Santayana, who is committed to doing only what it is possible for him to do as an individual rooted in history. In so doing, Santayana is able to thwart the denial of his own expectations or hopes. And yet Auden's ironic assessment of his own philosophic position (at least at this particular historical moment)—the liberal, humanitarian, secular, pragmatic probing of what will improve human life—carries its own kind of success. Freud's death not only leaves his life's work incomplete but also identifies him with the fate "common to us all" (*CSP,* 167). In a way, like Santayana, Freud faces at his death the "problems . . . about our dying" (*CSP,* 167) which can never be definitively subdued.

The reason for Freud's wish being denied him is rooted in the very interests that dominated his life and made his reputation, namely, "those he had studied, the fauna of the night" (*CSP,* 167). Through such striking images, Auden develops not so much an explanation as a kind of allegorized mini-drama of Freud's life and times. This avoidance of explanation is Auden's way of not making a definitive historical judgment on his and Freud's times and the general modern cultural context. It also allows him to introduce allusively real and important elements that cast Freud as a victim of history and a kind of tragic hero in Auden's mini-drama. That Freud should die in London rather than Vienna and that he

should be a cultural alien exiled by a racist-dominated home country are impor-
tant for Auden to mention.

They provide a transition from Freud the individual thinker and explorer of
the psyche to Freud the elusive enemy of the modern bourgeois world and its cul-
ture. This last is the real core of Auden's elegiac reflections on Freud. What he
does in the poem is to begin with Freud the man, "this doctor" (*CSP*, 166), and to
conflate him with what may be called "Freudianism." Essentially, this last is a
world compelled to confront and to respond to his ideas, methods, treatments,
and theories. In the process, the latter assumes priority largely because Auden
also has an ironic, satiric intent as well as an elegiac, mourning intent in the poem.
He wishes to expose the culture's opposition to Freudianism for what it is, a last
ditch defense of "conceit," "frustration," "the Generalised Life," and "the mono-
lith / of State" (*CSP*, 168). Unsurprisingly, these foes of Freud and his "rational
voice" (*CSP*, 170) are exactly those struggled against by Auden from his begin-
nings as a published poet.

Indeed, the affinities between Freud the "scientist" and Auden the poet be-
come as close to explicit as the latter can rhetorically risk or sustain when he says
of the former:

> Of course they called on God, but he went his way
> down among the lost people like Dante, down
> to the stinking fosse where the injured
> lead the ugly life of the rejected. (*CSP*, 168)

In the Freud-Dante-Auden linkage, a second level of dramatic allegory emerges,
which functions as an implicit justification for Auden's conception of the poet and
for his own poetic practice. Like Dante, his is an allegorical mind that has a place
for religion because it finds the notion of the quest central to mankind. He sees
the start of that quest to entail being present in Hell. From there, the quester
learns certain inescapable truths, one of which is the need for compassion for oth-
ers. Yet another truth learned is that of the limits of such compassion in the face
of the stark and awesome reality of the nature of self and others.

The "scientist," the dispassionate observer and explorer of reality, and the
poet, the empathic sympathizer with "the injured" and "the rejected" (*CSP*, 168),
are implicitly fused in this section of the poem. In turn, both are essentially iden-
tified with the writer of the elegy.[32] This identification provides the warrant for
Auden's extenuating of Freud's defects—his "autocratic poise," his "paternal

strictness" (*CSP,* 168), his frequent wrongness, and his occasional absurdity. These extenuations do two things. Most obviously, they suggest Freud belongs not on the pedestal of a tragic hero but rather on the plane of an ordinary courageous participant in life. They also provide a defense of the author-poet against the supposition that he is implicitly elevating himself above others. In effect, Auden suggests the poet-scientist (Auden-Freud) gains his ultimate value to mankind by providing individuals with a sense of calm, the assurance of escape from their dilemmas, and the return of things long-forgotten. By such a provision, they are united in themselves with a sense of an inherited "richness of feeling" (*CSP,* 169) and gain an enthusiasm for the mysteries of the unexplored.

This role devolves in the poem's last three stanzas into one of pathos for poet, "scientist," and mankind at large. Their actions and the world's inevitable response co-mingle them into the figure of the scapegoat, compounded as it is of the traitor, the victim, and the antagonist. The fate of this complex servant of "enlightenment" (*CSP,* 169) is, then, to be condemned by ourselves, mankind at large. As a result, the focus of the mourning shifts from the individual poet (Auden) lamenting the death of his culture hero (Freud) back to the allegorical figure of Impulse. It provides a concentrated image of grief, love, and understanding of the fate of the scapegoat who is the "rational voice" (*CSP,* 170):

> Over his grave
> the household of Impulse mourns one dearly loved:
> sad is Eros, builder of cities,
> and weeping, anarchic Aphrodite. (*CSP,* 170)

Just as the scapegoat figure is a complex and contradictory one, so is that of Impulse, containing as it does both Eros and Aphrodite, both the embodiment of civilization and the epitome of dissolution and chaos.

As the conclusion of the poem, this allows Auden to provide a balanced and noncommittal assessment of history itself. First, he recognizes the fact of the subtle and profound interaction of creation and destruction as motivating human affairs. Second, he also conveys the inevitability of man's response to the death of those and that which he loves and values. The only true response is to mourn genuinely (a combination of feeling and demeanor) the loss of the "rational voice" (*CSP,* 170). To move from mourning to blame or invective or to prophecy and prediction is to give way to the poet's temptations to rhetoric. To judge is to personalize the point of view and in so doing to thwart the purpose and achievements of that voice which the poem is honoring. For the rational voice of Freud aimed always to achieve but one thing:

> he merely told
> the unhappy Present to recite the Past
> like a poetry lesson till sooner
> or later it faltered at the line where
>
> long ago the accusations had begun,
> and suddenly knew by whom it had been judged. (*CSP,* 167)

The voice implicitly cautions he who would be a poet that his goal is not the imposition of his own views on a problem or situation but simply the recitation of the past. In short, the voice becomes that of history until the hearer discovers the source of his problem. This lies in the limited value there is in identifying the critical accusations with either others or the personal self. History, then, for Auden, at least here, is largely an inscrutable fact or series of facts which the individual is required to accept and take account of but neither to rail against nor to take as a warrant for self-inflation or self-deprecation.[33] The individual, the society, and the natural world are all debarred from speculation as to possible or probable explanations.

Because history cannot be altered and because explanation is straitening, the best that Auden can offer is an amoral assumption about human existence which lends the gravity of both certitude and uncertainty to the nature of life. His assumption is that our claims to knowledge are pretense and that these claims range from love to death. What Auden achieves here is the linkage of love and death as subject to the same unidentified and mysterious powers, as not the product of free choice or individual decision. At the same time, he also mounts the suggestion that this view may be erroneous. This last reintroduces uncertainty into the perspective and diminishes the proto-explanation implied here to the level of pure speculation. And with it, Auden returns history to its inscrutable futurity mingled with desire and hope and the postulation of knowledge as a possibility.

Figures of Popular Culture

A quite different focus on the nature of history and memory occurs in Vernon Watkins's "Elegy on the Heroine of Childhood," Frank O'Hara's "The Day Lady

Died," and Louis MacNeice's "Death of an Actress." Each provides an elegiac recognition not of major cultural or intellectual figures but of individuals from popular culture who have had a significant impact on their authors. Other figures from popular culture so elegized include Lucille Clifton's "malcolm," remembering the assassinated civil rights leader Malcolm X, Betty Adcock's tribute to modern jazz great Dizzy Gillespie, "Poem for Dizzy," Richard Blessing's "Elegy for Elvis," a recollection of perhaps the best known of all popular culture icons, Elvis Presley, and Sharon Olds's assessment of the famous movie star in "The Death of Marilyn Monroe." To shift from central political, philosophical, and intellectual figures to persons such as Pearl White and Billie Holiday is simultaneously to lose as well as to gain. The losses include a diminished sense of the ultimate importance of the person remembered, a puzzlement as to the relevance of the author's effort at recollection, and a marked decline in the traits of the traditional elegy.[34] The gains are more difficult to identify at the outset in part because of their relative novelty and lack of established context. Close examination of the poems in question will yield, it is hoped, a fuller sense of the benefits accruing to their approach, which is akin to that of contemporary historical methods that draw on popular culture and everyday life for perspectives on the present.

Watkins and O'Hara take radically different approaches to their subjects. The former assesses at some length the educational impact of a popular culture medium such as the movies on children like himself. The latter, on the other hand, creates a snapshot impression of the personal effect both in life and in death a single popular entertainer has had on him. By so doing, they suggest the range of responses the individual is capable of making to a significant occasion in his or her history. Watkins's use of an epigraph establishes his way of connecting the poetic speaker to the silent film star Pearl White.[35] In it, he underlines the close relationship between the star and her audience of children in that "we died in you" (4). By its applying to all members of the audience, the epigraph also gives the poet's personal recollection of her socio-cultural implications for the role movies had in the education of modern children. Essentially, he is concerned with the complex significance carried for him and his peers by such carefully structured and stereotypically plotted illusions.

Thus, Watkins develops a sympathetic assessment of the central role played by White and her movies in the introduction of the young to terror, fear, death, apprehension, and escape. His detailed evocation of the interactions of the young audience and White's dramatic incidents builds a sociological picture replete with his own personal memories. Her illusory adventures introduce the children to thrilling but safe dramatic encounters with death that presage their own subsequent actual involvement with it in all its diverse forms. Both in memory and present awareness the poet senses both the closeness and the dissimilarity existing between childhood, projected fantasy, and adult reality. Out of the imitation of reality superimposed on the actual fully recognized by his adult self, he gains a carefully conditioned nostalgia for both the intensity and the security realized by his childhood movie experiences. He is dramatically aware of the loss inherent in the gaining of maturity, the belated recognition of its make-believe quality, and the similarity that obtains between the childhood anticipation of the heroine's threatened demise and the adult confrontation with personal mortality. The fond shake of the head over childish excitements and thrills is subtly qualified by the poet's final awareness of "How silently at last the reel runs back / Through your three hundred deaths, now Death wears black" (6).

Watkins's six-line, ten-stanza recollection of an extended memory from childhood lies at the poetic extreme from O'Hara's brief series of punctiliously recorded objective statements about the events experienced by him alone in a single day. Operative here is the randomness of the events, their singularity and lack of broad social significance, their irrelevance to the critical recollection of an immediate past memory occasioned by seeing the newspaper picture of Billie Holiday announcing her death.[36] Only in the last four lines does O'Hara reveal the immediacy of the elegiac impact created by the confluence of the picture / death and the memory of his actual presence at one of her nightclub performances:

> and I am sweating a lot by now and thinking of
> leaning on the john door in the 5 SPOT
> while she whispered a song along the keyboard
> to Mal Waldron and everyone and I stopped breathing. (325)

It is his poem's title alone that announces her death, but what it triggers is a personal memory of a compelling experience and musical performance. Together, title and poem suggest that her death derives its meaning or significance from the past experience of the individual. Two factors, however, qualify or condition this perception. The first is that the individual memory of the uniquely powerful and touching performance was apparently shared by all of the spectators, for "*everyone* and I stopped breathing" (325; my italics). The second is that the death of a junkie, has-been jazz singer commands sufficient public attention to warrant tabloid newspaper notice, that is, to have a claim on society generally. When one considers the singer, her audience(s), and her death, clearly the aesthetic effect of her singing is one with her demise. In both cases, it is the cessation of breathing which marks the high point of the experience of the audience. What O'Hara, then, achieves is a minimalist elegy for a legendary popular singer. And in doing so, he defines her aesthetic achievement as essentially elegiac in character, a rendering of the style, character, and impact of death as an aesthetic experience and form.

The completion of the modern dismantling of the elegy of the past is perhaps best captured by Louis MacNeice in his "Death of an Actress."[37] There, the subject, the style, and the tone all combine to call in question the memorializing of such a death. The sudden death of an aged music hall artiste named Florrie Forde,[38] the conversational four-line stanzas, and a compassionate but realistic assessment of both the waste and the value of a not overly talented performer cohere in shaping a new elegiac mode. The poem neither celebrates nor laments the passing of any of her physical, emotional, intellectual, or social traits. Instead, MacNeice draws detailed attention to the pathos of her death, the ridiculousness of her demeanor, the hackneyed nature of her public performances, and the tastelessness of her role. The poet's challenge is to raise the subject's stature with his audience to a level commensurate with that it holds in the poet's view.

MacNeice does this largely by granting her limitations and shortcomings at the very outset and then by carefully suggesting their historical value. Her cultural role is that of satisfier of the public taste, compensator for the dullness and boredom of society, and provider of hope for small rewards for the all but hopeless, whether civilians or soldiers. This is what warrants her death being celebrated. The unabashed sentimentality, absurd flirtatiousness, and flagrant foolishness of her performances gave her audiences, MacNeice suggests, not simply what they wanted but what they needed if the nation was to survive two world wars. She is the embodiment of vaudeville, of music hall entertainment. As such, she forms part of the culture's history as lived rather than as contemplated at a distance by, say, Pound through literary works and classical myths.

It is her role as an emblem of national history, of "an older England" (178) of innocence, naiveté in facing international conflicts, simple pleasures offered to limited aspirations that make her deserving of celebration. And it is the fact—introduced in the last two stanzas—that she and her world are now fully part of the past rather than the present that generates the elegiac note of sorrow for their disappearance, loss, and death: "Let the wren and robin / Gently with leaves cover the Babes in the Wood" (178). The speaker looks on her with fond respect for her extended efforts: to buoy the human spirit in time of war and economic hardship; to give substance—shabby though it may be—to the dreams of a strait-ened society; and to maintain an image of cultural innocence compounded of children and sunlit days. Even her death is seen as an acknowledgment of the propriety endemic to her society, for she has "taken her bow and gone correctly away" (178).

Yet this attitude is only superficially of the same order as that expressed dur-ing World War I. The latter readily drifted into either sentimental maudlinity over the national past or critical disdain rooted in a preference for the turbulence of the present in which the future of the culture is still undecided. This is seen at the beginning of the last stanza, which repeats the word "correctly" from the penul-timate one. By so doing, it captures the fitting way in which the end of her life encapsulates the end of an historical era and so prepares for the elegiac regret and sadness of the poem's ending. It also reflects the detached, understated ironic view of the contemporary spectator—like MacNeice himself—reading the daily paper not for glimpses of the innocence of children but for information about the still on-going struggle of World War II. He thus also appraises Florrie Forde's swift collapse into death as the historically correct thing to occur. Her time is past, and however sad that may be in personal terms, it is still inevitable that it should be so and appropriate that it not be allowed to linger to degenerate into senti-mentality.

The social innocence and political naïveté of the world in which her career flourished, even as much as the gaucherie and tawdry values of the music hall it-self, are lost permanently in the speaker's opinion. Therefore, it is natural that the emblems of that state of the world—"the Babes in the Wood"—should also be submerged "gently with leaves" (178). Both "gently," as befits the elegiac temper of regret, and with fallen "leaves," a symbol of another death that occurs fittingly and naturally.

By their reflections, all three poets—Watkins, O'Hara, and MacNeice—raise the power of the casual and almost insignificant to intrude on the human psyche. It is remembered either as a life-shaping force or as a disruption of the ordinariness and humdrum quality of life. They also see the artistic performance as akin to experiencing death viscerally rather than simply metaphorically.

In Watkins's case, Pearl White's movies introduce their child audience to death at-a-remove and in advance of their actual experience of it. Thus, when as an adult the poet confronts death as a present and recurring phenomenon of life, he sees "how silently at last the reel runs back / Through your three hundred deaths" (6). In doing so, he recognizes two contradictory aspects of the movie experience. First, he perceives the illusory, artificial, and inaccurate nature of his childhood vision of death on the screen. Second, he admits its compelling power in shaping his preparation for living in an adult world. For O'Hara, it is the artistic performance of Holiday that is the encounter with death-at-a-remove *and* with reality rather than illusion. And it is her actual, physical death that creates the awareness that the fictional or metaphoric death of her art is now but a memory of death as a metaphor for art. Both the death implicit in her art and the memory of it are creations achieved through artifice and style.

MacNeice approaches the death-at-a-remove motif by focusing on the reported loss of another person known only at a distance, and that largely from a detached, somewhat skeptical standpoint. Florrie Forde's demise is, for him, not a reminder of a past illusion nor a personal encounter with a much admired artist. She is the appropriate end for an outworn culture. For all three writers, though implicitly, history and futurity are unpredictable and unfathomable in both pragmatic and absolute terms. As a result, only memory exists in a recoverable or achievable form beyond the immediate present. This priority of memory results in their not even essaying the explanatory models to which Auden finds himself turning.

Such a reduction of the elegy as a poetic form to the confines of the poet's reflective moment is the product of his recognition of history-as-event as fundamentally inscrutable. As a result, the reliance on tradition, in this case, the tradition of the elegy, is aborted or felt to be irrelevant. And yet memory—as indicated above—continues to exist for the poet so that at least the *idea* of the elegiac continues. Since memory functions as a personal dimension in these modern poems, it is understandable that the poets should turn their attention to the question of the relation of the elegiac to themselves as poets.

Dead Poets: The Role of the Poet

A few poets, such as Hart Crane in "At Melville's Tomb" and Auden in "At the Grave of Henry James," focus elegiac explorations on burial places in order to assess both themselves and past masters.[39] Others, however, turn their attention directly to a particular dead poet whose life and/or work commands their attention in a particular way. In doing so, they raise an issue haunting most of them, namely, the actual culture role of the poet today, and with that their collateral concern to formulate yet once again new and relevant defenses of poetry. Thus, poems by William Carlos Williams (on D. H. Lawrence), John Malcolm Brinnin (on Federico Garcia Lorca), George Barker (on Michael Roberts), Thomas Merton (on Ernest Hemingway and James Thurber), W. H. Auden (on William Butler Yeats), and James Wright (on Morgan Blum) present markedly different personal elegies.[40] They range from Williams's biologically or botanically grounded celebration and Merton's religiously oriented assessment to Auden's culturally focused appraisal and Barker's respectful remembrance of an intellectual mentor to Wright's self-appraisal in the light of the fate of younger poets struggling to become known and so remembered. In so doing, they demonstrate the multiplicity of responses to the death of a poet given rise to by the twentieth century. As we shall see, these responses raise anew the traditional issue of the cultural role of the poet and the defense of poetry it necessarily entails.

Virtually all of these poets—Wright is the exception—focus on famous to well-known writers whose careers have functioned as cultural icons for the modern literary world. Ironically, they appear to their memorializers as figures of pathos, flawed character, compelling achievement, synecdochic mystery, serene finality, and personal instruction. Only Barker's tribute to Michael Roberts explicitly identifies him with "the greatest" and "best" of mankind.[41] When these tributes are set over against earlier elegies, their praise of their subjects is clearly more sharply qualified. Renaissance elegies on Sir Philip Sidney, for instance, commemorated him as a Protestant champion, as a representative of a cause, as a public figure, and as an exemplary knight rather than as a poet. They contrast sharply with those of deceased modern poets insofar as their authors sense the poet's value to reside almost exclusively in his being a poet.[42] They emerge as efforts designed both to laud and to speak the truth, scrupulously omitting neither personal flaw nor aesthetic achievement.

The clearest instance of this is, of course, Auden's celebrated "In Memory of W. B. Yeats" and, in particular, the opening lines of Part II:

> You were silly like us; your gift survived it all:
> The parish of rich women, physical decay,
> Yourself. Mad Ireland hurt you into poetry. (*CSP,* 142)

To say that such an assessment reflects no more than Auden's ambivalence over Yeats's kind of poetry, his manner of living, and his psychological profile is to state the obvious. But Auden was also clearly aware that as a mid-twentieth-century poet acknowledging the demise of a powerful predecessor, he had to take into consideration the terms appropriate to the modern age for elegizing anyone. And such terms could not aspire to the honorifics and superlatives summoned up by, say, Shelley for Keats. Implicitly, therefore, Auden is assessing the significant difference between his time and that of the past. He dispassionately concludes that the difference between the poet and his public is considerably less than it had been in earlier times. No longer a transcendental quasi-divinity nor a profoundly isolated tragic hero, the poet today shares in the silliness of his fellow citizens, in the ordinariness or commonality of mankind.

This dedication to the full picture, to the hues and shadows of the poet's portrait, is not simply a break with the past history of the elegy. It is also a recasting of that tradition in a way that authenticates the legitimacy of the convention of memorializing itself. What is more sharply drawn than in earlier, Romantic elegies is the distinction between the individual and his works or art as a whole. For Auden, this distinction is no less than that between death and life, the person inevitably committed to mortality and the poetry which "survives, / A way of happening, a mouth" (*CSP*, 142).

Written as the poem was at the beginning of World War II, it is almost inevitable that a poet like Auden would conflate the silly mortal individual and the mass of European nations enmeshed in snarling animal-like hatreds. Together, they represent the eternal enemies of poetry. For Auden, poetry ultimately is the crystallization of values dedicated to healing and freeing humankind. Imaginative release from the imprisonment in the happenings that make up mortal life is a central function of poetry, he feels. Simultaneously, he sees poetry as healing its audience of the increasingly egotistical self-interest developed by ordinary life's daily events.

This juxtaposition of person and poetry is mediated only by the poet. He alone is capable of perceiving and sharing in the contemporary human condition of "intellectual disgrace" (*CSP*, 142), frozen pity, and lack of success. At the same time, he is still persisting in the perhaps almost doomed effort to encourage rejoicing amid a deeply constrained world and to teach the receptive person "how to praise" (*CSP*, 143). The logic of this role for the poet preserves Yeats the man as a figure deserving of public honor. It also assures Auden's own future as a person aspiring to surmount the historical and functional limitations of his age.

This is presented dramatically in Part III, where first "William Yeats is laid to rest" (*CSP*, 142) and then Auden enjoins an unidentified poet to "follow right / To the bottom of the night" (*CSP*, 143). Yeats, being dead, cannot be the poet addressed directly, even though his works may retroactively function as the "unconstraining voice" persuading their audience "to rejoice" (*CSP*, 143). As the remaining lines indicate, the living poet being so enjoined is Auden, whose location on the poetic spectrum virtually demands that he fuse the twin traditions of the vatic and the civic. And that essentially is what he symbolically, elliptically, and perhaps only semiconsciously does here.

A quite different tack to the memorialization of a fellow modern author is taken by William Carlos Williams in his elegy on D. H. Lawrence.[43] Here the focus is not on the textual or artistic characteristic of the works nor on the artist or poet as a distinct functional entity in the culture. Rather, Lawrence is presented as a natural force. He is a concentration of cultural energy operating in the natural world and dedicated to countering "waste and life's / coldness" (1:392). Auden's distinction between artist and work is tacitly ignored in favor of a biologically (and botanically) grounded continuum embracing the whole range of living creatures: "English women," "the serpent in the grotto," "unopened jonquils," "the frogs, speaking of / birds and insects," "rabbits," the sounding "cricket," "forsythia," and "the crinkled spice-bush" (1:393–395). It is this multiform living environment in which Lawrence too lived, struggled "with a fury of labor," and died in the hiatus between "spring's decay" (1:392–393) and the onset of summer with its blood-warming heat. Poet and setting—both natural and socio-historical— are part of a single world. Both are engaged in purely natural activities whether of static contemplation, simple being, or frenzied mental and physical action.

Such a vision of the dead poet eliminates the sardonically critical assessment of European and indeed the whole of modern society found in Auden. In its place stands an almost quietistic rendering of Lawrence's life-history as a purely natural phenomenon. Lawrence's struggle to vivify his world and its people earns him the reiterated sorrowful epithet of "poor Lawrence." Neither rage nor despair are part of the lament. Instead there is the calm acceptance of the inevitability of his labors ending prematurely and the equally reflective implication that this, too, is a natural part of life:

> But for Lawrence
> full praise in this
> half cold half season—
> before trees are in leaf and
> tufted grass stars
> unevenly the bare ground. (1:393)

Unlike Auden, Williams bestows "*full* praise" (my italics), that is, without differentiating the man from the writer.

The reason for this is not so much a matter of differing judgments about the intrinsic merits of Yeats and Lawrence. It lies rather in Williams's election of a biologically determined ground for his poem. This leads to his structuring his metaphoric narrative into a kind of natural allegory of Lawrence's life and works. As befits an elegiac narrative, Williams's begins with "Green points on the shrub / and poor Lawrence dead" (1:392). This situates his reflective effort to assess Lawrence's life in toto: "Dead now and it grows clearer / What bitterness drove him" (1:393).

The second stanza makes clear that Lawrence's cultural starting point is his view of and relationship with his own culture:

> so English
> he had thereby raised himself
> to an unenglish greatness. (1:392–393)

His sensitivity to the undercurrents and nuances of English life is matched by his conviction that it is highly limited in character, disintegrative in effect, and motivated by the lack of love:

> Poor Lawrence
> worn with a fury of sad labor
> to create summer from
> spring's decay. English
> women. Men driven not to love
> but to the ends of the earth. (1:393)

In particular, the last two lines suggest the biographical allegory of both Lawrence and his society. They encapsulate the motivation underlying the growth of an empire as well as Lawrence's own historical trajectory. He has sought to escape a temporal region in the process of a decay seen here in the manners and attitudes of modern women. By roaming the world in both familiar ("Mediterranean evenings" [1:393] and "the cities of / Mediterranean islands" [1:394]) and unfamiliar ("the scorched aridity of / the Mexican plateau" [1:394]) regions, he embarks on a quest as actual as it is metaphoric or symbolic. Literally and figuratively, he seeks sun-drenched climates capable of kindling a fire within human beings. In these brief phrases, Williams calls up memories of Lawrence's travels to Italy, Sardinia, Mexico, Australia, and the far west of the United States and allegorizes them into a concentrated thematic focus.

This quest, however, never achieves its goal of cultural and personal transformation. Yet Williams does not regard Lawrence as a failure. The intensity of his passion, the desperate straits in which the culture is lodged, and the fact that time and change are the products of extension rather than concentration all conspire in his thwarting:

> Febrile spring moves not to heat
> but always more slowly,
> burdened by a weight of leaves.
> Nothing now
> to burst the bounds—
> remains confined by them. (1:394)

Lawrence is, like the tragic hero, committed precisely and exclusively to the course of action he followed and to its being thwarted by the cyclical forces of life and death. These forces, Williams realizes, cannot be condemned—nor should they be railed against—since they are purely natural in their being.

For Williams, the elegiac nature of his poem consists in three factors. First, there is the poet's (and physician's) recognition of the necessity of the human struggle against decay. Second is the inherent failure to achieve or effect full self-realization. And finally, there is the concrete inscrutable actuality of nature. Coupled with this is his complementary awareness that nature, the world, and the social order of massed humanity inevitably outlast the individual human being no matter how strong, dedicated, or persistent he is about transforming the human condition. The result is an elegiac attitude founded less on grief or regret than on a heroic pity for both the struggling individual and the natural world steadily being itself and pursuing its unalterable course.

The serpent or snake matches the "satiric sun" (1:395) both as a presence and as an absent reality. The significance of both is coterminous with their actuality, thus leaving them with an indeterminacy of meaning. And this is the final perspective provided by the poem on the elegiac subject:

> Greep, greep, greep the cricket
> chants where the snake
> with agate eyes leaned to the water.
> Sorrow to the young
> that Lawrence has passed
> unwanted from England.
> And in the gardens forsythia
> and in the woods
> now the crinkled spiced-bush
> in flower. (1:395)

Natural creatures, human beings, and growing, flowering things all continue their ordinary, natural, daily activities apparently indifferent to the demise of the ostensible elegiac subject. This, however, does not diminish the validity of the elegiac temper, nor of the poet's willingness to raise his voice to record the situation that he is witnessing. The responses of the natural world are as they are and not to be questioned or criticized, for to do so would be pointless. Yet the individual truly perceiving the situation before him raises his voice in a muted celebratory pity that both nature and mankind are as they are and, biologically at least, are incapable of change.

Unlike Auden, Williams is not even covertly judgmental about Lawrence, his subject, the culture in which he lived and by which he was shaped, or even about himself, who is writing the elegy. His stance is more spectatorial than participatorial. Or if "spectatorial" sounds overly passive, perhaps "objective" more nearly captures Williams's elegiac temper toward a writer he admires and a world he can only acknowledge with respect for its unequivocal existence. As an elegist, he places himself close to the dispassionate center of actuality. Consequently, Williams's challenge is to retain the core of feeling for Lawrence and his world that initiates the elegy as a poetic act. He must avoid lapsing into quietistic indifference to pity for the heroism exhibited and ultimately disregarded by the world at large. It is as a compensation for this global disregard that the poet himself embarks on the elegy. He does so without thinking that such an effort will itself do more than marginally and fleetingly record the truth about the elegiac temper as seen from a biologically grounded perspective.

A somewhat similar attitude to a dead famous artist occurs in Thomas Merton's "In Memory of the Spanish Poet Federico Garcia Lorca." The chief differences, however, between Merton and Williams are noteworthy. The former, as his title indicates, limits his attention to the act of communal or national memory without claiming to invoke the elegy as a poetic form. Moreover, he grounds his attitude in a religious rather than a biological perspective. Both writers, however, convey their attitudes through natural or environmental images that function almost iconically as an encoded summation of their subject's life and its role or place in the national history. And both arrive at a sense of the puzzlement at the situation they have recalled. For them, it is as if the role of the memory itself is to heighten the awareness of the inherent inability to explain or justify the subject's death.

A subtle yet highly significant difference between the two poems lies in the

manner in which each eschews full and direct mourning as part of the poet's role.
Williams confines his direct expression of sorrow to the phrase "poor Lawrence."
In context, this places Lawrence in an essentially pitiable condition touched with
just a hint of irony at his own heroic folly in endeavoring to rescue his nation from
its own deathlike cultural state. Merton does not even go this far. He is content to
deflect the mourning impulse from his own voice to that of "the sharp guitars"
(44) and the singing woman whose "words come dressed as mourners" (45). For
him, the poet's role is not to mourn personally and eloquently as it is with Mil-
ton and Shelley. Instead, it is to record simply and economically the common, ha-
bitual actions of mourning for a national cultural hero struck down by his own
people. To Merton's mind, plangent guitars and a single woman singing amid ru-
ined houses and broken walls are both mourning Lorca's death and celebrating
their national heritage of profound sorrow and grief and deeply meaningful pas-
sions. And in doing so, they are not doing two things but one that appears in dif-
ferent guises. Betrayal, he implies, is endemic to and inherent in the culture of
Spain.

Williams develops his metaphors and symbolic images to chart the limits of
his biological perspective with its empirical grounding. Their combination of
power and limitation issue in his final almost phlegmatic view of reality and the
human condition. In contrast, Merton strives to achieve a mystery and signifi-
cance reaching beyond the biological as is revealed in his parenthetic and inter-
rogative refrain:

> (Under what crossless Calvary lie your lost bones, Garcia Lorca?
> What white Sierra hid your murder in a rocky valley?) (45)

The lost body of the murdered poet is linked metaphorically with that of the
slain god-man, Christ, in an effort to transcend Williams's resolutely physical and
natural point of view. In a way, the introduction of such a Christian perspective
enables him also to avoid the explicit judgmental and explanatory attitude found
in Auden's handling of Yeats's death and its significance for European culture. By
linking Lorca to Christ, Merton avoids having to take sides on the Spanish Civil
War and thereby explicitly politicizing Lorca's fabled role as murdered poet. To
have done so would have been to abandon or contradict the spectatorial, obser-
vational attitude conditioning his elegiac act of recollection. It would have trans-
lated Lorca's death from a profound human mystery lying beyond the bounds of
human inquiry into a historical event possessing a clear but limited meaning.

Instead he implicitly links Lorca's historical and political killers with Christ's ancient religious and secular slayers. The antiquity and almost archetypal nature of the latter enables Merton to confer a timeless and insoluble mystery on the fate of Lorca. Otherwise, Lorca's death could achieve but the status of a vexing puzzle that is but one of many in the continuum of history. Essentially, this collusion of Lorca and Christ enables Merton to make of Lorca's memory an aspect of a pattern and so to ensure that it will remain a living entity. From his religiously oriented perspective, Merton sees Christ's memory as ritually ordained to remain alive. In contrast, the memory of a historically murdered poet is almost certain sooner or later to be swallowed up in the maw of historical events and lost sight of with the passage of time. Only with their metaphorical linkage can the latter be ensured of being remembered and mourned over.

Strikingly enough, another of Merton's elegies suggests an apparently contradictory view of the relation of history and religion, of the individual and the universal. "An Elegy for Ernest Hemingway" focuses on the immediate response in the present to the death of a famous writer. It is as if Merton sees the actual moment of death and the responses both of the community and the individual poet as somehow sealing or permanently consolidating the historical reputation of the artist. Such a reputation constitutes the persistence of the life in human memory. And in so establishing it by his poem, he develops what is in fact an exception or qualification to the loss of personal memory over time presumed by his Lorca poem.

An even more paradoxical inflection to his view of Hemingway's death is his placing the suicide in a priestly context of convents and monasteries. Such a world might be expected to be either indifferent to or dismissive of the death, yet it is marked with a quiet acceptance and recognition of its significance. The poem begins by articulating the dependence of Hemingway's recognition by the Church on the fact of his death even though he finally is adjudged to have followed and embodied a "brave illusion" (316):

> Now for the first time on the night of your death
> your name is mentioned in convents, *ne cadas in obscurum.* (315)

It is his mistaken world-outlook, despite which he is seen as "a friend" (315) and "still famous" (316) by both other denizens of purgatory and by clerics, that provides the final paradox of the poem.

This outlook consists essentially of two traits—Hemingway's language described as "an idiom you made / great" (315–316) and his dedication to "the adventurous / self" (316)—each of which is seen by Merton as counterpoised against the other. Like Williams with Lawrence, Merton places Hemingway's language in an imagistic context that echoes key figures from the life and artistic career. Images of "a far country" (315), the rising sun, and a tolling bell serve as mnemonic devices. They both recall Hemingway's literary achievement and point to implications that undercut the legitimacy of his vision:

> How slowly this bell tolls in a monastery tower for a
> whole age, and for the quick death of an unready
> dynasty, and for that brave illusion: the adventurous
> self! (316)

Here the conventional linkage of the deceased elegiac subject with his age and culture is thwarted by the single word "illusion." It calls in question the whole concept of "the adventurous self" on which Hemingway based both his life and work. Hemingway is seen as someone who has failed his time by leading it in a false and unreal direction. He has inclined it toward a reliance on the concept of a separate, autonomous self able to venture into areas undetermined as to outcome by any power greater than man or nature. To the theological imagination, the dreadfulness of the folly is exposed by the stark actuality of the final line of the poem. It captures the awfulness of the venture even as it admiringly emulates the simple declarative tone of Hemingway's own idiom:

> For with one shot the whole hunt is ended! (122)

This elegy of Merton's, then, fuses an almost awestruck regard for the artist's handling of language with a stern moral judgment of his thought. In contrast, these two elements are separately explored as distinct elegiac components in short poems by Thomas Merton and John Malcolm Brinnin. The latter's "Little Elegy for Gertrude Stein" imitatively celebrates Stein's attitude toward and unconventional treatment of language.[44] Like Williams and Merton, he uses familiar phrases coined by the author—"pigeons on the grass" and "the rose that is a rose"—and wordplay based on repetition and rhyme. By so doing, he reconstructs mimetically her philosophy of language while also including an assessment of language's status and place in contemporary culture. Stressed in this reconstruction is her intellectual isolation from society, her artless innocence and simplicity in implementing her views, and the congruence of her verbal practices with the existential actuality of human life. Since "words in her hands grew smooth as stone" (98), her language came to presage the silent finality of death itself. In the face of death, the effort to say goodbye in a truly meaningful manner is physically impossible even as is the attempt to assign explicit meaning to Stein's use of words. To say goodbye is as profound and enigmatic as "a rose is a rose."

Such an approach to the elegiac is almost the polar opposite of that taken by the great Renaissance and Romantic poets. For them, the full resources of rhetoric are available and frequently invoked in order to match and reconcile the grief-stricken and the celebratory responses to the subject's death. Brinnin, in effect, diminishes the scope and potential of the elegiac form (hence the use of "little" in the title).[45] He does so not in order to argue the impossibility of creating an elegy so much as to strip down its language to its real essence. In so doing, he creates a *felt* rather than an *expressive* elegy, a form that comes as close as possible to standing outside or apart from language. This is underscored by having the farewell conveyed not by a poem but by the bells "tolling her past" (98). Music rather than speech or words is the language of farewell even as innocence becomes the trait of the dead. Both leave behind the explicitness of ordinary speech as the generator of the complexities of the living. Brinnin's final perspective, then, is that Stein's use of language is not simply experimental. It also is a deliberately extreme way of aspiring to a deathlike condition of freedom from expressive meaning and a celebration of an unspoken farewell:

> May every bell that says farewell,
> Tolling her past all telling tell
> What she, all told, knew very well. (98)

In the face of death, all speech is "smooth as stone" and "the word is worlds away" (98), leaving only the ritual bells whose significance is known to all and different, or at least incommunicable, for each. In short, Brinnin's elegy is not only little because of its relative brevity, as is Merwin's single line elegy, but because it is as close to the *felt* elegy of the bells as the *expressive* form of language can come.

Such a conceptual diminution of the elegy as a means of conveying loss manages to maintain the lyric component of the poetic form. A similar effect is achieved by Thomas Merton's "Elegy for James Thurber." It, however, emphasizes not the lyrical but the satiric or complaint component of the form. It does so in two-part progression. First, it focuses on the death of a writer famous for his comic wit and absurd or bizarre fantasies. Second, it suggests his death releases him from a contemporary world suddenly become devoid of laughter or humor. The tone is one of acerbic congratulation of the dead for having achieved that state and so of having avoided a life in which "fools seem to have won" and "humor is now totally abolished" (132). To the poet, death is far preferable than an existence in which there is "nothing to laugh at" (132):

> Leave us, good friend. Leave our awful celebration
> With pity and relief.
> You are not called to solemnize with us
> Our final madness. (132)

Such an injunction completely reverses the conventional elegiac strategy of deep mourning that is designed to bond the poet with his subject. By identifying the ceremonial farewell to Thurber as "awful" and a conclusive form of "madness" that does not require his presence, Merton instead creates a separation or disjunction between himself and Thurber. In peculiarly mordant fashion, it enshrines and elevates the comic and the witty to heights achieved only by Thurber in his work. Thus, Merton drives the apocalyptic vision of madness to the icy Popeian comic fury reached in *The Dunciad:*

> You have not been invited to hear
> The last words of everybody. (132)

The excruciating tedium of listening to "the last words of *everybody*" (my italics) is balanced by the relief inherent in the phrase's awesome import of the finality of human life itself. The compressed significance—partly comic or ironic and partly apocalyptic—of *"last words"* (my italics) moves the savage satiric tone of most of the poem into a more theological perspective. There, even dedication to final things and a restoration of the human being's place in the world becomes implicitly secondary and subordinate to that entity who has been "invited to hear / The last words of everybody" (132), namely, the Creator himself. Even the comedy of the human, as embodied by Thurber, is subsumed by the divine comedy of the Creator, who is destined to oversee the demise of that creation on which He lavished so much attention and concern. Presumably, Merton is arguing that the futility of such a creative venture engenders a wry and detached perception on the part of God. And such a cosmic irony, in turn, absorbs the savage satiric irony and bitterness felt by the human creator, the poet, at the world bereft of humor with the death of Thurber.

If modern poets such as Merton and Brinnin focus on comic or experimental figures such as Stein and Thurber, they do so both in order to test the conventional boundaries of the elegy and also to hint implicitly that its subject need not be well or widely known.[46] More unequivocal explorations of this strategy are found in George Barker's tribute to Michael Roberts and James Wright's low-keyed recollection of his tragi-comic farewell to Morgan Blum. Both of the men elegized were poets, but neither is particularly well-known or celebrated. As such, they call the reader's attention to the fate of most poets—to die without public recognition and to be remembered only or largely through the memorial verse of better-known fellow-artists. Neither Barker nor Wright, however, address this issue explicitly. To do so would be to turn the elegy into a quasi-philosophical reflection on their own achievement in which issues of luck, good fortune, greater skills, and genius would have to be addressed to the disadvantage of the ostensible subject. Instead they take two quite different positions to celebrating the friend who is essentially unknown. Barker praises Roberts rather extravagantly while coupling his praise with oblique and not so oblique criticisms cast as honest judgments. Wright, on the other hand, diminishes his own social or professional standing in an effort to reach an honest and direct assessment of the final situation of the largely unknown poet. Out of it, he turns his own isolation as an individual into a poignant expression of sorrow for the deaths of a whole class of individuals, namely, young unknown poets.

Of the two poems, the one by Barker resonates more fully with conventional elegiac elements, while Wright's is more personally lyrical in tone and attitude. Thus, Barker begins with the traditional interrogatory exclamation of shock and outrage at his subject's death—"how dare the greatest die?" (267)—which quickly modulates into the conventional lament compounded with scorn for a world that can countenance the injustice that leaves living those of far less talent and moral worth:

> So wasteful the world is with her few of best.
> . . . .
> The proud ride past us on their hippogryphs
> To lazy empires opulent with trophies
> Others caught up from the holocaust and the hazards
> At what a price. (267)

Such a traditional or conventional opening, naturally enough, generates the equally traditional response to the lament. After angrily grieving at Roberts's death, he immediately launches a denial of the world's having completely lost the

deceased. Thus, he flatly rejects his own elegiac question, which introduces the
contemplated loss of the person being mourned:

> . . . They do not die.
> Over my writing shoulder, now, guiding
> As many before he guided . . .
> He returns when the poem comes down from the sky
> With the truth in its claws. (268)

In short, Roberts survives as an imaginary and imaginative presence capable
of exercising his habitual role as teacher. And the critical lesson he teaches is that
death is not an escape but a challenge inevitably resulting in loss and defeat of
the challenged one. Mortality is a fact of nature, like falls in mountain climbing.
Both result not in refusal to make the effort but in insistence on extending the
challenge to its highest level.

Wright's poem implicitly begins where Barker's ends. It tacitly accepts the fi-
nality of the fact of mortality and the irrelevance of direct acts of mourning and
ritual expressions of grief. Thus, it begins simply and starkly by registering only
the fact and impact of the unknown poet's death:

> Morgan the lonely,
> Morgan the dead,
> Has followed his only
>
> Child into a vast
> Desolation. (145–146)

From there it modulates into a narrative of Wright's, the speaker's, desire to ac-
company Morgan on his Styx-like boat ride to the other side, his clandestine effort
to visit him in the hospital, his rejection for unexplained reasons by other poets, and
his final sense of endless loneliness. Wright's achievement here is to merge an anec-
dotal, almost comic narrative of the displacement of the ritual of final farewells
with a profoundly restrained lyric cry of isolation, longing, and change. The
speaker's desire is not so much to mourn the death of his friend, the unknown poet,
as it is through him to regret his own continuing to live, isolated in his private and
personal self, when his deepest desire is also to be dead. For him, to be dead, how-
ever, is not to be nescient or reduced to nothingness or freed from isolation. It is
only to be elsewhere in a stark, unfeeling world of darkness, coldness, and silence:

Where the dead rise
On the other shore.
And they hear only
The cold owls throwing
Salt over
Their secret shoulders. (146)

This desire is redeemed from self-indulgence or self-pity by the final perspective, which broadens out the view. It becomes a wider historical contrast between past and present that transmutes the personal longing for a change of place and condition of living into a generalized observation on the fate of poets:

And so a couple
Of years ago,
The old poets died
Young.

And now the young,
Scarlet on their wings, fly away
Over the marshes. (147)

This "observation" uses the neutrality of a generalization that, in being sharpened into a series of polar contrasts (youth—age, human—bird, acceptance—escape), moves beyond the personal without renouncing it. Behind or enveloped in the generalization lies the persistence of the speaker's individual longing for a world elsewhere. The big difference is that in tacitly desiring to emulate the blackbirds soaring beyond the marshes, he transforms the change from a static dead-end of persistent waiting into an active, free pursuit of fresh opportunities.

In doing so, however, Wright articulates not so much a passionate recognition of the availability of these opportunities. Instead, he conveys a desperate hope on the part of all young poets, whom he feels are basically isolated and lonely, that their profession may still remain viable in the contemporary world. Both he and Barker generate a sense of the generic poet as a historically endangered species. For them, the poet is subject to forces not so much focused on his extinction as largely oblivious to his existence or function.

Dylan Thomas and the Poet's Fate

The starkness of the possibility of the modern poet's cultural endangerment and irrelevance is not so much directly faced as subconsciously intruding upon their sensibilities. This can perhaps best be found in a series of elegies by various hands all focused on Dylan Thomas.[47] Poems by Edith Sitwell, Hugh MacDiarmid, Vernon Watkins, and George Barker take a quite different tack from that of Wright and Barker in the just cited elegies. The fact that Barker should be aligned on both sides of the question of the poet's fate testifies both to the complexity of the issue and to its importance in his mind. What these poems do is face directly the issue of what defines or characterizes the poet as a figure in society and the world. But they do so from an insider's position, one that is dedicated to defending aggressively the poet and his role.

Each of these poets presents a significantly different master-image of the poet as embodied in Thomas. Where they converge is in their insistence on the poet's perdurability as a figure central to the world and mankind. Edith Sitwell sees the poet as a major figure of myth; Hugh MacDiarmid sees him as a creature of historical legend; Vernon Watkins, who knew Thomas best, treats him as the embodiment of the force of nature itself; and George Barker asserts that he is the epitome of language most fully realized. All, almost instinctively, veer away from the poet as an individual rooted in a specific historical period. They avoid regarding the poet as a creature increasingly isolated by and from his society. This allows them to stress their own distinctive, value-laden image of the role of the poet in the world that they continue to inhabit. And it is on this "more-than-individual" quality that they, in effect, unite to mount yet another defense of poetry. For while they draw on distinctive traits or aspects of Thomas's personal being, they do so essentially to make them *exempla* of something larger than, other than, the man himself.

Sitwell transmutes Thomas, the Welsh country lad intoxicated with language, into a "Young country god, red as the laughing grapes" (423).[48] He becomes the key figure in her eclectic amalgam of nature and fertility myth borrowed from works of comparative religion, such as *The Golden Bough,* the biblical tales of Adam, Abraham, and Noah, and classical accounts of the Gorgons, the Minotaur, and Sisyphus. He is not only the embodiment but the latest version of the dying and reviving god who brings fertility to the world through magical song while ultimately having to face powerful enemies who entrap him in labyrinths of temptation, danger, and frustration.

Sitwell's syncretistic approach enables her to represent Thomas as a multidimensional, more-than-human figure capable of embodying mankind's aspiration to life and divinity. Unlike the traditional or conventional elegy, her poem opens

not with a lament for her subject's loss of life but with an almost serene accep-
tance of it as the fulfillment of his male erotic and moral goal:

> Black Venus of the Dead, what Sun of Night
> Lies twined in your embrace, cold as the vine?
> O heart, great Sun of Darkness, do you shine
>
> For her, to whom alone
> All men are faithful—faithless as the wave
> To all but her to whom they come after long wandering. . . .
>
> Black giantess who is calm as palm-trees, vast
> As Africa! In the shade of the giantess
> He lies in that eternal faithfulness. (422)

This implicitly identifies Thomas with a specific dying and reviving god, namely,
Adonis the young, handsome lover of a goddess. In doing so, Sitwell is able to dif-
ferentiate between male sexual and romantic behavior in life and in death. Thus,
she can include Thomas, the flagrantly promiscuous individual, in an all-inclu-
sive class or group that in moving from life to death shifts to the role of faithful
lover and companion.[49] From the very beginning, her concern is to expand his
role and to sharply delimit his individuality as a historical person.

Such a bipolar lover is in itself an ironic identification, one who embraces
both life and death. Yet he is also the very essence of the world as an original and
perfect entity "made of the pith and sap of the singing world—/ Green kernel
of a forgotten paradise" (422). As such, he embodies the persistence of the di-
vinity and unity of the natural, which includes in an evolutionary series the cre-
ation of plant, worm, beast, and man. It is his force and power as a figure of gi-
gantic and enormous creative capability central to the very emergence and
continuance of the universe that is celebrated. He, for Sitwell, is the embodiment
of the sacred vision of life as "the oneness of the world" (422). Through the con-
templation of him as a physical creature, this vision of change and unity—this
"holy living, holy dying" (422)—is learned. As such, Thomas becomes in a far-
reaching and profound sense "our hope in this universe of tears" (423).

What makes the poem an elegy, however, is only secondarily his centrality as a
symbol. It is the fact of his loss, the fact that "he is gone" (423) that creates a meta-
physical lament out of his previous glories. Now he is "a buried sun" (423) who "is
one with Adam, the first gardener" (423). No longer is he simply the creative, force-
ful, vital creature who functions as the divine fructifier of nature, the maker of

"frozen fire from gilded Parnassian hives" (423). He has moved from his purely physical and active role as the ritualistic Frazerian wild creature racing through life to preserve "the festival / of wheat" (423). In short, Sitwell implicitly depicts the death of the poet as a fundamental loss for all of mankind and all of history. In contrast to the imperiled position of the individual contemporary poet envisaged by Barker and even more by Wright, she harks back to the ancient, mythopoeic notion of the poet, his role and function. Thomas, like the original poets of ancient civilizations, "sang / Of the beginning of created things, the secret / Rays of the universe, and sang green hymns / Of the great waters to the tearless deserts" (423). Their role was to celebrate creation in its most fundamental state, to preserve life from sterility and the "dust of Death" (423). Quite literally, the poet's task is to revive contemporary society whose corruption, inanition, hatreds, monsters, and pervasive sterility reflect the imaginative horrors of classical myth.

Thomas's loss to the world through an early and sudden death is, of course, a profound one. But because of the way Sitwell construes death itself, it is one not bereft of benefit to Thomas. Death, for her, while associated with grayness and dust, burial and mourning, is also part of "the oneness of the world" (422) that couples absence with presence. Thus, it is a positive as well as a negative condition, one where "all are equal in the innocent sleep" and present in "the clime / Of our forgiveness" (423). Because of its very inescapability, "Death, like the holy Night / Makes all men brothers" (423) and inurement an entrance into "the wise and humbling Dark" (424). These tonalities born of Christian stoicism balance the Romantic grief associated with the too-soon extinguished life of the young poet (whether Chatterton, Keats, Shelley, or Thomas). They, in effect, turn Sitwell's attention back to life and to the poet's central achievement. In her metaphoric schema, the poet provides a counter to "the empires of the human filth" (424) by announcing the arrival of dawn, light, and "all glory hidden in small forms" (424). All of these forms are signs or symbols of the eternal Sun, which is both a natural and supernatural presence, and toward which man so encouraged endeavors to strive. The poet, for Sitwell, thus stands forth as the reminder of human origins in "a forgotten paradise" (422). Even more so is he an adorner and exalter of those already dead, a celebrator of perpetually new beginnings, and a recaller of the diffuse and myriad glories of being alive.

Hugh MacDiarmid reduces the attention on Thomas as a historical individual even further than does Sitwell. He restricts his focus to Celtic historical legend as the backdrop for a personally witnessed allegorical event bearing on the poet's death. The death, however, is conceived of as following from a mythic or legendary war involving deities, human beings, and birds. Approximately the first half of his poem centers on MacDiarmid's allegorical recollection of seeing an arrow shot into the air and, just as it is about to make its descent to earth, being seized by a crow that bears it off into the night. This picture is so remote from the specifics of Thomas's sudden death in New York that without the poem's title, "In Memoriam Dylan Thomas," it would be difficult to link the poet unequivocally with these lines.*

This, however, is part of MacDiarmid's intent, for he sees the arrow and crow as part of a persistent Celtic legend recounted in the stories of Valerius Corvus and "the great Irish epic of Ulster, / The *Tain Bo Chuailgne*" (413).[50] In doing so, he implicitly asserts his right as a cultural insider to comment on the abrupt cessation of Thomas's career as a poet embodying a Celtic tradition that includes not only the Welsh but also the Irish and the Scots. Such a strategy enables him to remove Thomas's death from the Romantic pathos of the young man untimely cut off at the peak of his powers and the emotional outpouring of grief that attends it. Instead, the course of the arrow against the setting sun is seen as a bifocal aesthetic vision: "a gesture of farewell, partly of triumph, / And beautiful!" (412)— about to be "dimmed by destiny" (412). The natural fall of the arrow is aborted by the crow's seizing it in his beak. This, he claims, makes it "a very old and recurring portent in our history" (413) and so not a unique occurrence but rather an integral part of the very fabric of Celtic history. Thomas is thus absorbed into the legendary integuments of the Celtic warrior-hero as the contemporary embodiment of Cuchulainn and Corvus. His allegorical status as arrow is overlaid with a legendary role as warrior and opponent of external and vastly more numerous forces. These last are expanded, too, from Celtic legendary powers by a remembered, actual classical vase and "scenes of the Trojan War" (413). Nor is the expansion limited to an increase in the cultures deployed and the historical time involved. The crow stands both for "battle / And the gods and goddesses of war" (413) so that Homeric divinities are included in addition to the human beings battling over the actions of a renegade wife and foreign adulterer. In effect, these images serve to link imaginatively, if not historically, Thomas, Celtic legend, and the Trojan War of Homer. In the process, as with Sitwell, Thomas's historical individuality as a poet is submerged in a welter of ancient and traditional associations.

The effect of this is to assuage the calamitous response of the contemporary artistic world to Thomas's death by moving it into a historico-mythic setting extending into the deepest reaches of time. Both Sitwell and MacDiarmid are suggesting that the historical cultural centrality of the figure of the poet is the true perspective because it is the original one. Against it, the contemporary world's casual dismissal of or indifference to the poet's role is implicitly seen as a historical and intellectual aberration not destined to prevail for long. This implication shifts the attention of both poems from the dead poet who is their ostensible subject to the living poets actually writing them. Sitwell's invocation of primitive, classical, and biblical allusions and symbols coupled with her use of a long, unrhymed line, an irregular verse form, and apostrophaic interrogatives create a hieratic tone that makes her voice rather than Thomas's demise the central concern. And this voice is one coming from the immemorial past when myth and ritual were both central and commonplace and the poet was a singer and priest as well as, in Auden's words, a player with words.

MacDiarmid's stance toward the dead poet is less spiritual or religious and less rooted in a Frazerian ritualistic pattern of vegetative death and revival. For him, from the very outset, the temporal focus of the key event is the present and his own response to it:

> I rejoiced when from Wales once again
> Came the ffff-putt of a triple-feathered arrow
> Which looked as if it had never moved. (412)

The poet is a historical observer who takes the death of a creator of bold, beautiful, natural phenomena—"soaring, swimming, / Aspiring towards heaven, steady, golden and superb" (412)—almost as secondary to his being deprived personally of more such creations. The crow of death who seizes the quintessential Thomas poem in his beak arouses in the speaker both anger and fear. The anger is in response to the deprivation of more such exquisitely crafted and powerful arrows of the imagination as MacDiarmid found Thomas's poems to be.

> . . . I was furious.
> I had loved the arrow's movement
> Its burning ambition in the sunlight,
> And it was such a splendid arrow,
> Perfectly-balanced, sharp, tight-feathered,
> Clean-nocked, and neither warped nor scraped. (413)

The fear and fright aroused by such a casual, clumsy, and unexpected act as that of the crow's stems from its injection of a foreboding past into the present. It ominously portends defeat by a contemptible, vulgar, and unprepossessing adversary no matter how deeply connected historically with "the gods and goddesses of war" (413). History thus becomes for MacDiarmid both a heroic cultural talisman and a grim reminder of perennial defeat.

With this, MacDiarmid, the nationalist rebel and political activist, assumes the key role supplanting Thomas and his poems. They become simply the most recent examples of "a very old and recurring portent in our history" (413). As a Scot, he is convinced of the disabling, thwarting, imprisoning effect of his nation's being subjected in a variety of ways over centuries to the dictates of another nation. Consequently, he must defy the power of the portent and assume the vigorous tone of the poet as warrior or defender of his country. But since the time of his own and his nation's triumph is not yet, he perforce has to couch his insistence on the ultimate triumph of the figure of the poet allegorically. The restoration of the arrow and the overcoming of the crow are a narrative emblem of the perdurability of poetry and its ability to counter the destructiveness of history:

> But the crow cannot quench the light
> With its outstretched wings forever
> Nor break the law of gravity
> Nor swallow the arrow.
> We shall get it back. Never fear!
> And how I shall rejoice when the War is over
> And there comes from Wales once again
> The fff-putt of a triple-feathered arrow
> Which looks as if it had never moved! (413)

Whether as priest or as warrior, the poet as seen by Sitwell and MacDiarmid is less an individual than a type, a *figura* of extended historical dimensions. It absorbs the ostensible subject and transmutes it from a person to a function selected by the elegizing poet in accord with his or her personal predisposition. Sitwell's transmutation of Thomas into a bardic priest intoning the origins of the world reflects her own later view of the modern poet's social role. Perhaps it also reflects her social status and her willingness to isolate herself culturally and psychologically from the immediacies of the contemporary world by affecting a preference for life in another, older universe whose values and perceptions she can communicate to those willing to respect them. In effect, she is willing to abandon the present to the contemporary world while implicitly elegiacally intoning her own demise and her role as poet. All that is left is the oracular anonymous voice murmuring tales of loss, change, and transformation of values. And yet it is these that invoke hesitantly the possibility of revival and restoration of the glories of the past.

MacDiarmid, on the other hand, resists the tendency to modernist elite withdrawal and quietistic surrender by adapting his poetic to his social outlook. Thus, he projects the contemporary poet in his own likeness as a historical observer of a scene he cannot refute or reject but only outlast. Such enduring accords with a historical determinism whose focus is literally aesthetic and allegorically sociopolitical. His assertions of resistance against the crow and all that it stands for reflect the faith of the poet as social or political rebel in the inevitability of change and victory for his values. In contrast, his memorial assessment of Thomas as a poet is fully celebrated only in the conviction of the persistence of the verbal craftsmanship of the poet, the launching of his poems as an exercise in ambitious aspiration doomed to limited achievement, and the hope for a world of unfettered freedom in which peace is achieved. And in that celebration, it is clear that it is the poet who is still alive, who persists in resisting with stubborn determination the efforts to overshadow and obliterate his role, rather than the dead poet, that commands the admiration and respect of himself and others like him.

By way of sharp contrast to both Sitwell's and MacDiarmid's handling of Dylan Thomas as elegiac subject are Vernon Watkins's two poems on his friend, "Elegiac Sonnet" and "A True Picture Restored." In both, he is concerned to mourn while celebrating the personal traits and achievements that made Thomas a unique individual. It is almost as though Watkins is determined to keep Thomas as a man whom he knew personally from being subsumed under mythic and legendary rubrics of the sort developed by Sitwell and MacDiarmid. It is not so much that he completely rejects their generalizing tendencies as that he scales them down. He does so by focusing on the traditional lament and consolation expressed by nature and felt by the survivors remembering the dead poet. This is captured succinctly and effectively in the Italian sonnet, which concentrates on three distinctive aspects of Thomas deeply felt by Watkins: his concern with "the living word," "his love of vanished things" (434), and his absence from the present scene.

Yet Watkins begins his sonnet not with the particulars of Thomas as an individual but with a generalizing cast to the scene of mourning. The setting's pathetic fallacy clearly suggests its affinities with the conventional elegiac opening:

> Over this universal grave the sky
> Brings to the grieving earth its great reward. (434)

In so doing, he links the individual, the poet as a function, and mankind, all of whom suffer death. Thomas, however, is not so much subsumed into larger classes of being as placed as but the most recent of an endless series of fatalities. And yet, coupled with the grief over his death, the speaker associates the earth with receiving "its great reward." The burial of Thomas in his native land, the bringing of him home, in effect, is how Wales is honored for having nurtured him.

The same duality of response to Thomas's death is continued in the second quatrain, though now concentrated on an intimation of the graveyard scene. The body is "sleeping," while it is the leaves of the trees that are "dead," and it is the poet's body that restores to them "the patient light" (434) produced by its own diminution through death. Restorative though it may be, the body is unblinkingly seen as impoverished in contrast to the richness and diversity of nature embodied in the trees. This mirroring is then transmuted from sight to sound so that the unchanging starkness of the inanimate body (the corpse) occasions the silence of grief, which in turn engenders the awakening "of the living word" (434), which is the expression of loss.

This emotion occasions the movement out of stasis and sleep identified with death and into movement, wakefulness, and renewed life. It also focuses on Watkins's memory of the poet's love of the past, of things lost or no longer present, and of his own elegizing nature. Both of these afford some measure of consolation, largely for their having existed and been shared with or witnessed by Watkins. Nevertheless, memories cannot fully compensate for death. They are overshadowed by the irreversible and irreplaceable loss of the poet who emotionally impacted all:

> It is not this that leaves the heart's way ploughed;
> It is the shade the sun no longer flings
> Of one who touched the humble and the proud. (434)

A less compressed tribute to Thomas is found in Watkins's longer elegiac poem. It stresses both the personal immediacy of their relationship and also Watkins's engagement in a sustained act of recollective assessment. In this last, he sums up the impact of his friend as a poet linked to the whole tradition of English poetry. Thus, the poem is both a correction of public perceptions and a series of specific recollections that exemplify the nature of the man. The dual and balanced nature of the poem's title indicates this at the very outset: "A True Picture Restored" and "memories of dylan thomas."

Perhaps one of the first corrections of the public image of Thomas is that he was the quintessential Romantic poet, one driven by the overflow of powerful emotions, a creature of impulse who lived a life of solitary and splendid isolation. Thus, Watkins opens by calling attention to Thomas's literary mentors, whom he, surprisingly enough, identifies as being two great Renaissance poets not readily associated with Thomas: "Fired first by Milton, then the dreams / Of Herbert's holy breast" (286). In doing so, Watkins calls attention to Thomas's intricate and sonorous diction and to his simple spiritual attention to the commonplace and ordinary in the natural world. These, he feels, place him in the central English literary tradition.

Thomas's literary heritage and affinities are immediately balanced by his identification in Watkins's mind with a local region of light, sunset, green mountains, and "the sky of changes now / On waters never still" (286). In addition to Thomas's principal concerns—to celebrate the world and the word—Watkins here presents the idyllic paradigm of universal natural change that undergirds the elegiac and the death of Thomas. This paradigm is a backdrop for his personal, almost homely, recollections of Thomas as a good and close friend. Out of these emerge Watkins's vision of Thomas as the archetypal giver or restorer of life, as the cause or the force of life in others: "The man I mourn can make it live, / Every fallen grain" (286).

The next fourteen stanzas are given over to a synoptic series of memories of Thomas in his Welsh setting of Swansea, to a combination of meticulous specificity of detail and generic rendering of a semiurban Welsh childhood and maturation. In charting Thomas's relationship to his hometown environment, Watkins has a delicate task to address: to praise the poet without discountenancing the prevailing societal mores, which were largely at odds with Thomas's own. This explains his stress on Thomas's sense of his craft as something to be learned through sedulous devotion to its nuances. He spent, Watkins recalls, countless hours behind "that working window at the top" (287) studying his craft and welcoming the roles both of "the neophyte and clown" (287) in order "to pull illusion down" (287).

Implicitly here Watkins is countering the community's suspicion of the poet's apparently casual and indolent lifestyle by underscoring the hard work invested in "compiling there his doomsday book / Or dictionary of doom" (288). At the same time, he counters the community's principal imaginative activities—the cinema and the church—by suggesting the poet's responses to both. Thomas, he suggests, was neither a secular hedonist nor a religious dogmatist. Instead, he was an active participant in both the world of fleshly entertainment and spiritual aspiration who saw clearly the limitations of both:

> The neophyte and clown
> Setting the reel and arc-light up
> To pull illusion down.
>
> . . . .
>
> The excess or strictness God allows
> In every devious fate,
> He honoured these with early vows
> And cursed the aloof with late. (287)

As Watkins sees it, the cinema and the strictness of God as manifested in the Welsh chapel-goers' beliefs are bipolar factors in Thomas's maturation as a poet and a person. Together, they show two key facets of his being. One is his passion to produce and also to expose illusion. The other is his acceptance of a power or authority that exceeds human understanding. In effect, the cinema and the church are joint images by which Thomas captures the nature of poetry. For him, it is both the creation and the destruction of illusion and the honoring of the spiritual that transcends the narrow limits of the religion he knew. It is this very expansiveness of temperament, this insistence on respecting both the human delight in illusion and mankind's insistence on felt truths, that drives Watkins to his first direct lament for the poet's passing:

> The latest dead, the latest dead,
> How should he have died,
> He in whom Eden's morning
> Had left its ancient pride,
> Adam, God, and maiden,
> Love, and the yearning side? (287)

Thomas's linkage to the spiritual antedates any church, subsisting as it does with Adam and Eve and the prelapsarian world of Eden. Given these religio-archetypal affinities, Thomas's death becomes incomprehensible. For one thing, it represents a profound loss of someone of supreme value. And for another, it signals the unlikelihood of his recurrence. Someone able to respond to the aesthetic and spiritual dimensions of the immediate natural world who also is able to maintain the basic simplicity of the heart's aspiration is, in Watkins's view, improbable to recur. The enormity of this unlikelihood is captured by his blunt interrogative directed at their nation itself: "And Wales, when shall you have again / One so true as he?" (287) The rhetorical form of this question clearly suggests that the only true answer is "Never."

This gloomy and foreboding query captures one facet of the elegiac temper—the almost despairing sense of the irretrievability of the person whose loss has just been suffered. There is, however, another facet that traditionally offsets the sense of loss with a wisdom compounded of despair and memory. This dimension, strikingly enough, Watkins begins to incorporate in his very question about the uniqueness of the community's and nation's loss. Iterated there are Thomas's intuitive oneness with nature in its distinctively Welsh forms of mountain, sea, and bird; his preservation of it in "its pristine state" (287); and his sensitivity to and love for the less than perfect members of mankind. By using images found in Thomas's own poems, Watkins effectively blurs the issue of whether these traits are expressed directly by the man himself or indirectly through his poems. In so doing, he is able to fuse man and poem in his elegiac tribute, thereby avoiding the situation encountered by Sitwell and MacDiarmid where they sacrifice the individual in order to concentrate on the role as poet.

Yet because Thomas as individual was so in tune with the elements of the natural world, especially water, the very fact that "all rivers run / Back to the birth of light" (287), he too is felt to share in this movement. Through his identity with nature as moving waters that follow the course of light and birth and by having him aware of the changes endemic to the world at large, Watkins is able to effect the transformation of the dead friend into a resurrectionary figure. His emblematic role as the human representative of the natural world is fraught with apprehension as well as exaltation since "among the living he was one / Who felt the world in flight" (287). The term "flight" is heavy with ambiguity, suggesting both soaring movement and change as well as desertion and escape from, perhaps, the endless alternation of death and birth. Thus, it arouses concern for the disappearance of life as we know it coupled with an implicit question as to how we are aware of this concern and how we share it with others.

At this juncture the poem suddenly focuses on Thomas as poet when Watkins recollects his nighttime visits to Thomas working on his poems. Summoned up here is his legendary dramatic persona as a reader of poetry. For Watkins, hearing him read his poems was a personal and private experience, not a public performance. Consequently, his response is even more intense he implies. Thomas's reading obliterated time and rendered space simultaneously empty and full, and made the private scene into "the centre of the world . . . the hub of time" (288). At this moment, in the act of reading or speaking his own words at once complex, simple, and sublime, Thomas miraculously counters the inevitable human march toward death. Simultaneously, Watkins declares the poet and friend "showed me his nature then as now, / The life he gave the dead" (288). It is the two—the person and his words, arrived at "after toil and plumbing" (288)—that transform the elegiac from a lament to a celebration of the fact that for Thomas "it was the dying earth he gave / To heaven in living verse" (288). For Watkins, the poet is not a creature separate from his personal individuality existing solely as a mythic or legendary figure. Rather, he is a unique being known intimately who faces the life known to all of us and "in the one death his eye discerned / The death all deaths must die" (289).

In drawing attention to Thomas as reciter, Watkins succeeds in fusing the man and the poet and in regaining both through a clear memory of him as a speaking voice rather than a dead body:

> Nor by the black of London's blinds
> Or coffin's rattling cord,
> But by the stillness of that voice
> The picture is restored. (289)

And yet it is not the energy or profligacy or exuberance of the poet's speaking voice celebrating the works of others and of the ages that proves restorative. Instead it is the very absence, the permanent cessation of it that shifts the controlling image of memory back from the fluidity of sound to the precision of the picture.

Consolidating that restoration is the prayer-like recognition by Watkins that Thomas was dedicated to geographical locality as the authentication of the reality of the individual:

> Let each whose soul is in one place
> Still to the place be true.
> The man I mourn could honour such
> With every breath he drew.
> I never heard him wish to take
> A life from where it grew. (289)

Such an encomiastic tribute subtly links Thomas as poet of the world with Thomas as Welshman. Thereby it draws the nation into Watkins's elegiac remembrance of greatness and gratitude that ends fittingly with something other than a conventional celebration of the poet's life. He concludes, rather, with the simple intensity of the sorrow at the loss sustained by an individual friend, the mass of mankind, and even nature:

> And yet the man I mourn is gone,
> He who could give the rest
> So much to live for till the grave,
> And do it all in jest.
> Hard it must be, beyond this day,
> For even the grass to rest. (289)

In the end, the restoration of the vision of the reality of Thomas is disrupted. Instead, presented in full naked finality is the terrible fissure of loss created by a friend and fellow-poet gone forever. So overwhelming is the fact that this sustainer of life is irreparably absent that even the grass will have to struggle to suspend its customary labors.

George Barker, like Watkins, attends both to the individual man and the poet as spiritual revivifier in his "At the Wake of Dylan Thomas."[51] For him, however, it is language extended to its fullest through the energy of joy and music and image that comprises the defining nature of his personal acquaintance and of the ideal poet.[52] Where Watkins concentrates on nature as sensory ground and subject of Thomas's poems, Barker finds language itself to embody Thomas's defining trait as a poet. Thus, he begins his elegiac tribute by declaring his own reluctance to use language "even for such a purpose / As to honour this death by act of passion" (308). His reluctance is attributed to his recognition that speech has been abandoned by the now deceased Thomas, "that master of the house," and that consequently "the air is full of dead verbs" and "there are ashes / In every dumbstruck mouth" (308). In place of language and the expression of grief there is only death, silence, and the sea prevailing:

> Silence is what we hear in the roaring shell.
> That first sea whence we rose and to which shall
> Go down when all the words and all the heroes
>
> Striking their lyres and attitudes in the middle
> Of that burning sea which was a cradle,
> Go down under that silence of that sea. (308)

The implications of this are elegiac in a double sense. With the master of language, Thomas, silenced and with those who survive hearing only silence, poetry itself is silenced and with it Barker's own career as a poet. This is a premonitory vision of the ultimate end for every hero of language, every poet, when death calls him down into its perennial silence. Silence is that from which man comes at the time of the world's creation and to which he returns inevitably. And it is against this vision that Barker must struggle if he is to continue to use language, to write poetry, and to mourn elegiacally the friend whose wake he has just attended. In celebrating that ceremony, Barker is faced not only with grieving the loss of a fellow-poet but also affirming his own aliveness and continuing existence as a poet, a user of language.

His affirmation is achieved through a metaphoric act of memory in which he recalls Thomas's symbolic act of creation designed to replace the pain of existence with the joy of being:

> This son of pearl was walking beside water
> Taking the pain of sand out of the oyster:
> "We will make poems," he said, "simply from joy." (309)

It is Thomas's simple, childlike, innocent delight in the creation of poetry and the apprehension of the physical world that spurs Barker here to mime Thomas's use of language as an exuberant, joyous magical act: "all joy is magical" (309). His own frenzied escalation of language to a veritable whirl of words is designed to counter the silence, both physical and metaphysical, that has beset the world with Thomas's death and the victory of the sea.

Barker employs an amalgam of biological, chemical, religious, and literary images to capture Thomas's mixture of the sophistication of the baroque and the artlessness of the naive:

> And with the same wonder that the first amoeba
> Stepped out of hydrogen and saw God's labour,
> He goggled at glory as though it had just begun.
>
> That burning babe! Crying from a bushel
> Where he hid all his knowledge in the vessel
> Of a divine and a divining image,
>
> He triumphed up the trumpets of a cherub.
> What is more for ever and more terrible
> Than Abraham's kid and babe singing together? (309)

Here, Thomas's innocent enthusiasm for life and language is not linked with the prelapsarian world as it is by Watkins. Rather, it is allied with the classical god of fertility, who is living and dying in a postlapsarian universe:

> He is as old as that forgotten garden
> Where only he and all the spellbound children
> May freely in delight forget a fall. (309)

Barker's recollection of his fellow-poet and his ability to revive the spirits of others through communicating his own joy in living is clear-eyed enough to face the duality inherent in the situation symbolized by the wake. To remember creative vitality and to take heart from the recollection entails, by the very fact of its being an act of memory, the stark recognition that Thomas is now a corpse incapable of returning in human form. As such, he raises the persisting question as to the inexpungibility of his vitality, freedom, and resourcefulness. Barker senses the shadow of his own mortality as a person and poet, so that "the images of death begin to glitter / Like falling icicles of an immanent / End" (310). His oscillatory attitude toward Thomas's demise forces his consideration of his own relation to Thomas, his death, and what it may presage.

Through his overt identification with Thomas, he is able to feel that his own poem "speaks / A crown of joy or courage among cold rocks" (310). In effect, through his elegiac remembrance the continuity of the proud voice of the poet as recaller of the past and celebrator of the present is established forever: "'My voice and my grave open. I cannot die'" (311). He feels Thomas lives through his poem as a force or power investing its language with joy and courage and immortality. At the same time, Thomas as a person exists only as a ghost descending to the grave and the underworld. In admitting this, Barker draws for himself and presumably all living poets a somber but bold prospect. His metaphoric declaration of immortality is language's own utterance, one that accompanies the descent of the dead in a spirit of proud invincibility:

> But his ghost puts by this poem and goes down
> Shaking its locks loudly into the dark,
> And every word of the tongue follows him proudly. (311)

Anonymous and Apocryphal Individuals

Acquaintances, Soldiers, Old Ladies

*P*ersons unknown to the mass of mankind and perhaps only casually familiar to the poet constitute a significantly different subject from the varied historical figures just considered. For one thing, they arouse a different set of expectations in the poetic audience, one largely marked by the absence of any immediate expectations at all. Such a neutral response mirrors that of the ordinary contemporary reader for the multitude of historical noteworthies honored by many poets of centuries ago. Thus, how one is to take the celebrations of their several deaths is built up by the very unfolding of the individual poems themselves and the attitudes engendered by the poet. Such poems, at least in part, frequently occasion a self-questioning by the poet. For instance, there is the query as to whether one is actually writing an elegy or not. This, in turn, involves an assessing of the customary nature of the genre and whether such an effort should even be essayed given the modern poet's often detached or ambiguous attitudes toward the subjects presenting themselves.

This is seen best perhaps in two poems by Robert Lowell and Ronald Bottrall that function as a kind of transition between the historical and the anonymous. Both identify their subjects by name and so as actual individuals while simultaneously raising for the reader a concern as to their identities and natures. Lowell's "Alfred Corning Clark (1916–1961)" and Bottrall's "One Cornishman to Another— Peace Alfred Wallis!" name their subjects explicitly, but this does little to establish their personal natures or to mute the sense of anonymity they initially carry for the reader.[1] In so doing, both poems intensify interest in the poet's precise relation to his subject. At the same time, they render suspect his right to voice a full elegiac response to the person he is remembering.

As a school classmate, Clark obviously was familiar to Lowell, and yet it is the very scope and reality of this familiarity Lowell questions.[2] Thus, Clark begins as a stranger, a "foreigner" to Lowell as narrator, and virtually everything detailed in the poem intensifies this impression. At its end, Clark remains inscrutable or unknowable "as a lizard in the sun" (21). In effect, he appears to be all surface and removed from the schoolboy world of the author's recollections. Lowell's memory and his habit of contemplating the past for personal resonances both moral and psychological have been jogged into play by casually noticing Clark's newspaper obituary. As a result, by the time Lowell claims to "feel the pain" behind Clark's face and "hardly recognizable photograph" (20), the recording of superficial details of his life gives a tone of polite diffidence to the declaration. Only by the balanced antithesis of the next line—"You were alive. You are dead." (20)—together with its full stop punctuation is the event engrafted with a certain solemnity acknowledged by the poet as appropriate and fitting to the death of a childhood acquaintance, of someone whom one once knew and knows no longer.

The temporal gap between the two periods of time and the attendant reflections on time, familiarity, and history they occasion underlie the sense of loss created by Clark's death. This loss, however, clearly cannot be for the passing of a close friend. Instead, it is for the impossibility of ever repaying an emotional debt owed to a person so different from the poet as to be secretly envied. Clark's "triumphant diffidence" and his "refusal of exertion" (21) are the antithesis of the manic poet's demeanor then and now. Where they resemble one another is in their intelligence: for the one, a casual assumption from birth; for the other, a passionate pursuit of achievement. Lowell's praise for Clark's mind and attitude—"quick and cool to laugh" (21)—is suffused with self-deprecating envy: "I was befogged, / And you were too bored" (21). Clark's superiority is not simply a product of Lowell's introverted and self-chastening mind as is seen by their schoolboy games of chess which, Lowell remembers, Clark "usually won" (21) without excitement or apparent effort.

All of this is Lowell's hesitant, circuitous effort to sketch how contemporary poetry proceeds to entertain writing an elegy on a person largely unknown to the general public. First comes a reiteration of a newspaper's "dry / obituary" (20). Then, there is a checking of Clark's remembered traits against his own poetic impulses. And finally, there is the somewhat reluctant (and unstated) decision against such an effort. Though Clark is ultimately worthy of praise despite a life largely unrealized, such praise cannot exceed the limited, personal recognition presented here. Lowell's negative judgment is ultimately not based on any sense of his own greater achievement or even on his obliquely revealed envy of Clark's nature and abilities. It derives from his admiration for someone who could live his life so fully in accord with his own values while remaining indifferent to those of the world in general.

In effect, it is almost as if Lowell senses intuitively that Clark from his childhood lived in a manner more appropriate to one bearing such an august name as Lowell than did Lowell himself. And yet if Lowell had been able to live in such a fashion, he would not have become the world famous poet he did. Thus, for him to offer elegiac praise of Clark would implicitly entail a disavowal of himself and his role as poet. Substantially, then, the poem he does write in remembrance of Clark is less an elegy in the traditional sense than a disavowal of the elegy as a form appropriate for him to essay in this situation.

Bottrall's poem uses a quite different strategy for essentially the same end. It deflects the elegiac temper into a remembrance of an idiosyncratic individual worthy of recollections. Where Lowell bases his memories of Clark on the accident of their schooltime acquaintance, Bottrall sets his fuller recollection of Wallis in the geographical and ancestral context of their joint residence in Cornwall.[3] In this regard, he recalls Watkins's reminiscences of living, like Thomas, in Swansea. Where they differ, however, is in their occupations or professions. Wallis, the older man, spent his life by the sea as a fisherman and caustic student of religion as well as—ultimately—a painter, while Bottrall as a child played, listening entranced to the multi-toned sounds of strange tongues that presaged his becoming a poet:

> You heard religious voices disputing
> And accusing; seated above Porthmeor
> On the Man's Head, that rifted rock jutting
> Into the opal shallows, in my keyed ear
> > Jewelled word-patterns shone,
> Commanding in strange Caliban shapes from sea and sun. (119)

Despite their differences in age and occupation, Wallis and Bottrall share a readiness to use language for the rhetorical purpose of advancing their own deeply held opinions, the one religious, the other literary:

> I also underwent the meal-time thrust
> And bitter counterthrust of text and precept,
> Citations from Hosea adduced to invest
> A cutting word with a fresh barb—myself adept
> > At setting well-ground themes
> To Wellsian tunes and kindling passionate family flames. (120)

For Bottrall, the commendable qualities of Wallis are his energy and vigor of advocacy even, or particularly, when that advocacy is at odds with or different from views held by Bottrall as a youth. In his process of translating physical activity and energy into metaphor through human effort, Wallis invests the physical with the imaginative in his seeing the actual ships as "hounds at play" (118). That this is part of an extended analogy between the religious and the poetic views is suggested by the succeeding stanzas. They move from praise of the metaphoric to disdain for the intellectually weak and conventional to admiration for a loosely Blakean rejection of the common sense of group opinion. All of these are tacitly points of admiration in Bottrall's recollective tribute to his fellow Cornishman. Wallis's method of arguing from "a holy rite / Of bible texts" (118) is wholly alien to Watkins's own reliance as a youth on the rationalistic and scientific "Wellsian tunes" (120). Nevertheless, in Bottrall's view, the vigor and full-throated commitment to a definite point of view is the same in both.

And yet this similarity in the two men is by no means identity of interest or attitude. This is dramatically evident when Watkins shifts from Wallis to himself as child visitor to the former's fishing village. In doing so, he sets youth over against age, mining town over against fishing village, and life of the mind over against that of the body. Implicitly he draws Wallis's energetic commitment to an individualistic and iconoclastic repudiation of "the superficial daubs / Of elderly academic nincompoops" (118) into his own way of thinking. But he does so through language heard. Wallis's religious language is markedly different from Bottrall's artistic and imaginative speech. It becomes, the poet now sees, a basis for dialectical agons of contention between the sacred and the secular.

A secondary dialectic is also presented, this one between the views and responses to life of D. H. Lawrence and Wallis. In this polarization between the exotic, the distant, and the primitive, on the one hand, and the native, the near or present, and the local, on the other, Bottrall clearly sides with Wallis's defense of the latter. They share a common geographical ancestry to which, unlike Lawrence's restless wanderings, they cling steadfastly. They do so because it encapsulates their racial heritage of living "near / To death, from shoal, mine, tempest" (120). This daily, soul-penetrating contact with and awareness of death as an ordinary, commonplace, and frequent phenomenon is fundamental to the Cornish psyche and temperament. By not grasping this, Lawrence has mistaken the Cornishman as "hard-backed with squashy souls / That stepped-on oozed white guts" (120). In reaching such a conclusion, he has founded his preference for the exotic on not realizing that "disgust / is often measured by similitude of dust" (120). In short, Lawrence's recoil from the living reality of personal origins is assessed in terms of the commonality of death. Against this measuring rod, the intensity of the emotion is seen as both erroneous and excessive to the reality of the human condition. The reality is, Bottrall suggests, that the dialectic of exotic and local share in that both have secrets of a preternatural or awesome order. Cornwall equally with the American Southwest possesses opportunities for interacting with the forces of evil, death, and deprivation. And out of his native context of struggle, danger, and poverty, Wallis was able "to make the moving things of flesh and soil seem one" (121).

It is in this dynamic harmony between man and environment that Wallis's great achievement lies, one which presumably Bottrall hopes to match if only in being able to remember it as a shaping force in his own quite different life:

> Now our tender land enfolds you, in rest
> Beside the sea that pulls with its high tide
> The anchors of our being, There may no blast
> Of jazzed-out progress intrude its brassy pride
>> And distort or untune
> The living tone-fall that springs from every carn and towan. (121)

While Bottrall comes closer than Lowell to the general elegiac mood, he too deflects his attention away from the note of mourning that ordinarily dominates in the elegy. His attitude to Wallis's death is more one of acceptance than of loss deeply felt. He concludes, therefore, with satisfaction that Wallis's final resting place perpetuates the balance of land and sea, steadiness and movement. In so doing, it reflects permanently Wallis's imaginative vision of life lived in conjunctive struggle with the natural world. Ultimately, the poem resolves the tensions between two radically different views of life through their being rooted in the same geographical location. The peace which he enjoins on Wallis in the poem's title is the truce that can come only with death and memory entwined. And as the remaining living member of the dialectic, Bottrall ultimately must celebrate the memory of Cornwall rather than mourn the death of Wallis. Place rather than person is at the core of the poem, thereby rendering it a memorial to the poet's own living and growth rather than an elegy for the loss of an admired antagonist to death.

Both Lowell and Bottrall exemplify the poet's unwitting encounter with the difficulty of knowing someone well or fully enough to elegize them. Such an act entails not only knowledge of another but also of self. The elegiac effort necessarily demands examination of one's own identity and recognition of the self's at least partial anonymity. Out of it is defined how specifically it relates to the elegiac subject, to the other who is both known and unknown. In the poems considered, both poets deflect the challenge of elegizing the anonymous sub-ject precisely because they are unable fully to deal with the anonymity of the known.

Other modern poets, however, come at the issue not from the standpoint of ren-dering the known individual anonymous through recognizing the limitations of that knowledge. Instead, poets from Siegfried Sassoon to John Crowe Ransom seek in a variety of ways to elegize those who are fully anonymous. Siegfried Sassoon and Wallace Stevens take up the familiar task of memorializing the fallen warrior, the soldier who is unknown as an individual because he stands as the symbol of all who have fallen. The differences in tone and authorial at-titude between their two versions implicitly capture the contrasts between En-glish and American, soldier and civilian, and their responses to the deaths of thousands.

Sassoon's "To Any Dead Officer" is casual, anecdotal, and bitter in its reminis-cences. Its five stanzas allow sufficient scope for a mixture of detailed recollec-tions of typical behavior and savage reflections on the reasons for soldiers' deaths.[4] He presents them as if in a letter or telephone conversation to an absent friend, sharing news, hitherto undivulged memories and thoughts, and responses to the absence itself.[5] By this, he is able fictively to individualize his subject while incorporating generic traits found in the wartime situation. In effect, the poem's title and the attitude expressed by the speaker are at odds for ironic purposes. The former generalizes the figure while the speaker explicitly individualizes his sub-ject. The irony central to Sassoon's historical intent is created by the shifting of attention from the one to the many.[6] By so doing, he suggests that all dead offi-cers were individuals badly dealt with by life and by death. In the former, they were subjected to the less-than-human existence in the trenches of World War I. Whereas in the latter, they are wasted in an insignificant struggle, a bogus battle as it were. The burden of the poem is borne by the speaker's anger and bitter frustration at the society's political maladroitness and blind stupidity exercised in the conduct of the war. It is not so much that young men are being called on to fight, but that they are being denied a chance to win through blind, headstrong, and inefficient leaders who heedlessly sacrifice their lives in vain.[7]

   Given such a situation and official attitude, the poet's challenge in elegizing such a death is twofold. He must avoid sentimentalizing it while refraining from trivializing it. The one requires attending to the individual as victim, and the other to the group as victim. Sassoon de-sentimentalizes the death by emphasizing the ordinary, nonheroic nature of war life and by underscoring its accidental, pointless nature. At the same time, he avoids trivializing the death by stressing several facets of the situation. These include the intensity of the victim's love of life and his desire to survive, the underlying normalcy of his response to war, the sense of what the circumstances need or demand, and the understanding of the suffering attendant upon the official description "'wounded and missing'" (85).

These competing demands on the poet result in a strategy for memorializing the death that changes the traditional elegy's balance between anger and sorrow, satire and lyric so as to give greater weight to the former. Thus, Sassoon shifts the focus on the death by satirizing its place in the larger, political scheme of things and the official language and attitudes toward it. He captures the ironic and contemptuous attitude of the survivor in much the same way as MacLeish does while memorializing his brother. Sassoon, however, allows a single, brief revelation of the intensity of the sorrow at the waste and folly of it:

> Remember me to God,
> And tell Him that our Politicians swear
> They won't give in till Prussian Rule's been trod
> Under the Heel of England . . . Are you there?
> But we've got stacks of men . . . I'm blind with tears,
> Staring into the dark. (85)

The barely suppressed anger and frustrated sorrow caught in these last lines is virtually the only sign of the elegiac temper's customary response to death. In its stead are placed a disgusted rage at the inevitability of death in a thoroughly mismanaged conflict, at the indifferent utilization of human beings as raw materials like cordwood, and at the creation of multiple victims. What Sassoon dramatizes, then, is the need for such a tonal shift in an elegiac effort when its subject is plural and its role that of individual, helpless victim.

Sassoon's poem epitomizes the response to death by war made by many of the participants in World War I. A far different treatment is that of Wallace Stevens's "The Death of a Soldier." Not only was it written by a noncombatant at the time of World War I and by an American rather than an Englishman, but it aspires to viewing the event *sub specie aeternitatis*.[8] Its tone is philosophical, its attitude essentially fatalistic and detached, and its manner calmly declarative[9]:

> Life contracts and death is expected,
> As in a season of autumn.
> The soldier falls. (97)

The demise here involves not the suddenness of accident but the predictability of life. And the question of its cause is skirted, though alluded to indirectly and obliquely. Consequently, it is seen as a natural, inevitable event emblemizing the course of human life. The death of warriors is but one instance of the endless cessations of personal existence. By reducing the millions of such events to a single figure, Stevens ruthlessly strips the event of public recognition and recollection and the person of any trait other than his humanness:

> He does not become a three-days personage,
> Imposing his separation,
> Calling for pomp.
>
> Death is absolute and without memorial,
> As in a season of autumn,
> When the wind stops. (97)

The uninflected flat directness of the statements, the simplicity of the diction, the repetition of the autumnal reference, the variation of line length, all contribute to a careful neutrality of judgment concerning the event. The overt effect is that of an anti-elegiac poem whose studied composure and emotional control pares away centuries of traditional literary, historical, and social conventions. As a result, it avoids metaphoric and highly wrought rhetorical language for factual, declarative utterance.

As the last stanza reveals, this sort of speech has been steadily building throughout the entire poem. It creates a covert effect grounded in a commonsense reality:

> When the wind stops and, over the heavens,
> The clouds go, nevertheless,
> In their direction. (97)

This second effect restores the elegiac temper through reliance solely on the perceived facts of death: life both stops and continues despite what its spectators feel. Both the stoppage and the continuance are part of its natural and normal rhythm. The measured recognition of this is, for Stevens, the just, appropriate, and only elegy needed or possible. Seen as the culmination of a shaping of sympathies begun with Sassoon, cultivated and shaped by Hemingway, and finally compressed by Stevens, the poem is a modern epitome of the elegiac as the laconic disavowal of the expressing of grief. The control required to repress mourning is the revelation of the depth of feeling contained therein. As such, it may be the inevitable form for the elegiac in an age so dominated by profound loss expressed in so many ways and conditions. ·

As we have seen, the modern period has suffered enormous personal losses through its worldwide experience of multiple wars, insurgencies, revolutions, police actions, and reprisals. At the same time, it has also witnessed the lengthening of individual lives through the discoveries and significantly improved and expanded practices of medical, nutritional, agricultural, and environmental care. As a result, it is no surprise to discover poets attending to the death of the aged as well as of the young. Sassoon, Louis MacNeice, and Thomas Merton all chart the range of the modern elegiac temper in poems dealing with the end of elderly women. In many ways, they serve a role as central to the elegiac temper as that of soldiers. Young men and old ladies both focus the mind, though in quite different ways, on the significance of death, personal mortality, and the idea of loss.

Sassoon's "To an Old Lady Dead" conveys by its very title something of the multiplicity of poetic functions it serves. The use of "To" captures, first, the dramatic informality of a personal monologue. By suggesting a direct address to the woman, even though she is beyond hearing it, the poet ironically defines his awareness of the difference between his visits to her while alive and now that she is dead. The invocatory "To" also functions partly as a salutation of honor or homage, as in a toast of recognition. As a result, the poem also celebrates the achievements of her long life—a serene elegance of taste, a natural politeness of manner, and an informed conversational ability. All of these testify to gracious living at its most civilized. And finally, the "To" functions as a meditative memorial based on the acute difference between living and dying as seen in one individual.

   This difference is struck immediately in the first line by the epithet "old lady" with which the poem opens. It suggests a brusquer mode of address, one less polite or circumspect than has been the speaker's practice when she was alive. Implicitly, this also suggests the poet's initial attitude contains a measure of deceit, perhaps dictated by self-interest. This notion is underscored by his candid description of his demeanor: "last year I sipped your tea / And wooed you with my deference" (184). Modifying to some degree this attitudinal coldness is the fact that the epithet also indicates that she is cast as a type or function of chronological age rather than of individuality. In what follows, there is a depiction of the covert difference between she and the poet founded upon their respective ages and social status: "These moments are 'experience' for me; / But not for you; not for a mutual 'us'" (184).

In many ways, the poem reflects the prewar society chronicled by Henry James and reflected in an American setting by T. S. Eliot's "Portrait of a Lady," which similarly explores the mixed and ambiguous motives and values of a dramatic speaker.[10] Thus, why he metaphorically "wooed" her is a tangled set of possibilities. Included are: for the experience of gaining her favor; of observing a kind of social curiosity for his own ironic purposes; and of somewhat cynically improving his social position and gaining inclusion in a special circle or society. Sassoon here shares with James and Eliot the same clear-eyed, dispassionate self-assessment discovered almost unconsciously by their speakers. In all, one's self-interest is noted with little embarrassment or chagrin.

The very fact of her death, however, initiates both this self-assessment and the sharp differences he notes in her when living and dead. These differences point up the puzzle or enigma he faces in assimilating the contrast and its significance. On the one hand, there is her undeniable power and success as a social figure and, on the other, its transformation into a memorial to an artifice of unreality, emptiness, and nothingness. They work together to become a kind of *memento mori* of the social persona:

> You lived your life in grove and garden shady
> Of social Academe, good talk and taste;
> But now you are a very quiet old lady,
> Stiff, sacrosanct, and alabaster-faced,
> > And, while I tip-toe awe-struck from your room,
> > I fail to synthesize your earth-success
> > With this, your semblance to a sculptured tomb
> > That clasps a rosary of nothingness. (184)

Essentially Sassoon inverts or pulls inside out the elegiac pattern. In it, the customary sense of loss articulated by the speaker for the deceased usually intensifies the latter's significance, and the final note expressed is one of acceptance of or reconciliation with the fact of the death. Here, he explicitly testifies to the relative absence of meaningfulness in the dead woman compared to her while living. This underscores his inability to feel any continuity between the two. In effect, death is the victor not only over the woman but also over the speaker, who is unable to voice an elegiac farewell or to feel the elegiac temper of loss. Instead, he is left simply with a hard-edged realistic assessment of the triviality of the upper-class life of gentility to which he has aspired so willingly. Here Sassoon signals the first signs of the dissolution of his society's conventional respect for such a life and the traditional elegiac way of honoring it. Not to write an elegy is an authorial choice, but to write a not-elegy is a cultural decision with far reaching consequences.

A later instance of the same general phenomenon is Louis MacNeice's "Death of an Old Lady." Though it avoids the Browningesque gradual disclosure of the speaker's character, it shares with Sassoon's poem a kind of wry, studied, almost clinical interest in and reflection on death.[11] While both are struck by its finality, it is MacNeice who captures more fully both its inevitability and its accidental or unpredictable quality.[12] He does so by linking the old woman as a child with the Titanic about to leave the shipyard in which it has been built.

The poem begins in MacNeice's characteristic version of the middle style, a low-keyed narrative that builds significance through the accumulation of details in a past scene. But in beginning the second stanza with a verbal quibble—"Named or called? For a name is a call" (463)—he casually raises the motif of voices and language. In a self-conscious and reflective way, it provides an incipient rationale for metaphor and with this for the old lady's identification with the Titanic, the ship of grandeur and disaster:

> Shipyard voices at five in the morning,
> As now for this old tired lady who sails
> Towards her own iceberg calm and slow. (463)

The irony inherent in linking the two—the old woman and the new ship—is accentuated by the final stanza. It suggests that the voices mentioned in the previous stanzas, though originally from her childhood, are actually recollected on her deathbed:

> They called and ceased. Later the night nurse
> Handed over, the day went down
> To the sea in a ship, it was grey April,
> The daffodils in her garden waited
> To make her a wreath, the iceberg waited;
> At eight in the evening the ship went down. (463)

This irony is heightened by the allusion to John Masefield's line, which creates an implicit juxtaposition of a past noble tradition and the present sense of an isolated or final occurrence. For MacNeice, the embarkation is on a disastrously interrupted and death-filled voyage rather than a successfully completed journey. The poem's tone as a whole is neutral regarding death, whether of the old lady or of the Titanic's passengers, and the only sadness expressed is the normal regret for the fact of death's inevitability. The speaker is recollective and spectatorial rather than passionately committed to the elegiac act of mourning the loss attendant on death.[13]

If Sassoon's attitude is ironic and puzzled and MacNeice's gravely sympathetic but fanciful via his equation of old lady and ship, then Merton's is almost macabre or grotesque in its matter and manner. And yet his poem alone proclaims itself an elegy and documents its historicity by commenting on the deaths of a series of actual old ladies. "An Elegy for Five Old Ladies" dispassionately records their inept encounter with machinery (*"a driverless car"* [310]), the bizarre nature of human events, and the purposiveness of the accidental to create a baroquely comic scene that, nevertheless, receives a spiritual rationale.

As with Hopkins's "The Wreck of the Deutschland," Merton has to counter both the event's appearing to be wholly fortuitous and inexplicable and the ladies' responsibility for their own irresponsibility.[14] Only by so doing can he square his religious perspective with his claim to be writing an elegy. He does so by investing the event with the aura of a divinely ordained or permitted event and by linking the women with nuns as bridal partners:

> Let us forget that it is spring and celebrate the rider-
> less will of five victims.
>
> . . . .
>
> Let us accordingly pay homage to five now legendary
> persons, the very chaste daughters of one unlucky
> ride.
> Let the perversity of a machine become our common
> study, while I name loudly five loyal spouses of
> death! (310)

Also contributory to this linkage is a species of indirect narration and language choice that allows him to represent the implied point of view of the women and their fellows. Thus, he implicitly calls on his readers to contemplate the theological mystery of the occurrence of bad events in a divinely ordained universe. From the ordinary daily secular point of view, the women are seen to be "waifs" and "orphans" (310), pathetic victims of their abandoned and hopeless condition as residents in a nursing home. His religious perspective, however, contains a willingness to risk the appearance of absurdity. And this enables him to elevate the confused and helplessly inept elderly women to the status of "loyal spouses of death" (310). In so doing, Merton grounds his elegy in his religious faith, in his theology of obedience and acceptance that can transform the most baroque of events into an acceptance of a rationally inexplicable occurrence. It does so through the formal rhetoric of injunctive prayer caught in the repeated phrase "Let us" (310). This extends the poem's elegiac temper to the hopefulness of a request addressed to God by human beings contemplating the death of fellows known to them only through the pages of the *New York Times*.

Widows, Mothers, Children, Maidens

Much more immediate and personal in character is a group of poems dealing with various sorts of familial losses that strive to explore and test the boundaries of the modern elegiac temper. An interesting case is William Carlos Williams's "The Widow's Lament in Springtime."[15] Several of its elements suggest its affinities are with the conventional elegiac form. Thus, the widow singles out the death of one individual, her longtime husband, as the supreme occasion of personal sorrow surpassing all others in a lifetime of sorrow. She frames her lament in a garden setting of flowers and fruit redolent with life. And finally, her reflections point up a clear contrast between past joy and present sorrow. However, what keeps Williams from developing a conventional elegy per se is his use of a first person dramatic speaker, which differs significantly from that deployed, say, by Tennyson with *In Memoriam*. The widow concentrates exclusively on her own emotional pain at the disruption of her life rather than on the loss of the deceased to her, his family, and the community. Nor does the poem contain anything resembling the elegy's characteristic acceptance of the loss sustained by the world at large.

In short, Williams focuses on the personal nature of her grief, her relative inarticulateness of expression, and the virtual banality of her wished-for gesture of resolution being cast as an abandonment to despair and death itself:

> I feel that I would like
> to go there
> and fall into those flowers
> and sink into the marsh near them. (1:171)

The poem thus deals with an almost pre-elegiac state of numbness and shock at the very fact of the death rather than with the celebratory elegiac rendering of the momentousness of the event for all those still living.

Or to put it another way, the poem engages directly the kind of response made not by a poet but an average person capable only of personal, not communal or public, sentiments. Consequently, its challenge is to convey the intensity of her grief without rendering it overwrought or embarrassing. And it meets this challenge by a process of elision that moves from metaphor to concrete detail to direct statement. A fairly elaborate metaphor linking her sorrow and her garden segues into familiar specific details of plum and cherry blossoms and then emerges as a direct statement contrasting her former response to nature to her present one:

> but the grief in my heart
> is stronger than they
> for though they were my joy
> formerly, today I notice them
> and turned away forgetting. (1:171)

A far different use of the first person lament is found in Edith Sitwell's "A Mother on Her Dead Child."[16] Williams is restrained, simple, and direct in his effort to make the formality of the traditional elegy bend to capturing the immediate dramatic sensibility of a distraught individual who is not a fully conscious or articulate character. Sitwell takes the opposite tack. Her character, the mother, is heightened, rhetorically extravagant, elaborate, and archetypally imagined. She is not so much an individual parent as all mothers who have lost an offspring. In a sense, she feels herself as such and sees her situation in relation to the far larger one of the earth, the sun, the seasons, and the Fall of Man.

Her reflective attitude is consonant with the poem's title, the purpose of which is to sum up all that she knows and feels about the child rather than merely to mourn its loss. The loss, however, is part of her knowledge and not a separate alternative to it. This comes clear when the child appears to come alive with the arrival of spring and "the warmth of the affirming sun" (279). The child metaphorically is part of the world and the earth. Yet it is the mother's very doubt as to the reality of the rebirth that motivates her initial plea of the dead child:

> O Sun of my life, return to the waiting earth
> Of your mother's breast, the heart, the empty arms.
> Come soon, for the time is passing, and when I am old
> The night of my body will be too thick and cold
> For the sun of your growing heart. (279)

Both death and rebirth are dependent upon time for the appropriateness of the occasion. The uncertainty of rebirth is heightened by the mother's apprehension that it may occur too late for her to be able to play her original role of nurturer, bonder, and mourner. The loss she is concerned with is not only that of the child but of her own physical abilities to function as a mother. In effect, she is voicing an elegiac concern both for the loss of her child and for the loss of herself as mother.

The specifics of the loss to motherhood through aging and time's effects are spelled out by projecting them not on to the living actual mother but rather on to the metaphorical mother, which is death, the earth that presently holds the child:

> Return from your new mother
> The earth: she is too old for your little body,
> Too old for the small tendernesses, the kissings
> In the soft tendrils of your hair. The earth is so old
> She can only think of darkness and sleep, forgetting
> That children are restless like the small spring shadows. (279)

Essentially, the mother is arguing that to delay the rebirth until she too is old will be to deny the child the personal attention compounded of soft affection, gentleness, understanding, and patience that defines motherhood. In so doing, Sitwell implicitly creates a fissure between her original declaration of the unity of seasons, earth, sun, and living creatures and this view, which polarizes the birth mother, the speaker, against the death mother, the earth.

This fissure between unity and division, harmony and jealousy, undercuts or aborts the initial hopeful plea for rebirth and restoration of the loss of the child. Time and change cannot honor the plea to redress the fact of death:

> But the huge pangs of winter and the pain
> Of the spring's birth, the endless centuries of rain
> Will not lay bare your trusting smile, your tress,
> Or lay your heart bare to my heart again
> In your small earthly dress. (279)

The loss is permanent, as is the anguish at separation; only the longing persists. So intense is it that the denizens of the world, "the lost men, the rejected of life" (279), conspire to prevent the mother from identifying her child's pitiful voice with those of a fallen world rife with "fever" (280), darkness, and disintegration both physical and moral. This appears to be an incipiently humanitarian identification with the lot of mankind through the longing to maintain the child's memory. Yet it is foregone as the child's smile is transformed into "a gap into darkness" that "rends the soul with the sign of its destitution" (280). The world is essentially a loveless condition of deprivation and suffering antipathetic to the soul. Nevertheless, it recognizes that to identify the dead child and the suffering of the world is ultimately to foster the profoundest of illusions on the part of the mother. Better not to link personal suffering and universal deprivation than to submerge the former in the latter. That would delude the mother into feeling that trying to save "the lost men" (280) is the same as loving her lost child.

This is not to say that Sitwell feels the world is to be ignored, nor that its ills and suffering should be denied. Bringing light, peace, holiness, and love to suffering mankind is both possible and enjoined. What must be denied is that this is identical with or a substitute for the mother-love felt for the child. Maintaining such a denial, in effect, continues to affirm the fissure between love and loss, unity and separation. And more. It requires the mother to recognize the obligation laid upon mankind to alleviate, to the extent possible, its general suffering regardless of whether it can ever be totally eradicated.

Consequently, she admits her willingness to sacrifice her child to death yet once again: "And, knowing this, I would give you again, my day's darling" (280). Such a sacrifice, however, is as impossible as the child's rebirth. What redeems it—and indeed the very reason for it—from mere words, a pointless protestation, is its preservation of the mother's most profound grief, that which outlasts time and the world:

> O grief, that your heart should know the tears that seem empty years
> And the worlds that are falling! (280)

Only through such a protracted contemplation of the complexities of the situation of living mother and dead child is Sitwell able to articulate finally and directly the mother's sorrow and sense of elegiac loss. This loss is complex and extends beyond the immediate situation. It begins with grief for the loss of her child and extends to her imagined awareness of all the sorrow inherent in living. Finally, it entails the sense that her own immediately felt loss is identical with the destruction of the ordered, organic unity of life itself. Thus, she stands as the polar opposite of Williams's widow, who is limited to rendering her grief in terms immediately familiar to her and her physical surroundings.

A somewhat similar polarization is found in Seamus Heaney's "Elegy for a Still-Born Child" and John Crowe Ransom's celebrated "Bells for John Whiteside's Daughter," though with one key difference. Certainly Heaney's poem shares the qualities of immediacy and intimacy with that of Williams in almost the same measure as Ransom's aligns itself with Sitwell's drawing on the traits of impersonality, philosophical reflectiveness, and unusualness of attitude. Where Heaney and Ransom differ—and it is a significant difference—from Williams and Sitwell is in their speakers's relationship to the object of loss. The former two have no familial connection to their poems's subjects; as friends or neighbors, they stand at a remove from the possibilities of heartfelt agony sustained by family members whether mother or wife.

As a result, they approach their elegiac task through descriptively recalling the lost children and the concrete differences their loss has made in the lives of those remaining. Heaney even goes so far as to address the child directly, informing him or her of the perceptible physical change in the mother's step and posture wrought by its delivery:[17]

> Your mother walks light as an empty creel
> Unlearning the intimate nudge and pull
>
> Your trussed-up weight of seed-flesh and bone-curd
> Had insisted on. (61)

Through the homely idioms of fish basket and firmly tied living package, he is able to fuse the physical awkwardness and embryonic appearance of pregnancy. In this way, he merges the sense of relief and wonder that occurs with the delivery. The result is a marvelously understated yet poignant rendering of both mother and child. The mother's immediate delight at the birth itself—its being concluded and over with—is primary and physical. But it merges with the presence of the not yet wholly formed infant—its concrete presence and on-going self-definition—to suggest simultaneously both its normal futurity and the cataclysmic impact of its actual fate.

Succinct though it is, nevertheless, twice as many lines are devoted to the mother as to the poet's friend, the father. Warrant for this lies, of course, in the greater physical intimacy experienced by the mother and in her need to physically recoup while the father can only anticipate and speculate on the nature of the emerging being. None of these lines in the poem's first section strays, however, from the involved yet spectatorial stance of the poet-speaker.[18] It manages, but barely, to maintain the decorum of restraint inherently imposed by the developing situation:

> Doomsday struck when your collapsed sphere
> Extinguished itself in our atmosphere. (61)

Indeed, so austere is the likening of the infant to a "collapsed sphere" that even the full semantic weight of "doomsday" does not offset the shock of the image. The human impact of the loss of the child, which modifies or focuses the shock of the sphere image, is reserved for the succeeding line: "Your mother heavy with the lightness in her" (61). The apparent paradox yields to logical inference based on the child's loss. The heaviness possessed by the mother is emotional and follows from the child's being born not into life but death. The interchange of physical for emotional weight is predicated on the change from birth to death and the suddenness of the loss compared to the brevity of the life.

Yet even here it is the speaker's perception, not the parents' reaction, that dominates the elegiac effort. He signals his empathy and conveys his own sorrow and sense of the pathos of the event through a contemplative exercise of memory by reviewing almost ritualistically the details testifying to the grotesqueness of the occasion and the mode of publicly recognizing it. The third and last section of the poem foregrounds the poet's own largely unconscious actions—"I drive by remote control" (62)—over against a landscape that mimes the sense of absence, deprivation, futility, and chilling repetitiveness felt by parents and spectatorial friends alike. By so doing, the poet creates an elegy-at-a-remove, a poem that expresses the loss and heartbreak felt by all but neither celebrated nor compensated for by any witness:

> I drive by remote control on this bare road
> Under a drizzling sky, a circling rook,
>
> Past mountain fields, full to the brim with cloud,
> White waves riding home on a wintry lough. (62)

These lines embody not so much the pathetic fallacy as the mourner's perception that the lonely journey he as a human being is continually taking in life is through a world that is the familiar home of personal grief and human suffering. It implicitly becomes, in effect, a lament for all through focusing on the loss of one.[19]

John Crowe Ransom's poem also adopts the impersonality or ostensible detachment of the observer or spectator. To it, however, he also brings a tone cunningly modulated out of a diction compounded of light bemusement and sober or serious solemnity. So casually reflective of the child's nature and behavior is the poem that it requires the title, "Bells for John Whiteside's Daughter," to establish the central question as to whether it is a celebration of her life or an elegiac mourning of her loss.[20] The crux of this question exists in the opening and closing repetitions of the phrase "brown study" (8). It maintains the tone of quick, lively, delicate movement coupled with the attitude of bemusement and astonishment at its cessation. It also captures the hope or expectation that it is merely an interim or momentary departure from customary behavior, a momentary intrusion of reflection on a pattern of ceaseless, purposeful activity.

Ransom avoids the very fact of the child's death in two ways. First, this metaphor diminishes the event's solemnity and all but eliminates its sorrowfulness. Second, abbreviated pastoral descriptions recall the child's liveliness, vigor, and imperiousness. These last function in attenuated fashion in a manner similar to the pastoral convention of the Renaissance elegy. In the orchard she is accompanied by her shadow while by the pond the geese cry "Alas, / For the tireless heart within the little lady" (8). On the surface, both contribute to the naturalness of the descriptive effort and to the adult point of view of indulgent tolerance for the child's playful activities. At the same time, they also suggest the cessation of these games. The shadow is both the metaphorical one cast by death as well as the physical one made by life. And the goose cry of sadness contains a premonition of the impending reality even while capturing the mock-solemn tone of the adult ascription of speech to the bird "who cried in goose, Alas" (8).

The complex image of child and geese works to idealize and aestheticize the scene, to distance the death by dwelling on other, less compelling, nonhuman problems.[21] It also develops a more playful and fondly benign attitude toward the child, which contrasts sharply with the more traditionally solemn, late nineteenth-century approach of, say, Robert Bridges in his poem on a dead child.[22] From the poet-speaker's perspective, the girl appears to treat the geese like a humorously conceived tyrant, driving them "from their noon apple-dreams" and forcing them to "scuttle / Goose-fashion under the skies" (8). Yet this mildly indulgent attitude toward the child is disturbing and even disconcerting in view of her death. To maintain such an easy familiarity with and fondness for the child as a figure of play seems almost condescension and a kind of over-civilized indifference to the fact of her death.[23] Further reflection, particularly in view of the last stanza, suggests the image of the child as a busily engrossed mock-tyrant contains the Browningesque motive for the speaker's attitude throughout the poem. Death itself is a tyrant but a seriously functioning one driving the speaker and everyone else toward mortality. The speaker and mankind in general cannot or will not face this real tyrant except obliquely through the "brown study" image, which makes of death a mere momentary reflection on the passing idyllic scene.

What keeps the poem from being a dramatic evasion of the starkness and irremediability of death is the last stanza.[24] There the mourners are "sternly stopped" and say "we are vexed" at the child's still circumspectly described state of a "brown study" (8).[25] It is in John Whiteside's house, his daughter's home, where the body lies before the funeral is to begin. Ransom's irony at the fact that the child's home in death is the same as in life reflects not critically but compassionately on the speaker's polite, civilized, cultivated distancing from the physical reality of death. It is the sight of the child herself that breaks through the avoidance mechanism of fond recollection and substitute-assumption to assert the solemnity of the occasion. The mourners are momentarily in the position of the "sleepy and proud" (8) geese being relentlessly forced out of their comfortable, familiar world. They are subject to a far less playful though serious tyrant. At the same time, they are at once children and parents/adults. As the former, they are "sternly stopped" (8) and rebuked for dreamy inattentiveness. As the latter, they express their disapproval among themselves of the child's unchildlike and uncharacteristic contemplativeness and ruminativeness.

In being "so primly propped" (8), with its aura of stiffness and artificiality, she is the antithesis of herself, who is all speed, lightness, movement, and mercurial purposiveness. The mourners "are ready" (8) now to face the fact that the stillness of the former, not the vitality of the latter, is now the child's reality. And this reality they can only contemplate and mourn silently. With this, we see that Ransom has presented us with a poem about death that is not an elegy in the traditional or conventional sense because it does not publicly or explicitly mourn anyone or anything. Yet it is, nevertheless, suffused with the elegiac temper.[26] This consists of the recollection of happier days, emotional shock repressed for cultural reasons, and disbelief leading to denial. The consolation of the traditional elegy is transmuted into a light tone that compassionately and without criticism reveals the human limitations of the attitude expressed explicitly by the speaker.

Another elegiac poem that moves even further into impersonality and control of the speaker's feelings is Ezra Pound's "Ione, Dead the Long Year." He generates this impersonality by situating his subject not in the present nor the contemporary world but in the classical past of Greece and its mythology. The impersonality is also underscored by the lack of any identifiable specific relationship between the poem's speaker and its subject, Ione the Nereid.

The effect is a timeless one generated by an unknown speaker mourning explicitly the loss and absence of a mythological creature. The impossibility of such a lament increases the sense of the enormous historical distance obtaining between the modern poet and his dramatic speaker. When coupled with the poem's brevity and tonal restraint, this looking back over vast temporal vistas to an isolated scene deeply mourned arouses a feeling of almost archaeological discovery. The poem suggests it is a self-contained fragment magically recaptured from a far distant and significantly different civilization. It reads as if it were something to be found today in *The Greek Anthology:* devoid of context, uncertain as to the total action of which it is a part, declarative in mood, simple in diction, and yet, somehow, strangely moving and complete in its expression.

For Pound, the mournful celebration of the loss of a minor sea nymph is dedicated to achieving and carefully controlling a tone of ineffable sadness and profound regret. This tone he creates through word and line repetition, quasi-internal rhyme, and a line length that is not so much varied as varying:

> EMPTY are the ways,
> Empty are the ways of this land
> And the flowers
> Bend over with heavy heads.
> They bend in vain. (112)

Here the pathetic fallacy is developed unabashedly to capture poignantly the speaker's own unstated feelings of loss and absence.

In a sense, over against this imputation of a lone voice heard from afar both spatially and temporally is the last line. It focuses explicitly on the nymph Ione rather than on the speaker:

> Empty are the ways of this land
> Where Ione
> Walked once, and now does not walk
> But seems like a person just gone. (112)

Her absence is intensified through shortening its duration and makes it appear she is almost still present. The unbelievability of her loss or death signals it has not yet been fully accepted by the speaker, whose relationship to her remains completely uncertain. By refusing to explain the loss in any substantial way, Pound turns our attention wholly to its emotional consequences. These are expressed simply, sorrowfully, and obliquely. External and internal desolation are matched so that foreground and background are subsumed by the equating of emptiness with absence or loss. The Nereid is raised to the status of a crucial aspect or element of life from her rather insignificant classical role as one of a number of off-spring born to Doris and Nereus, both of whom are offspring of the sea.[27] It is perhaps in this association with the ocean that Pound finds the rationale for Ione's centrality to the speaker, a nameless voice from the most distant civilized past of mankind. She, to a degree like Ransom's child, embodies the fluid movement, changing aspects or miens, and ceaseless vitality of life itself. With her no longer present, the speaker can only lament her absence, which leaves life and its cultural customs empty, sterile, and changeless. He grieves, in essence, for the change in his world wrought by the absence of change itself.

In this poem on Ione, Pound provides a simulated textual fragment that gives a tantalizing glimpse of a culture quite different from that of the contemporary Western world. In so doing, it only hints at one of his central themes or motifs, namely, the changes inherent in and continually being wrought by cultural history and the fact that it fundamentally elicits an elegiac temper in him.

Further development of his ongoing contemplation of history is found in representative pieces such as "VI" and "VIII" from *Homage to Sextus Propertius*.[28] In general, Pound sees it as a philosophical and aesthetic subject arousing awed curiosity, surprised recognition of points of resemblance between past and present, and lambent pity for the human fate of defeat, death, and remembrance.[29] "VI" intermingles the personal and the historical, making of the latter an introductory background for the speaker's anticipation of his own death.[30] Thus, the first two verse paragraphs commingle the socio-historical winner (Marius) and loser (Jugurtha) in their suffering of death's transit as "one tangle of shadows" (218). History's course is altered, but not that of human life nor of its culmination. Tibet may indeed become "full of Roman policemen" and the Parthians may "acquire a Roman religion" (219), but Marius and Jugurtha cross "naked over Acheron / Upon the one raft" (218).[31] The commingling of the two figures undercuts the achievement of history's alteration of events and cultures. In doing so, it does not so much deny the achievement of human history as it puts it in a transcendental or meta-perspective. The irony of historical triumph is not its temporality but its short-livededness, like the life of the individual:

> One raft on the veiled flood of Acheron
> Marius and Jugurtha together.
>
> Nor at my funeral either will there be any long trail,
> bearing ancestral lares and images. (219)[32]

The speaker, an anonymous poet-scholar ultimately identifiable with Propertius, reflects on the contrast between his anticipated funeral and the traditional or conventional ones of public notables. Dispassionately, he points up the hollowness, the pointlessness of elaborate ceremonials, and their lack of efficacy. He does so because he is aware of the commonality of death regardless of an individual's achievement. Marius and Jugurtha, victor and vanquished, travel to the underworld together.[33] As a result, the speaker concludes that having "a small plebeian procession" as his funeral will be "enough, enough and in plenty" (219). This points up his desire to be seen as an ordinary person characterized by the self-aware humility and the aesthetic remove attained as a poet / scholar. Coupled with this declared modesty, however, is a sense of pride that is both explicit and implicit. Clearly, he is proudly satisfied at being able to carry presentation copies of his books to Persephone, the queen of the underworld. A more tacit pride emerges in his recognition of the pointlessness of elaborate ceremony. His anticipation of the gift of the books emphasizes the dramatic expectation that an afterlife exists into which one enters through ritual observances appropriate only to the individual. Books fully as much as "ancient lares" (219) ease the entrance into death.

The quiet arrogance of the intellectual may be preferable to the bold forays of military and political leaders and may provide a wiser perspective on one's own culture and the role of history in human affairs. But it is still not the ultimate achievement wrought by contemplating the past and its impact on one's own life. That, for Pound, is gained only in verse paragraphs four and five. There, the speaker directly addresses Cynthia, his beloved. He offers predictive directives to her as to the details of the funeral ritual. These are founded on some sense of genuine personal feeling or decorum and duty or of all intermingled. The confidence he expresses in her anticipated observing of the burial customs—following the body, lamenting him by name, and bestowing "the last kiss on my lips"

(219)—is, however, not arrogance or an exercise of personal power. Rather, it follows from his hopeful conviction of her love for him set over against a sardonic recognition of its likely fleeting nature:

> "He who is now vacant dust
> "Was once the slave of one passion:"
> Give that much inscription
> "Death why tardily come?" (219)

Yet even here Pound's goal is not to mount a love-conquers-all answer to the inevitability of mortality. This the final verse paragraph ironically reveals in several ways. Even her laments at his death, though perhaps deeply felt at the time, are, he insists, but a custom reaching back into prehistory and the goddess's grief-stricken frenzy at Adonis's violent and sudden death.[34] Once again, Pound finds both motive and meaning for contemporary behavior in the deepest recesses of past history. The motive is personal need of the most intense order. The meaning is the ultimate failure of individuals to counter death and the transformations it wreaks on human beings:

> In vain, you call back the shade,
> In vain, Cynthia. Vain call to unanswering shadow,
> Small talk comes from small bones. (219)

What Pound does here is to array a full panoply of historical events set over against a personal anticipation of death in order to celebrate both love and its limits in the face of mortality.[35] The ritual of mourning recurs, though likely to be of growing infrequency not so much because of the subsiding of personal grief as of social convention mythically sanctioned. Its effort to undo death is recognized as futile and incapable of begetting anything but silence. The view is ostensibly skeptical and stoical, as befits a disbelieving pagan. Yet at the same time, because it is anticipatory in outlook and dramatic in address, it also possesses a skillful and somewhat sadistically calculating effort to elicit from his beloved sympathy, consideration, and obeisance to his still living wishes in the present.

In effect, Pound develops a proto-elegy delivered by the subject himself and thus restrained in tone and avoiding any sense of magnitude in a loss that has not yet occurred. The poem's goal is to reveal the elegy itself as a cultural custom, a "vain call to unanswering shadow" (219). Nevertheless, it is articulated out of being "'the slave of one passion'" (219), love. This motivation balances the vanity of the effort by the feeling for the subject. To understand both facets of the elegiac situation requires, Pound suggests, the perspective of the infinitely receding vistas of history viewed as timeless because still living.

The dominant note of pathos in "VI" emerges from the discovery of the limitations of cultural custom. It, however, is partially balanced by the poem's last line, which provides a profoundly ironic evaluation of the place of mankind in the totality of the universe: "Small talk comes from small bones" (219). The effect is twofold. First, it prevents the pathos from sliding into sentimentality. Second, and perhaps more important, it qualifies the pervading impression that the length of the historical view lends abiding significance and solemnity to human affairs.

"VIII" takes a markedly different approach to the topic of possible impending death. Overall, it adopts a mock-solemn, playful, and ironic tone concerning human and divine frailties and the ways in which they are exposed through myths and figures. Pound's speaker focuses on possible fates for persons that may occur prior to the need for either an elegiac temper or an elegy itself. His tone, however, dissipates the need for either by melding a Euripidean ironic questioning of the gods of Olympus with an Aristophanic narrative vigor.

The poem's invocatory opening suggests it is a mock-prayer or beseechment on behalf of someone other than the speaker couched in a comic mode of burlesque.[36] In asking as he does for mercy for a young woman who, like many others, failed to "respect all the gods" (221), the speaker minimizes her offense by arguing it is a common enough one. He suggests Jove's sanctioning her death will be seen as the product of an unnecessary artificiality and formality of attitude and response.[37] In contrast to divine arbitrariness, nature habitually dismisses the offense.

The second verse paragraph presents a series of questions addressed to Jove. These give the poem the appearance of a proto-dramatic dialogue in which the god's answers are presumed rather than delivered. Taken as a whole, they create a rhetorical account of misadventure and of relief finally arrived at. These condensed mythic narratives of initial misfortunes and rescue constitute an implicit argument for death as the only or ultimate surcease of misfortunes. Death is seen as a quiet, peaceful, pleasant alternative to the multiple perils and vexations of life. Rape, madness, murder, suicide, and sacrificial victimization are but some of the consequences of life that lead the speaker to suggest to "that unfortunate woman" (221) that "You may find interment pleasing" (222). This linking of the anonymous woman with the fates detailed in the various goddesses' myths is a way of quietly intimating a way-of-the-world attitude toward the lot of women. By so doing, it devalues the significance of death and the need for an elegiac remembrance.

At the same time, "VIII" counters the reliance placed upon love in "VI" by making the recounted mythic episodes a way of equating human seduction with divine lust. After pointing up the horrors of female existence—the actions of vengeful wives, flights from insane husbands, victimization by monsters, transformation into wild beasts—the speaker suggests that each of the goddesses finally is compensated for her suffering.[38] The effect of this is to mitigate the demeaning physical violence inflicted upon them. Similarly, the speaker, almost mockingly, holds out to his listener the prospect of alleviation for her sin (not respecting the gods) by her accepting the human-divine equation:

> You will say that you succumbed to a danger identical,
>   charmingly identical, with Semele's. (222)

The irony of "charmingly" reveals the danger of seeing human behavior in terms of divine narrative or mythic plot. To identify one's experience with actions and events recounted in myths is to deny the nature of history and human involvement in it. It is to engage in a self-delusory elevation of one's own behavior beyond its true bounds. To fail to see this is to risk failing to secure the ultimate release of death bestowed by the gods or fate. One must recognize that one's complicity in one's fate is part of that fate. Only then is it possible to "bear fate's stroke unperturbed" (222). Imputing it to some macro-mythic plot of suffering and pain and disadvantage is delusory.

The last two paragraphs provide an ironic refutation of the possibility of a quiet conclusion to affairs of the heart. Thus, to consider the poem as elegiac derives from the fact that it deals with the possible death of a person betrayed by sexual desire. The very fact, however, that it is only a possibility coupled with the playful ironies concerning Jove and his conduct suggest that it is a special form of the elegy. It functions as a comic or mock-elegy revolving around the woman's desire to die out of romantic frustration. So driven, the events become the material for yet another mythic bedroom farce, which is the generic polar opposite of the love elegy.

A quite different way of playing with the notion of the love elegy can be found in T. S. Eliot's "La Figlia Che Piange." Through its Italian title and Latin epigraph, the poem suggests its focus is romantic rather than elegiac, though seen from a distance and with the detachment of a spectator. He muses on a scene from the past while considering how he might have transformed it into an ultimately ironic elegy to the loss of love. Eliot's tone and setting are more those of Henry James during his Italian travels than the savage irony and comic attitude of Pound's classical models.

Thus, the first of the three paragraphs deftly captures the Jamesian luxuriating in the melding of aesthetic scene and subdued dramatic revelation coupled with a Tennysonian lingering on the euphony of language adapted to the modern idiom:

> Stand on the highest pavement of the stair—
> Lean on a garden urn—
> Weave, weave the sunlight in your hair—
> Clasp your flowers to you with a pained surprise—
> Fling them to the ground and turn
> With a fugitive resentment in your eyes:
> But weave, weave the sunlight in your hair. (20)

Physical and natural beauty, disappointment and pain, and verbal repetition combine to create the nostalgia for a past vision of romantic loss central to the love elegy. The language hints at a performance being staged at the same time as the vividness of the images and their typifying role is foregrounded to ensure identification with the scene for the reader, though not for the speaker.

The second paragraph reveals that the artifice of the elegy is seen from the perspective of a Jamesian persona—detachedly contemplative and aesthetically reflective, in full awareness of his directorial creativeness, and aspiring to an ironic civilized acknowledging of personal betrayal. This paragraph undercuts the artifice of poignancy created in the first. It does so by revealing that the initial scene is an imaginative extrapolation from a much less fully understood situation. The undercutting is achieved by shifting the tone from the romantic poignancy of unrequited love to sophisticated worldly diffidence, by shifting the gender identification from female to male with a concomitant increase in self-centeredness, by altering the speaker's role from involved director to co-conspirator in the betrayal, and by eliding from serious engagement to ironic observer and creator.

That Eliot's intent is not to deny the aesthetic validity of the initial elegiac picture nor to criticize the casualness of the spectatorial creator's adaptation of his experience is seen in the final paragraph. In effect, it shifts the focus from the loss occasioned by unrequited love to the incompleteness and open-endedness of imaginative contemplation in which dramatic / narrative closure are not achieved. The glimpse of reality that becomes the catalyst for imaginative extrapolations is set over against the possible fullness of quotidian reality carried to narrative fulfillment. This juxtaposition confirms the speaker as poet / artist for whom the loss of art and the loss of life provoke introspection and anxiety as to the choice of loss made even in the very act of choosing. It also suggests the reason for the underlying note of sadness inhering throughout in that the poet / artist is always inevitably dealing with loss as his or her emotional commodity.

Thus, Eliot, like Pound, goes behind the elegiac form to reveal its formality as a response to human experience, its artifice consciously created by an artist. Where Eliot goes beyond Pound is in his making out of this revelatory exposure an elegy for or on the artist and his function of always having to experience loss either in art or in life. The understated regret at this fact does not solidify into sorrow, as with the traditional elegy. This is largely because the imagination's persistent contemplation of the interaction of loss and gain continues to "still amaze / The troubled midnight and the noon's repose" (20). In other words, the artist's elegy for the loss inherent in his function is balanced by his endless ability to contemplate and wonder at the diverse possibilities of art and life. His loss, though undeniably a loss, is nevertheless also a gain, and in this subdued fact he has the consolation explicitly provided in the traditional elegy.

II

Other Elegiac Modes

4

The Love Elegy's Transformations

*T*he love elegy, of course, has a long tradition reaching back at least to the Roman one of Tibullus, Propertius, and Ovid. Clearly, this tradition extends, though with marked changes, through Renaissance writers such as John Donne and Ben Jonson to modern poets such as Edna St. Vincent Millay and Ezra Pound's *Homage to Sextus Propertius*. Pound's series of poems serves both to remind us of the Roman tradition and to indicate the significant differences between it and modern exemplars like Millay. Yet these and other modern love elegists also are subject to another tradition that materially gives them overall a quite different tone and elegiac attitude. This second tradition consists of the romantic notion of love, with its exalting of sexual passion, its countenancing of adultery while ostensibly honoring monogamy, and its acceptance of acute disappointment and grief as the virtually inevitable result of loving. Essentially, it softens the harder edge of the Roman tradition by viewing the lover's sensibility as more psychologically than rhetorically fragile while implicitly denying the likelihood of such a relationship being repeated with yet another partner. In what follows, "personal relationships" refers exclusively to those of romantic love, marriage, and related extra-legal connections. All, whether consciously or unconsciously acknowledged, involve some sort of gender or sexual basis. Historically speaking, these relationships have more commonly been expressed in a lyric rather than an elegiac voice. Exceptions exist of course, as with Hardy's *Poems of 1912–1913* and Tennyson's *In Memoriam*. Tennyson's extended lament, however, raises too many complicated issues about socially suppressed gender drives to warrant ready inclusion in the love elegy per se.

How this merging of two relatively divergent traditions works itself out in modern literature can be seen by comparing Edna St. Vincent Millay's *Fatal Interview* (1931) with Edith Sitwell's *Three Rustic Elegies* (1927). The former deploys a sonnet sequence to chronicle, through the use of a variety of literary traditions and influences, the rise and fall of a personal love affair.[1] This variety, in effect, serves to depersonalize the highly wrought intimacy of the relationship. Such a depersonalization through a submersion of it in well-established forms and attitudes contrasts sharply with the immediacy and intimacy found, say, in similar topics addressed by so-called confessional poets, such as Anne Sexton.

Sitwell, on the other hand, avoids even the literary use of the first person with all of its puzzles about personal identity, autobiography, and poetic personae. Instead she grounds her three poems—"The Little Ghost Who Died for Love," "The Hambone and the Heart," and "The Ghost Whose Lips Were Warm"— in seventeenth-century historical incidents. These are cast as dramatic dialogues between quasi-allegorical or personified entities. The effect is to distance even further characters from the personal and, in so doing, to point up the difference between the lyric and the dramatic voices. Both poets, however, engraft on to these radically different voices their distinctive adaptations of the elegiac temper. The result is a striking variation in the conventional or traditional elegy as a mode of poetic expression. What both address is not so much the loss of a beloved as the loss of love itself. For Millay this loss is rhetorically tantamount to death itself, while for Sitwell it becomes grounds for analytic exploration of the nature and kind of love that has been lost.

Millay's once-considerable reputation was largely built on her use of traditional forms and techniques to develop frank attitudes toward romantic love considered innovative in the first quarter of the century. Yet she also reveals a considerable preoccupation with the theme of death and with forms such as the epitaph, the dirge, and the lament traditionally associated with the elegy per se.[2] Taken together, these foci lead her to an exploration of love as a state marked by change and loss. In it, the ultimate human loss, life itself, is enjoined as a pervasive image or metaphor for the absence or withdrawal of the beloved. This use of death as metaphor, literary sign, or *figura* directs many of her poems back to the poetic persona and the concern with the speaker's voice and sentiments.

Thus, her "Elegy Before Death" begins with the stoical observation that vegetative nature and the seasons will continue after the human being's death and "Nothing will know you are gone" (69). The absence of any direct identification of the person with a lover suggests this is an anticipatory elegy for the poet. It operates as a kind of dispassionate lyric that eschews the elegiac conventions of profound lament and imaginative transcendence of the loss experienced. Having articulated a view that implicitly denies the elegiac opportunity, Millay then contrives to whittle away at the absoluteness of this view. Ultimately she is able to replace or augment it with an elegiac attitude founded on simple but momentous losses in nature. These testify to the speaker's anticipated absence or separation from life through death:

> Oh there will pass with your great passing
> Little of beauty not your own,—
> Only the light from common water,
> Only the grace from simple stone! (70)

In brief compass, what Millay does is to move from denial of elegizing to an understated and controlled acknowledgment of the elegiac fact. Because the death is only anticipated, it acquires both emotional strength and weakness. Taken together, they meld the stoicism of the original denial of the elegiac opportunity with the exercising of it in the final stanza. The strength given to the fact of death is achieved by its heightening the sense of apprehension and controlled devastation at its anticipated occurrence. At the same time, the very fact that the death is a futurity distances the speaker from the immediacy of the envisaged situation. This, in turn, makes the death appear artificial and "literary" or rhetorical rather than genuine and intimately encountered.

This rhetorical or loosely philosophical attitude to death permits Millay to treat it predominantly as a conceptual loss when applied to instances of a personal friend (as in "Memorial to D. C."), human beings in general (as in "Dirge Without Music"), or ostensible historical occasions (as in "Epitaph").[3] Even so, such poems contribute individual insights or facets of human experience. These enable her in *Fatal Interview* to move death from a conceptual reality to a metaphor for the change in a personal relationship and the ultimate loss of love. Thus, "Memorial to D. C.," which does possess a personal context, brings to the speaker or poet a sorrowful recognition of death as preeminently an irretrievable loss for the survivor.[4]

Such a loss is not only unalterable but universal, a kind of recurrent habit in human affairs, as "Dirge Without Music" solemnly asserts: "So it is, and so it will be, for so it has been, time out of mind" (240). But Millay's personal response is not that of the traditional elegiac acceptance and transcendence of the loss. Rather, it is a Dickinsonian rejection of the conventional elegiac temper that still acknowledges the fact of death and loss of all those valued in life—the wise, the lovely, the beautiful, the tender, the kind, the intelligent, the witty, and the brave.

Her rejection takes the form of an understated yet powerful whimsical irony. It is embodied in two statements made in response to the fact of death and its universality, namely, "I am not resigned" and "I do not approve." The lightness of tone here pulls against the somber lament of the loss found in the traditional elegiac attitude. At the same time, it intensifies the impact of the loss through the very futility or pointlessness of the utterances. This is all that the poet can proclaim on behalf of mankind: a verbal protest and disclaimer against the fact of universal mortality, against its reasonableness or fairness or deservedness. It denies not so much the fact as the acceptability of the loss and waste that death occasions. And it does so in a mild but firm manner that places in opposition to the nature of existence the only thing available, namely, the personal identity of the individual human being.

In "Epitaph," Millay uses a classical imitation to explore the impact of death on this identity and to argue for the avoidance of grief and lamentation. Her principal discovery here is that death entails not only the absence of life but also of consciousness: "empty is his skull" (295). This fact removes the personifications of Pity and Dread but also of Joy. It is this last which forces the final admission and recognition that "no man can have all" (295). Claudius, the deceased individual, is held, in Sophoclean fashion, to be better off dead even if he must lose Joy or personal happiness.[5] Such an insight is developed more slowly and fully in the *Fatal Interview* sequence. There, the loss of happiness, of another individual through the severing of a personal relationship, is seen to involve a death-like experience of separation that leaves the individual with a life still to live.[6]

Fatal Interview is a relatively early instance of the modern love-elegy and so stands in opposition to the traditional death-elegy in all but the formality of its verse structure. And even with this, Millay elects the sonnet sequence rather than the conventional elegiac lament. Her fifty-two Shakespearean sonnets, while a novel form for elegiac expression, also serve to establish a linkage to Renaissance sonnet cycles that bemoan the unrequitedness or loss of love. In effect, the use of the death metaphor plumbs the extremes of lost love. The impact of the metaphor on the loser serves both to associate the love- and death-elegy forms and to differentiate them. Indeed, it is through the multiple differentiations that Millay serves to give a new inflection to the modern love-elegy.

Perhaps the first difference to strike someone who is not a principal in the relationship being chronicled is that the love-elegy deals with an essentially transitory condition in contrast to the permanence of death. As Millay suggests in the second sonnet of the sequence, love, though productive of bliss, is not permanent like death but "will be gone by spring" (631). Yet it leaves scars that will condition and perhaps interfere with such subsequent relationships. Consequently, the poet's sorrow for the loss of love perforce must appear less momentous than Milton's or Shelley's response to the impact of death. Recovery, no matter how conditioned, is always possible for the love-sick but not for the deceased. Looked at with a cool eye, the loss of love is likely to be one of a series of such experiences and as such it contrasts with the uniqueness of the death phenomenon for the conventional elegist.

Millay even compounds this difference by suggesting that the mere and briefest of separations of the lovers creates a death-like experience. Conversely, the diminution of the love experience points up the exaggeration of language, the increase of rhetorical obviousness that enters into the love-elegy. In so doing, the linguistic artifice calls in question the sincerity not challenged in the traditional death-elegy. Here, the lyric voice that deals with love conflicts with the elegiac voice that laments a unique and unredeemable loss of life and presence.

By imitating the Petrarchan convention of the abused, suffering lover, Millay may seek to minimize the issue of personal sincerity by escaping into a patently artificial and highly rhetorical tradition. Unfortunately, a modern reliance on such a historical anachronism as the Court of Love and associated forms of verbal behavior is at odds with current customs and social realities, including those by which she herself was endeavoring to live.[7] As originally employed, the Court of Love convention created a beloved existing at an emotional distance from the lover. Yet the romantic love experience she is recounting documents an emotional and physical intimacy that is the opposite of the Renaissance lyricist's beleaguered, unrequited, and spurned lover.

Another difference between the two forms of elegy is in the focus of the subject. The death-elegy concentrates on the missing other and how its absence contrasts vividly with its prior presence. The love-elegy, on the other hand, zeroes in on the individual speaker's personal, physical pain occasioned by the loss of the beloved. Nor is this pain a single, unique phenomenon. Rather, being in love occasions multiple sufferings at the time as well as after the relationship ceases to exist. As *Fatal Interview* repeatedly documents, the love-elegy is self-focused whereas the death-elegy is other-focused. The former's concentration on individual, personal pain makes it an exercise in romantic egoism whose secondary attention is concentrated on the loss of the beloved. In order to maintain the primacy of the lover's ego, Millay is compelled to see the other, the beloved, as imperfect, cruel, heartless, and less committed to a relationship than the lover. In striking contrast, the death-elegy concentrates on the loss of the other as the consequence of death. In so doing, it views the dead individual as greater, nobler, closer to perfection, and almost more godlike than anyone else. Such judgments are cast as universal rather than particular assessments. Consequently, the issue of rhetorical excess is swallowed up in cultural pronouncements supported, it is suggested, by the bulk of the particular society and thereby gaining an acceptance greater than the merely personal. As a result, the reader of the death-elegy tends to share the sorrow and lamentation of the elegist while that of the love-elegy is inclined to view the grief and despair expressed therein as the feelings of another to be viewed at least with reservations and at most with skepticism.

Contributing to these attitudes is the difference in range of response to the climactic event in each case: loss of love and the death of a deeply valued individual. The postlude to romantic love consists of a more diversified and less coherent set of emotions and feelings. They are more uncertain and possess a greater range of oscillation: grief at separation and loss, anger at the beloved's failure to meet all one's expectations, attack of the beloved's shortcomings, longing for death as a cessation of the pain of loss, and despair at isolation. Only after this range has been explored do they settle into a stripped-down determination to endure the experience.

In contrast, the death-elegy coheres the feelings of shock, sorrow, fear of a future lacking the valued individual, loss of the unique presence into a focused lamentation. This mourning yields to an ultimate transcendence of grief through the invocation of the solace of time, religion, and philosophy. The death-elegist in general strikes the note of having come to terms with his sorrow and apprehension about the future. In contrast, the love-elegist admits that the ending of love, however painful, traumatic, and persistent, is implicitly a repeatable experience that is tacitly anticipatable despite a rhetoric of disclaimers. Death, on the other hand, is a single, unique event that for the elegist is not experienced personally but only at a remove as the experience of another.

The limiting characteristics of Millay's elegiac work largely follow from her reliance on a first person narrator, her involvement with an autobiographical context, and her historical position as a poetic premodernist. They, however, are countered to some degree in the three elegies of Edith Sitwell mentioned earlier. In grouping these poems together under the rubric of "rustic elegies," Sitwell would seem to be suggesting that they are simple rather than complex in the manner of *Lycidas* or *Adonais,* direct and straightforward in theme and language rather than oblique and elaborate, and rural or lower class rather than urban and sophisticated in focus and attitude.[8] These implications suggest the poems are the exercises or sketches of an unsophisticated craftsman rather than efforts like those of Milton and Shelley that seek to draw on the full resources of the elegy.

Set over against these qualities are those invoked by the easy mastery and interrelation of stanza and verse forms (principally quatrains and couplets), varied line lengths from four to seven feet, intricate shifting and balancing of end-stopped and run-on lines, Grand Guignol imagery and settings, and invocatory symbolism that is rich, allusive, profoundly rhetorical, and musical. All of these call up a sense of unequivocal urbanity, artifice as aesthetic pleasure, and upper-class sensibilities that delight in envisaging intricate speculations about basically simple human situations.[9]

In a sense, these traits suggest the perspective of a Marie Antoinette conscious of the fate of herself and her world, amused at the threats from the outside world, and yet prophetically decrying the lies and ambiguities that inhere in the language and social rhetoric of her own world. There is a very real sense in which these two emphases encompass both the premodernist and the modernist poetic strains with which Millay, too, was confronted but which she was unable to reconcile or even address. Sitwell, as we shall see, does address their dichotomy, though not so much with the intent of reconciling or fusing them. Instead she creates two different, almost opposed perspectives, each of which prevents the other from establishing a clear priority of value and truth.

The premodernist strain is found in the poems's reliance on a narrative base that tells a simple story of lost love calculated to do two things. First, it arouses in its audience a feeling of shocked recoil from the horrors possible in ordinary life. And second, it generates an easy ballad-like sentimentality and pity for the speaker or protagonist. The modernist strain, on the other hand, is exhibited by the stress on craftsmanship, the tantalizing creation of untraditional and subtle implications, the deft echoes of historical and religious allusions, and the generation of symbolic associations. All of these nudge the elegies from historical recollections that give rise to musing reflections on the ambiguous state of human affairs to imaginative prophecies. In utilizing these two strains in a highly individual manner, Sitwell achieves a greater accommodation to the rise of poetic modernism than Millay was ever able to achieve.

The first of her "rustic elegies" is entitled "The Little Ghost Who Died for Love." Its unidentified epigraph recounts the sad story of a seventeenth-century woman sentenced to death in place of her lover, who had been involved in a duel.[10] It is a dramatic monologue spoken by Deborah Churchill from the grave to other young women enjoying romantic love or contemplating doing so. Her opening lines provide a somber warning concerning the fate to which her love has brought her: the cold isolation of being dead, the absence of time, the forgetting of love, and the corruption and disintegration of body and soul. Nor was her single impulsive act, she says, intended so much to save his life as to save for herself his love as an actual physical presence.

Ironically, the consequence of this act is both the loss of his love and of him, too, as well as of her own life. This last occurred as then-legal compensation for his having killed his dueling opponent and fled to avoid facing the law. Her being scapegoated in this fashion is recounted so as to create a dramatic paradigm of the instinctive commitment to love and its consequences, namely, loss and death. She implies that death is the result of love and with it the experience of loss, the collapse of memory, and physical dissolution. All that survives even minimally is the participant's voice and consciousness. And these are condemned to an apparently eternal existence marked by cold, darkness, and a persistent incomprehension of her fate or its rationale.

The starkness of the death scene in the first fourteen lines (a combination of two quatrains and three couplets) is sharply contrasted to the succeeding twelve lines (all couplets). The former concentrate on the pitiable fate of the female protagonist; the latter focus on her enjoining the maidens to welcome spring and its fruits. A ripe, natural richness together with a geographical and astronomical exotic remoteness and splendor combine to create a scene "filled with sweetness like the bags of bees" (174).

The unity of nature and the young maidens—ground and figures—contrasts sharply with Deborah's situation. It creates a scene of human beings at their most fully realized—physically attractive, emotionally ripe—searching for physical pleasure in a way that deftly manages to imply simultaneously innocence and bodily fulfillment. Over against it stands the forlorn Deborah, a figure consigned to contemplating lost love, the consequences of acting on impulse, the fate of death by hanging, and an existence marked by perpetual desolation and isolation.[11] This juxtaposition suggests that metaphoric, imagistic, indirect fulfillment is preferable to literal, actual dependency on another. Silver snows buried in sweet cherries are better than any male lover who will desert one at a critical moment. As a result, Deborah enjoins the maidens to forget her fate and so to dismiss the idea of embracing romantic love and a physical lover.

Romantic love is polarized between its grim fate for the lover and the pursuit of its surrogate in the fruits of nature. The abandoned participant embodies the one while the first person narrator articulates the other. The effect of this is to heighten the pathos surrounding the narrator. Her lot is a forbidding one, deserving of being ignored and forgotten, so long as it is not emulated. Since this view is expressed by Deborah herself, it carries some of the same self-pitying notes as Millay expresses in *Fatal Interview*. Sitwell, however, differs from her by deliberately making her narrator a figure of pathos to the maidens. She is the abandoned woman who is said to "creep to the doctors bare / Booth" (174) in search of a drug to alleviate a fate to which she has, she feels, unfairly and unwarrantedly been consigned. The poet calls attention to the pathos of the woman's situation while maintaining a detached or restrained attitude toward it. Thus, Sitwell is able to dramatize it into a moral parable that in large measure blunts Millay's note of personal complaint. Consequently, her poem escapes the limitations of the individual lament.

This escape is seen most sharply when she has Deborah reveal that the medicine sought is not for her nor the love-sick country maid afflicted with "country sins and old stupidities" (174). It is a much more potent medicine than that used for abortions, since it is directed at "this old world" which "is sick and soon must die!" (175). It occasions death directly and immediately. The identification of the world as something moving toward death is based on its incomprehensible (to her) killing of one who had lived and acted only for love. Nor is her unwarranted fate held to be simply the loss of life; it also entails her transformation from a nightingale into a harpy. A small, quick, delicate, elusive bird of great vocal beauty becomes a raucous, unreal, rapacious, scolding, bad-tempered old woman. Her fate is both metamorphic and graphic; ultimately unloved by anyone but feared by all, she is destined to live among the dead after love itself is "'grown dead and rotten'" (174).

Deborah refuses to accept society's scapegoating of her, she accusatorially diagnoses the responsibility for love's loss as lying with the world rather than the individual, and she persists in continuing to mourn "among the ruins" (175). All of these add a tonic of stubborn courage and persistent resistance to the piteous figure of almost stylized pathos she has conjured up for herself in the first two-thirds of the poem. She recognizes that false signals of hope—"cockcrow marches" and new days "crying of false dawns" (175)—threaten to overwhelm and quiet her lamenting voice. Nevertheless, she insists that she will still continue to mourn. The elegiac lament for lost love is eternal despite its no longer being heard by anyone still alive and even after the disappearance of the world in death. What it mourns for forever is her unwarranted sad fate, the irony of the world's hypocrisy and corruption, and ultimately the end of the world as the source of love's betrayal.

By transferring the blame for lost love from the beloved to the world, Sitwell here is able to establish romantic love as eternal even though lost and to elevate it above death and the world. In this, she contrasts with Millay, who sees love as temporary, the fault as the beloved's, and the only resort against such loss the personal voice of self-pity trying to reconcile itself to enduring what it claimed to know was inescapable.

The first of these rustic elegies imaginatively speculates on a historical incident of romantic love and its elegiac implications. In so doing, it raises them to a kind of philosophical universal. The second elects a quite different strategy. "The Hambone and the Heart" is a quasi-allegorical dramatic dialogue between "A Girl" and "The Heart" over the betrayals of love.[12] These range from the romantic and sexual to the parental and religious. In the course of the dialogue, a series of polarities are developed: girl and lover, body and soul, Venus and the Worm, Judas's mother and her son, and, by implication, Christ and Judas. These, in turn, are subsumed under the figure of the Clown, who holds in his hands both the Heart and the Hambone (the soul and the body). By so doing, the Clown symbolizes Man, the human being, who stands over against the Heavenly creature, Christ, whose love is abiding rather than transitory.

The girl opens the elegy lamenting a lost love and her own envelopment by "Death alone" (176). Grotesque images reminiscent of the Renaissance *memento mori* tradition depict the girl as finding herself existing in a place where the living are ruthlessly and indiscriminately sacrificed to an alien god (Gehenna), leaving only the skeletal mortal remains. She is there because she had "dreamed that the bare heart could feed / One who with death's corruption loved to breed" (176). Her loss of her lover is seen not as due to a growing indifference to or boredom with her but to his death. This she allegorizes to mean that the human heart in general contains a Worm, an impulse of disintegrative corruption. It is even stronger, more basic, and more compulsive than love for another person. What brings warmth, light, and gladness to a person is the love felt by another. But it is less powerful and compelling than the desire for the corruption of the flesh— symbolized by dust, cold, ravening hunger, and the grave—felt by the other, the lover.

The attraction of bodily corruption, however, lies not only with the lover. It is not simply, for Sitwell, a personal or individual drive but one that is lodged deep and perennial and perpetual in the grave itself, which strives ceaselessly to satisfy this need. Love, therefore, of and for the mortal, as embodied by Venus, is not merely aesthetically and physically satisfying. It is also a drive to consume the mortal as found in the image of the Worm. As such, it is identified with death:

> The Worm's a pallid thing to kiss!
> She is the hungering grave that is
>
> Not filled, that is not satisfied!
> Not all the sunken Dead that lies
> Corrupt there, chills her luxuries. (177)

The insatiability of love is ultimately identified with the inevitability of death.

Clearly, this realization is the culmination of living through a romantic relationship and discovering its essential consequences and their reasons. In contrast to it, the girl's voice abruptly moves back from this grotesque scene of the grave, dust, corruption, despair, and the extinction of passion. It turns to the physically beautiful and delicately romantic setting of lovers prior to their discovery of the obligatory fate of their love. Yet even here, the future darkness which will enshroud the relationship is hinted at in her retrospective recognition of the implications of their shadows "beneath the twisted rose-boughs of the heat" (177). Now she sees the import of "their whispered warning" and of their having reminded her of "small unhappy children dressed in mourning" (177). All that she and her lover really saw initially was the Clown (symbolic of mankind) poised between the golden town of Heaven and the mortal world of corruption and isolation, between the ideal and the real, the desired and the loathsome. The Clown holds in his hands both "a Heart, and a Hambone" (177) symbolizing the soul (or consciousness) and the body. The duality of man's nature and his seeking of both the immortal (the spiritual) and the mortal (the physical) thus focus the girl's attention as the transition to the voice of the Heart occurs.

The Heart gradually reveals in its ballad-like narrative tale that it is the voice of Judas's mother. She bemoans his betrayal and the murder of herself at the behest of a sinister, hellish temptress whose traits are those of a vampire, traitor, and seducer of the once innocent child. Judas's love for the temptress—a woman other than his loving mother, one who is preeminently a sexual rather than a nurturing being—entails his willingness to sacrifice both his love for his mother and her actual life. Thus, romantic love preempts parental love even though it is unable to destroy either the mother's affection for her child or her conscious desire to nurture him still. What the Heart of the mother of the ultimate betrayer ultimately reveals is three things. First, her heart is consigned to forgiving its betrayers. Second, it still has to live with the awareness that others who are mortals, inherently possessed of corruption and therefore "servitors of Death" (180), know of her betrayal. Third, they recognize her soul's eternal anguish and grief and with it the irony that she both mourns and keeps the memory of his betrayal alive.

Implicit here—through the lines "'His body is a blackened rag / Upon the tree—a monstrous flag'" (179)—is the conclusion that Judas's betrayal of Christ, his master, was made possible as a result of his betrayal of his mother. The one who gave him life is sacrificed in order that he may occasion the taking of the life who offers him the new life. Intensifying the Heart's, the life-giver's and nurturer's, lament for her dead son is the bitterly ironic fact that she rejects the sardonic contempt and bitter humiliation of history and its mortal purveyors. She does so by proclaiming her willingness to sacrifice herself again to quench his thirst for the corruption of mortality, to deny his having sinned, and to assume the blame because "'the love / I bore him was not deep enough'" (180). The pathos of this assertion depends on the willingness of love to blind itself to reality; to take on itself more than is required or called for; to, in effect, keep on sacrificing itself for the beloved when such sacrifice is neither appropriate, true, or beneficial to anyone. The self-abnegatory dimension of love ironically compounds the questionable nature of mortal sacrifice. In so doing, it makes the desire to commit the ultimate deed appear absurd and foolhardy. It is as if love, whether taken or given, entails death either as imposed or sought.

This pathetic and ironic confession of love as responsibility is seen in its full horror and absurdity as the truth about love sought and lost. In the face of it, the girl responds to the Heart's confession. She declares her identification with the experiences of the Heart—sacrifice, tears for loss of love, and lamentation of and for mortality. At the same time, she articulates her own personal perspective on the tragic fact of death as crucially and inherently intermixed with the course of love. Mankind, "the tattered Clown" (180), insistently focuses on the mortal nature of the Hambone, "life-pink carrion" (180), and its involvement with the grotesque animalistic nature of life. Thus, the girl admits her beloved's preference for it to her: "Then you, my sun, left me and ran to it / Through pigs, dogs, grave-worms' ramparted tall waves" (180). The squalid ugliness of this admission is like the story of Judas's mother. It, however, does not provoke the girl to proclaim her sacrificial culpability in the action. She develops rather a secular answer or contrast to the essentially religious focus on the sacrifice of Judas's mother.

Against a backdrop of her self-contemplated death regarded as imminent, the girl only expresses puzzlement as to how she shall recognize her lover in the grave. She is convinced of its possibility despite her being able to embrace only the Worm, which is all that remains of him. By so doing, she faces "that last, less chasm-deep farewell" (181). Her acceptance of the inevitability of the last farewell is quite unlike the mother's refusal to accept the ultimate reality inhering in love, namely, that it has its limits and, ultimately, ends. The farewell seen by the girl is one that follows on death and is more profound than death. It occurs only after both the lover and the beloved are physically extinct, reduced to a state where the relationship of love can have no meaning.

The last of these three rustic elegies is entitled "The Ghost Whose Lips Were Warm," and it throws additional light on the theme of romantic love and its loss as well as on the very notion of elegizing itself. Essentially, this is a bipartite poem. It consists, first, of an elegiac lament by an old man for the death of his wife, and, second, of his dramatic account of his nighttime visitation by her after she has died. It thus both contrasts with and continues elements in the first elegy. It does the former by dealing with old age and married love rather than youth and un-married love, with requited and unrequited love, thereby completing a putative cycle of human relations. It continues, on the other hand, Sitwell's mining of the supernatural dimension thought to inhere in the love motif. By aspiring to raise the possibility of the persistence of the motif beyond time and mortality, it entertains a futurity beyond the individual.

Through basing her poem on an incident drawn from Aubrey's *Miscellanies* of the late seventeenth century, Sitwell gives it a more anthropological and historical cast than its immediate predecessor.[13] "The Hambone and the Heart" draws more on a religious context for its lament over romantic love. In historicizing the scene of the meeting of the old man and his dead wife, Sitwell is able to introduce the supernatural motif without straining the credulity of her modern audience. At the same time, the historical dimension enables her to avoid the quasi-allegorical perspective of "The Hambone and the Heart." As a result, she confers a kind of credible strangeness on the scene and its events akin to an anthropological encounter with a culture radically different from one's own.

The rhymed couplets develop a loose verse structure that also resembles "The Little Ghost Who Died for Love." The opening stanza quickly establishes the difference between the dead and the living, the natural and the human worlds.[14] The frozen tears of the dead never melt, while the ice in nature weeps and dissolves. These images indirectly celebrate the steadfastness and permanency of the dead's sorrow for the blighting of their original, living bliss of romantic enchantment. What links the human and natural worlds, the dead and the living, is the ability of the former to recall with pleasure, even though dead, that "one / Kiss that we take to be our grave's long sun" (182). It serves as a symbol of the whole transformative effect of romantic love that creates entirely new fruitful worlds for the lover:

> Once Time was but the beat of heart to heart;
> And one kiss burnt the imperfect woof apart
>
> Of this dead world, and summer broke from this:
> We built new worlds with one immortal kiss. (182)

Unlike Millay's *Fatal Interview*, Sitwell does not attribute the disruption of this state to one of the participants, the beloved. It is not human faithlessness that destroys romantic love but rather death which takes the beloved "to warm the dead" (183), leaving the husband-lover to "go sunless in their stead" (183). Death alters and darkens the bright, warm, living, fruitful state of romantic love. It also makes of the still loving lover a disintegrating, rotting, shriveled animal bereft of the beloved who stands as the very soul, the principle of life itself, for the lover. Or so he protestingly laments throughout the final couplets of the poem's first half. The poem begins as a fond recollection of the past conditions and pleasures of love. It follows this with a retrospective solace for what has been lost due to the exigencies of life. Then, it turns in the closing couplets of the first half into a lament by the lover for the consequences of love. He laments both the loss of the beloved—a loss which is tantamount to life itself—and also the radical diminution of his own being to a state even worse than that of the dead beloved.

In seeing himself as "more cold than she is in her grave's long night, / That hath my heart for covering, warmth, and light" (183), the husband suggests simultaneously a twofold perspective. First, romantic love still held by the living lover is a worse, more paralyzing, and more frigid condition than death itself. Second, and ironically enough, it is a better, more protective and nurturing, and more sustaining state than death because it persists into and beyond the grave. This persistence of his love mutes and partially deflects the egocentricity of his claim that life without reciprocated love is worse than death. It testifies also to the intensity, centrality, and extreme painfulness of love no longer reciprocable and to its similarity to death in its effects on the survivor—separation of body and soul, deprivation of warmth and companionship, and eternal isolation.

This protestation of the excruciating loss and the almost unconscious transition into self-punishment and egocentricity occasioned by love when disrupted by death is seen in quite a different light in the second half of the poem. Actions rather than words dominate the moral tone even as self-confession and personal paralysis dominate the events. The dominant note here is the pointed contrast between words and deeds. This produces a resultant calling in question of his earlier protestations as being but turns of rhetoric. In the face of his fearful responses to the visitation from the grave of his beloved, his assertions are seen as either fraudulent or excessive. They serve as warnings against asserting more than one can deliver or as indictments of false claims:

> . . . For this
> Dead man in my dress dared not kiss
>
> Her who laid by death's cold, lest I
> Should feel it when she came to lie
> Beside my heart. . . . (183–184)

It is only when one contemplates closely the startling and profoundly disturbing nature of the experience he undergoes that the criticism of his earlier protestations has its own sense of moral superiority questioned. Only when viewed as an actual scene rather than a purely literary one does its macabre quality fully shape our judgment as to the appropriate or likely human response. Shocked as he is by her kiss from beyond the grave being warm, he cannot face the prospect of determining whether her heart too may be warm: "I feared it, dared not touch and see / If still her heart were warm" (183). The logic of his fear is rooted in the fact that the possibility of her heart's being warm will be a de facto denial of death. And with it will come the destruction of his elegiac lament with its revelation of his egocentricity and rhetorical embellishing of his own pain, grief, and sorrow at his beloved's death.

But more than a reluctance to act in the face of his dead beloved's approach is operative here. For, as he admits, he does act—but in a shockingly self-centered, obsessive fashion. In effect, he places "the endless cold" of "all the earth of death" (183) between him and his beloved's heart in order to chill its warmth into the icy coldness appropriate to the deceased. He does so in order to prevent his living death—"this / Dead man in my dress" (183)—turning into an actual death. The latter will follow, he feels, should he actually embrace the nighttime apparition of his beloved and discover it too to be cold. Despite the elegiac and rhetorical lamentations of the first half of the poem, he cannot face the logical and experiential dislocations that would follow "when she came to lie / Beside my heart" (183–184). The moral contumely that ostensibly is his due as a result should not be leveled, however, until the full significance of his confrontation with the possibility of embracing his dead wife is recognized. It would entail his denying easily and willingly the laws of nature, the virtually universal taboos against necrophilia, and his own expressed sense of loss and the emotions surrounding it.

Coupled with these moral and psychological traumas, there is also his simple admission of the profound guilt already present in his relationship with the apparition. For what he finally sees he has done is to accept willingly his dead wife's kiss, which was "'the only light / She had to warm her eternal night'" (184). He has already made her lose the one thing reminding her of their love and life together. To deprive her of even more by lying close to her and feeling the warmth of her heart would be to take from her the one thing still reminding her of her past life, namely, her love for him and his for her. Thus, ultimately, Sitwell concludes, in denying her an apparitional and momentary relationship, he maintains their real and permanent love, which thereby is seen as capable of enduring even death. In doing so, she effects the final bond existing between all three poems, that which sees sacrifice as essential to all elegiac expressions of personal love. Deborah Churchill sacrificed herself to the state and the law for her lover; Judas's mother posthumously accepted her victimization at the hand of her son, the archetypal betrayer; and Aubrey's husband sacrificed his chimerical opportunity for fully regaining his beloved on behalf of his past reciprocated love.

When this last elegy is set over against the quotation from Aubrey which constitutes its epigraph, it is clear just how much irony has been invested in these elegies being characterized as "rustic." The settings and dramatic incidents of the poems derive from their epigraphs. These are characterized by an easy, conversational, nonreflective language and tone that essentially sum up the simplicity and directness of the rustic. The sophistication inherent in the poet's attitude toward her subjects is conveyed by her long, rhetorically laden lines with their rich patterns of imagery, judicious and restrained use of avowedly literary modes of allegory and personification, and ironic turns of complex thought and attitudes.

5

The Cultural Elegy and the Past

*T*he modern elegiac temper's continually expanding scope is reflected by increasingly diverse and mixed literary forms. The traditional lament for the death of individuals expands to include the separation of lovers and the disintegration of love, and the transformation of institutions such as marriage. The hitherto dominant lyric and elegiac tone now takes on the flatness of sociological discovery, the ironic withholding of capitulation to unrestrained grief, and the satiric indictment of what is ultimately the time-haunted state of the human condition. If the history of the elegy from classical to modern times reveals anything, it is the steady expansion of subject matter and diversification of voices with which that matter is expressed. The elegy starts from a lament for the death of a personal friend or a public figure. Now, however, the elegiac spirit embraces, through its affective and expressive movement, a polyvocal ritual of accommodation and transcendence of loss in all its forms. This represents an elision from a distinct and distinctive literary form to a multifocused attitude or temper. In effect, this movement reflects a growing awareness that loss, ruptures in expectancies and responses, and existential discontinuities may be engendered not only by individual persons but by families, relationships, cultures, and historical ages, as well as by philosophical *topoi* such as time, self, war, and spiritual consolation. One cannot help but sense a steady accrual of objects of loss, lamentation, reflective regret, and disquieted foreboding.

Coupled with this has come a multiplication of attitudinal tonalities or voices, ranging from the tragic note of desolation through the pathetic expression of separation and isolation to the satiric or ludic assessment of what remains. Concomitant with these expansions of the resources of the elegy proper there has come a loosening of the formal concept of genre itself. A conventional form such as the elegy is modulated into a discernible set of voices speaking in and through unrestricted kinds of texts on topics possessing family resemblances. So pervasive and powerful has this interactive nexus of loss, sorrow, rage, and recognition become that one is tempted to see the period as a whole as a threnodic age par excellence. In it, the complexly cadenced elegiac voice speaks not simply to what has occurred but what is to come. It was this elegiac propensity of attitude, implication, form, and style that forged the modernist connection. With it the concepts of myth, ritual, culture, and the past, both historic and prehistoric, gave rise to a literature of meditative self-discovery, revelation, and illumination. Modernist literary texts are strikingly, if often obliquely, elegiac because so many nonliterary texts of the era, such as Frazer's *The Golden Bough*, were also elegiac in form, attitude, and cultural conditioning.[1] The voice or voices heard in these works both generate elegiac resonances and are the occasion for elegiac reflections. Imaginative writers as well as all who are aware of history as their emergent, immanent destiny could scarcely not find in such works haunting and saddening evocations of the mutability of culture, history, myth, knowledge, and, ultimately, the self.

This is not the place to attempt to address exhaustively the whole range of features and intonations that make up the complex phenomenon of modernism.[2] For our immediate purposes, it is perhaps sufficient to single out four forms that it has taken since the beginning of the twentieth century. These can be called simply the classical, the comparative, the rococo, and the regional, though such designations are far from mutually exclusive. On the contrary, they almost certainly overlap with one another far more than they exist as thoroughly distinct entities or kinds.

The first of these embraces writers such as T. S. Eliot, Ford Madox Ford, and James Joyce and is founded on a matrix of Western Christianity, an approximation of the comparative method of classical anthropology, and an implicit reliance on or presumption of the relevance of a classical education. The second is best embodied by the work of Ezra Pound and Charles Olson. Like the first, it derives from the comparative method but differs from it in being essentially directed to multiple, non-European cultures of varying historical periods. Through this method and focus, it is assumed that a conceptual cultural amalgam can be formed as the basis for a palimpsestic contemporary worldview that is truly new.

The remaining two forms of modernism—the rococo and the regional—are both less strikingly original and historically more secondary than the others. They are less original in that they suggest literary antecedents with whom they may be said to have certain affinities even as they stand in a less dominant and self-consciously cultural role than do the classical and comparative species.[3] The rococo type of modernism is most fully embodied by the work of Edith Sitwell, especially her early and middle poetry. It embodies an elaborate counterpointing of linguistic elegance, ornamentation, and fluency with a heavy reliance on classical allusion and reference of a sort that predates the influence of the Cambridge School of Anthropology as embodied by Sir James Frazer and Jane Harrison. In this, it calls to mind the poetic work and role of Algernon Swinburne in its devotion to poetry as essentially an art of aural and oracular properties.[4] Through the use of sound heavily layered into patterns, this poetry challenges the immediacy of meaning while preserving it as a deliberately sought goal or intent.[5] Her poetry, like that of Swinburne, underscores the complex relations between past and present. Simultaneously, the past continues into the present even as its tacit disappearance is lamented. The sorrow inherent in the loss of any culture, no matter how frivolous or trivial in appearance it may be, is celebrated by contrasting past and present and by the elegiac regret of the poetic speaker.

The regional mode is variously embodied in Sherwood Anderson's *Winesburg, Ohio* (1919), William Faulkner's *The Sound and the Fury* (1929), *Absalom, Absalom!* (1936), and stories such as "The Bear" and "Red Leaves." For our present purposes, however, it is best defined by Allen Tate's "Ode to the Confederate Dead," and Robert Lowell's "For the Union Dead." Particularly in Anderson and Faulkner, it generates a heavily nostalgic concentration on flawed but deeply treasured subcultures, such as the small town, the wilderness, and the American South as a region. These have or are being eroded slowly and remorselessly, save in the memories of those who have known them. As the century wears on, the nostalgia becomes increasingly infused with irony directed both at the subject and the nostalgia itself.

Radically different though these various modes of modernism may be, their essentially elegiac attitude comprises a number of traits that generate intricate sets of crossovers between them. At the same time, it is clear that a number of these traits are far from mutually consistent with one another. Indeed, one of the identifying traits of modernism in general is precisely this clash of incompatibles. Out of it emerged both its ironic stance toward unreflective certitudes and its passionate pursuit of new grounds for, and modes of, conviction or belief.

One of the most obvious of these traits is the backward look at cultural history perceived as a sequence of receding vistas and superimpositional perspectives. In their several ways, T. S. Eliot, Ezra Pound, William Faulkner, and Ford Madox Ford all testify to the celebratory regret and the unblinking farewell such a look arouses in the anthropopoetic mind. For Eliot in particular, as in *The Waste Land* (1922), intertextuality is made to serve not only the ends of an interplay of literary voices sometimes polyphonic and sometimes antiphonal in character. It also functions as cultural and historical indices of value and attitude united in their subjection to the vicissitudes of human fortune grounded as it is in temporality:

> What is the city over the mountains
> Cracks and reforms and bursts in the violet air
> Falling towers
> Jerusalem Athens Alexandria
> Vienna London
> Unreal (48)

Pivotal points of various human cultures, such as the middle Eastern, the classical Greek, and the European, struggle in *The Waste Land* to maintain their eminence even as they move toward the unreality of the present. This unreality is compounded of the passage of time and the failure to realize the centrality of religious consciousness provided by a historically aware Christianity.[6] The exclusion of Rome from the above list of major world cities obliquely testifies to Eliot's conviction that, unlike the squalid secularism of contemporary London, there does exist a city whose cultural centrality and permanence is a consequence of its spiritual focus. Eliot, however, is too subtle a mind to risk explicitly identifying Rome in this way. That would entail a denial or concealment of its actual historical reality and the human shortcomings it has contained. Rome for him exists as an emblem or symbol of full religious consciousness rather than as a geographical and geopolitical entity. It functions as a counter to human cultures, to history, and to time itself by invoking the image of a still point in a turning world. In effect, it summarizes the elegiac attitude redeemed from history as an endless series of human unrealities.

Pound deploys many of the same techniques, but his elegiac focus is less upon the recurring loss of and struggle for religious consciousness. For him, the center of attention is upon the enormous historical, cultural, and educational lacunas between *virtu* and viciousness. As a result, poems like "Hugh Selwyn Mauberley" invoke a complex satiric irony directed at the contemporary English culture of the early 1900s and, by extension, at his own poetic career up to that time.[7] His contempt for the aesthetics of this world is founded on his awareness of his own mistake in endeavoring to resuscitate historically older cultures through imitating their forms of art:

> He strove to resuscitate the dead art
> Of poetry; to maintain "the sublime"
> In the old sense. Wrong from the start—(187)

In effect, Pound here acknowledges the futility of cultural restoration projects of whatever order. No matter how beautiful, appealing, and compelling the past is, it sings but a siren song leading to disaster and oblivion for the contemporary mind. Past cultures exist for him, as the *Cantos* demonstrate, not as contemporary realities but as models of and for living. They exist for him as *exempla* rescued from obscurity by artists, historians, and scholars, by, in short, all those who explore the past in order to correct the mistakes and to shape the directions of the present. It is for this reason that Pound, like Eliot, only much more so, invokes fragments from the past and makes recondite allusions to it in all its variegated historical reality. In "Hugh Selwyn Mauberley" the allusions are restricted to writers from French and classical cultures such as Ronsard, Flaubert, Homer, Pindar, Cicero, and Horace. They suggest that Pound is taking a bifocal view of the modern artist and the culture in which he lives. On the one hand, he has mistaken the relationship between past and present, and so his own role as poet. By extrapolating from high aesthetic points of past cultures and setting them over against the contemporary world as infinitely superior to it, he has implicitly cut off the aesthetic from the more broadly cultural forms of expression in order to elevate or privilege it. And by the same token, he reads the aesthetic as purely a phenomenon of the past, so that his attitude toward the present can only be satiric rather than elegiac.[8]

On the other hand, his allusions do single out nodes of extreme aesthetic value available to the poet from the several cultures. These do not lose their intrinsic worth by being cited in the present for the ironic purpose of satirically contrasting them to the English culture of the turn of the century. As a result, they function as emblems from the past that persist in the present and so refute his implicit polarization of present and past. This duality of perspective allows "Hugh Selwyn Mauberley" to be both a critical indictment of the present as embodied in English culture of the early 1900s and an implicitly elegiac remembrance of the past as the locus of elements of enduring cultural value regardless of what the contemporary world consists.

What enables these two perspectives to converge is the cultural fragment as a concept. The first regards the fragment as purely that, a fragment from a past no longer relevant in the eyes of the present culture. The second, on the other hand, sees it as a touchstone of enduring value. The self-indictment of the poetic persona named Mauberley rests on his treating of the aesthetic fragment from a past culture as the equivalent of the entire present culture of London and England. Mauberley's mistake lies in his equating of the part with the whole and of his resolute bifurcating of past and present into autonomous entities. Both of these Pound devoted the remainder of his life to correcting, at least to his satisfaction, in the *Cantos*. There, one of the major results is the development of a full-bodied elegiac attitude toward the past, which, for Pound, consists of a whole range of cultures—classical, European, American, and Chinese. Included are their socio-political, historical, economic, and biographical as well as aesthetic fragments. These last are also extended from the purely literary to include the visual arts, architecture and sculpture, and music. Were this the whole role or function of the *Cantos,* they would stand simply as an abortive and incomplete cultural encyclopedia. They are redeemed from this by also directing their elegiac attitude toward the individual. It is he who as human being is consigned to struggle to reconcile his aspirations to *virtu* with his perceptions of the myriad forms of viciousness that infect mankind and all of his cultures without exception.

A second trait, closely linked to the backward glance and often mistakenly identified with it, is the identification of a prior time of such diversified cultural or intellectual, moral, or aesthetic superiority as to warrant the mythic label of "Golden Age."[9] The prime exemplar of this, of course, is Ezra Pound. He certainly employs the backward glance to record his memories of aesthetic touchstones, of cultural fragments prized for their beauty, wisdom, or probity, that stand as a chart of his reading and thinking about the poet's place in the contemporary world. He also uses it in a more sustained and less individualistic way as a means of locating those civilizations and eras that possess educational and pedagogical potential for the century and culture(s) in which he lived.

The greatest concentration of Golden Ages rendered longitudinally through a text is undeniably in the *Cantos*. Yet it is important to note how early and how extensive, if how uncertain, was Pound's attraction to the ideality of an earlier elsewhere. There are signs of it in *Canzoni* (1911) and *Ripostes* (1912). By *Cathay* (1915) and *Lustra* (1916) it is a fully established geocultural *figura* that functions emblematically as well as heuristically and ironically, that is to say, educatively in Pound's sense of that often misunderstood term. Poems such as "The Tree," "Apparuit," and "The River Song" render iconically the sense of a Golden Age. The *Cantos* develop in a more sustained and extended sense the same basic concept historically and cross-culturally. Thus, in the first of these poems, the dedicated spiritual absorption of and empathetic identification with a totally foreign object, namely, a tree, is capable of investing a tale or story or myth from a remote culture with "the truth of things unseen before" (3). To the modern mind, an account of a person's transformation or literal identification with a tree cannot be accepted as true. Yet by the imaginative effort to accept the cultural postulates of another civilization, new insight becomes possible: "And many a new thing understood / That was rank folly to my head before" (3). What is understood is less the likelihood of such a transformation's actually occurring than how and why a culture other than one's own could so think and believe and the implications of that conviction. For Pound, the expansion of possibility is one of the critical marks of learning and education even as is the exercising of attention.

"Apparuit" sketches in greater detail and imagistic opulence a similar though strikingly more spiritual imaginative transformation. Drawing on Sappho and Dante, Pound merges the figure of a young woman with the natural pastoral landscape in order to render the poet's vision of the actuality of the ideal and of his awed response to it. What is made manifest to the poet as narrator is both a vision and an accompanying attitude or emotion. First, he realizes that the "loveli- / est of all things" (68) is the image of a woman in a natural setting. Then he implicitly echoes Dante's view in *La Vita Nuova* that the only appropriate emotion is love, love of and for a creature whose divine nature is a compound of the human and heavenly. Such a vision is part of the education of the poet in that it determines his role in his culture, a role that he must maintain throughout his career.

This is not to say that the image of a young woman as the focal point of his universe remains the object of his concentration. It is only the initial image of his controlling vision of the immanent nature of the divine. Nor is it irrelevant to find Pound even at this stage of his life drawing on classical and medieval cultures rooted in two different countries—Greece and Italy—and two radically different kinds of poet—Sappho and Dante—to shape and focus his own vision of the poet's mission. The aesthetic allusions seek to establish, albeit tangentially, a historical continuity in the poet's apprehension of his cultural role. In so doing, they carry an inherent elegiac attitude toward the vision and significance of the image of the young woman. This derives from the vision's momentary and fleeting nature, perceived as being "a / portent" and "swift in departing," yet so real as to leave the witness "caught at the wonder" (68). The glimpse of the eternal focuses the aspirations of the poet even as it evokes regret and longing, twin aspects of the elegiac attitude, for its very brevity.

"The River Song" takes a different approach to the issue of cultural education by absorbing the Western reader wholly into a foreign, ancient, and unfamiliar culture. In so doing, it inadvertently points up the role of the accidental in Pound's efforts to recapture other cultures's aesthetic responses to their own history. As such, it balances by its erroneous assumptions and translations Pound's penchant for *ex cathedra* pronouncements on other cultures and their products.[10]

More central for our purposes here, however, is Pound's effort to recreate the elegiac attitude that he finds in the originals of Li Po. By summoning up an Asian version of the poet's role as court figure in the Chu state, Pound endeavors to create in his Western reader an appreciation for the precision and acuteness of the anonymous poet speaker's perceptions of the external world, his delight in language, and—what contrasts with these—his subordinate, almost menial position in relation to the emperor. Amid the splendor of the court, with its elaborate boats, house, gardens, and birds, the poet observes the passage of time, the inevitability of change, and the transitoriness of glory or earthly fame. These last create an undercurrent that controls both the external world and the poem itself. It moves the poem to accept them as more permanent than even these perceptions that appear to dominate his consciousness. The very tranquility in the face of the transformation of "King So's terraced palace" (128) and the splendors of the court to "now but barren hill" (128) and the wry wish that "glory could last forever" (129) convey an elegiac attitude that is the polar opposite of what Pound is to express in "Hugh Selwyn Mauberley." The one is bereft of the satiric impulse to change and transform, the other redolent with discontent at the status quo. In so being, they implicitly contrast the role and status of the poet in their respective cultures. In Li Po's world, the poet has "joy in these words / like the joy of blue islands" (129); in Pound's London, the poet ironically asks, "What god, man, or hero / Shall I place a tin wreath upon?" (189)

From this, it would appear that Pound was destined to spend most of his career struggling to differentiate between his sense of the ideal role of the poet and his own personal and temperamental invocations of verbal power designed to make his own contemporary cultural reality square with that ideal. And indeed, that is very much what the *Cantos* reveals: his bitter struggles to invest fragments of past cultures with meaning and value for his assessment of his own modern multicultural imaginative environment. To find what is beyond history through history is his central goal. Thus, Kung's apothegms on order in Canto XIII embody not only useful knowledge and practical wisdom but also an absence of reliance on any human condition entailing futurity:

> If a man have not order within him
> He can not spread order about him;
> And if a man have not order within him

> His family will not act with due order;
> And if the prince have not order within him
> He can not put order in his dominions.
> And Kung gave the words "order"
> and "brotherly deference"
> And said nothing of the "life after death."
> And he said
>   "Anyone can run to excesses,
> It is easy to shoot past the mark,
> It is hard to stand firm in the middle." (59)

In addition, these apothegms gain both a plangency and an intensification of their temporal remoteness and cultural unavailability when seen in varied and attitudinally diversified contexts. They resonate with the futility of desire when read against the scabrous invective concerning his own cultural inheritance leveled in the cantos immediately following as well as the more philosophical judgment on the consequences of usury rendered in Canto XLV.

Pound's furious and persistent ransacking of European, English, and American history to locate nodes of cultural achievement represents the importation of context into text. With it occurs the generation of a bitter, satiric contrast between states of being and nonbeing that forms the structuring carapace without which the elegiac voice would be unable to sustain its stoical threnody. The burden of this oblique lament is developed through the isolate poet's voice affirming the occurrence of achievements of Golden Ages by grammatically negating their functional antithesis, usury, as in Cantos XLV and LI:

> With usura hath no man a house of good stone
> each block cut smooth and well fitting
> that design might cover their face,
> with usura
> hath no man a painted paradise on his church wall
> . . . .
> with usura is no clear demarcation
> and no man can find site for his dwelling.
> . . . .
> WITH USURA
> wool comes not to market
> sheep bringeth no gain with usura (XLV, 23)

With usury has no man a good house
made of stone, no paradise on his church wall
. . . .
Neither Ambrogio Praedis nor Angelico
had their skill by usura
Nor St Trophime its cloisters;
Nor St Hilaire its proportion.
Usury rusts the man and his chisel
It destroys the craftsman, destroying craft; (LI,44)

The greater the geohistorical distance between voice and age and the greater the communicative static, the greater the weight of the loss and the poignancy of the elegiac voice.

The Cultural Elegy on the Present and Future

The modernist elegiac temper is also shaped by another attitude. Confronted with an imperfect past, an inscrutable and problematic present, and a disappearing self, the modernist sensibility could easily have retreated. It could have withdrawn into a self-pitying cultivation of its tragically historical uniqueness or into a solipsistic imaginative denial of the contemporary realities it had so arduously discovered. To its credit it did neither, although ideologically blinkered successors have on more than one occasion mounted such assertions. Instead, as the later W. H. Auden perhaps best demonstrates, it set itself to forge a bifocal vision of man's fate. Collectively, it expressed the vanity of all cultures' achievements in the face of inevitable oblivion. But it also coupled this with the impulse to lament that otherwise unattended "long decay" (the phrase is Edmund Spenser's) and necrology of other persons, places, and things.

For instance, *The Sea and the Mirror* has Caliban conclude: "it is just here, among the ruins and the bones, that we may rejoice in the perfected Work which is not ours" (*CLP,* 250). And against that postulated spiritual ideality Ariel replies with the foreknowledge of "what we shall become," namely, "One evaporating sigh" (*CLP,* 252). Clio, the Muse of history, is found to be one who each time "had nothing to say" because she is engaged in "defending with silence / Some world of [her] beholding" (*CSP,* 309).

Here, the elegiac voice of modernism faces human imperfection and the inscrutability of time and history. In so doing, it deepens from the traditional mourning of the metaphorically elaborated protagonist and the conventional railing against a multifarious but triumphantly antagonistic fate. The focus falls on erring, fallible, mortal creatures who are memorialized and mourned for maintaining their individual human capabilities. By their faith, hope, blind conviction, and determination, they persist in their work, seen as *the* quintessentially human occupation or task. Thus, Voltaire continues to write because "all over Europe stood the horrible nurses / Itching to boil their children" (*CSP,* 145). And

Yeats's silliness does not prevent him from persuading "us to rejoice" or teaching "the free man how to praise" (*CSP,* 143).

This elegiac voice is given over to quietly celebrating those who, like Freud and Henry James, work within the parameters of human activity as if limits, conditions, and restrictions did not exist either behaviorally or temporally. In tonality and intensity, this voice drops to a minimalism of expectancy couched in a contemporary equivalent of the middle style:

> . . . though one cannot always
> Remember exactly why one has been happy,
> There is no forgetting that one was. (*CSP,* 341)

In the very act of acceptance there still sounds the note of received sorrow. It functions as the ground-base of the elegiac uttered in the primary and essential isolation of the human condition:

> The dripping mill-wheel is again turning;
> Among the leaves the small birds sing:
> *In solitude, for company. (CSP,* 338; Auden's italics)

Such a *topos* brings the elegiac impulse full circle historically by recapturing in a manner both self-aware and self-critical its recapitulation of the late medieval "ubi sunt," Spenser's haunting phrase "the ruins of time," and the Vergilian "lacrimae rerum."

This recapitulation of the various historical tonalities of the elegiac temper is not, however, univocal or confined to a single author. Indeed, it is its very polyvocality that marks the modern approach to the elegy, thereby transforming it from a single genre to an entire range of attitudes. For our purposes, this can perhaps best be seen by turning to poems of a highly diverse order written by Edith Sitwell, Allen Tate, Geoffrey Hill, and Robert Duncan. Two of these poets from two major cultures embody historically and thematically a number of the major traits of modernism per se. The other two represent in very different ways some of the strategies and attitudes of postmodernist poetry. By considering them together, it may be possible to better apprehend the full scope of the modern elegiac temper, to sense the variegated pattern of modernism, and to appreciate how its successors were able to contribute strikingly different tones and attitudes.

Edith Sitwell's rococo modernism differs from the stylistically revolutionary version of Eliot and Pound precisely in its language and its uses. Whereas they insist on making it new verbally, she relies on such traditional strategies as rhymed couplets, conventional classical allusions, alliteration, assonance, and esoteric specialized vocabularies. This is seen vividly in her "Elegy on Dead Fashion."[1] Under its late nineteenth-century sumptuous verbal splendor, it, nevertheless, still advances certain of the modernist reflections on time, the past, myth, loss, and death:

> . . . those epochs gone,
> Our eyeless statues weep from blinded stone.
>
> And far are we from the innocence of man,
> When Time's vast sculptures from rough dust began,
> And natural law and moral were but one—
> Derived from the rich wisdom of the sun.
>
> In those deep ages the most primitive
> And roughest and uncouthest shapes did live
> Knowing the memory of before their birth,
> And their soul's life before this uncouth earth. (198)

The elegiac awareness of the differences between past and present, the omnipresence of death and mortality in human consciousness, the permanence of the divine despite its historically changing shapes and forms, and the narrative voice's reflective sadness and sense of the persistence of loss as a constant in human affairs all emerge relentlessly from a context ostensibly dedicated to the ephemeralities of fashion in clothing, manners, and natural settings.

The poem opens in a mockingly fond manner by suggesting that scholars of romance and fashion are engaged in a somewhat trivial but pleasant aesthetic pursuit. They study simply what ordinary people of the past have talked about and been concerned over, namely, the clothes and styles of various times and places. The past focused on is essentially tripartite: the nineteenth-century English formal gardens and great houses such as Sitwell herself occupied as a child; eighteenth-century French nobility and high society affecting to be nymphs, shepherdesses, and others from an earlier pastoral world; and the classical world of Olympus and its occupants such as Venus, Adonis, Cupid, Jupiter, and Juno.

The surface beauty, pleasantness, and fancifulness of these contexts are challenged by the historians' mulling over such matters as Venus's age, her likelihood of remembering Adonis's kiss, and her present condition of being "dead and rotten" (193). Their research cannot be more than an exploration of the dead; it cannot restore to life the ancient philosophers and poets, such as Plato and Aristophanes. As dead individuals, they must necessarily abandon the classical myths or stories and their characters embodying the human focus on love, sex, and romance.

From the standpoint of the narrative voice, the mythic nymphs are likened to summer flowers both by now being dead and as recollected as being no longer present. Their past elegance is set over against their present elegiac air, which consists of a gentle sorrow for the loss of such living forms of beauty, elegance, and artifice:

> Yet once on these lone crags nymphs bright as queens
>
> Walked with elegant footsteps through light leaves,
> Where only elegiac air now grieves—
> For the light leaves are sere and whisper dead
> Echoes of elegance lost and fled. (193)

What is recollected, however, is not the original nymphs of classical times but their simulations playfully enacted by the members of a high society which, too, has vanished. All that is left are the memories, whether actual or a part of the historical record. These subsequent stanzas suggest a gradual and general diminution of human life by tracing the transition of nature—trees, flowers, woods, owls, snow—from summer to winter. This transition reflects that from past to present, from high to ordinary or low society, from nobility to servants, and from stylistic affectation in dress to clothing intended for warmth and protection. The closer one comes to the present the more mundane and dedicated to its perpetuation life becomes.

In effect, at this stage of the poem Sitwell sees the relation of past to present essentially as do Eliot and Pound, but from the opposite end of the social scale. Where Eliot adapts the urban squalor of Baudelaire and the provincial elegances of Boston to his elevation of the Renaissance past, Sitwell invokes the splendors of nineteenth-century English high society with its shooting-boxes, castles, and country parks, but only as limited approximations to the Olympian grandeur of the classical world.

While Eliot and Pound balance their elegiacism for the past with astringent irony and satire for the present, Sitwell takes a milder stance by seeing the children of the remembered past in a quasi-comic light. They play in their still stylish clothes and carry on their simple or innocent flirtations amid a rougher, more natural landscape than did the nymphs of the more distant past. Their grandfather, Jupiter, is metaphorically likened to a nineteenth-century Scots nobleman or member of the gentry. Similarly, Sitwell's intermingling of Roman and Greek deities juxtaposes the urbanities of a late nineteenth-century classical education against the heavier documentation and more professional comparative method of its anthropologically oriented successor. The shift in tone is from the light gracefulness of the gentleman amateur to the multi-disciplinary concentration of the professional scholar. This reflects the gradual deepening of the poem's sense of "dead fashion." The referential scope of the phrase increases from contemporary shifts in clothing styles to historical modulations in the understanding of the ties and differences ever obtaining between past and present.

Thus, the children's discovery of rocks holding fading flowers as winter approaches comes to be seen as a bucolic comedy containing "the secret of how hell and heaven grew" (195). The natural cycle reflects and recapitulates the historical cycle of new and old fashions and the spiritual cycle of death and life. Similarly, the gods—Jupiter and Juno—are played by the owners of the country estate, thereby establishing the nobility as the equivalent of the divine Olympian hierarchy, a comparison that is both embraced and made sport of by Sitwell. Juno's world is that of the dairy and garden in contrast to Jupiter's concern with the hunt—his shooting-box over against her farm, physical destruction and death contrasting with physical nurture, fructification, and life. The extension of the gods-nobility metaphor leads to a recognition of its limits. Clearly, the implausibility of identifying the nineteenth-century British upper class with gods and goddesses is beyond the imaginative bounds of even the most extreme of right-wing Tory thinking, such as that of Evelyn Waugh. At the same time, this metaphor forces us to recognize that the temporal difference between past and present exposes the loss of one sort of artifice and fashion for another inherent in the latter. To reduce Olympian deities to upper-class property owners clearly spells a loss in grandeur, but from the poem's narrative focus and its appearing in 1926 so does the singling out of such property owners for such an inflation in status. The implicit elegiac sense of loss in the shift from gods to property owners is balanced by the slyly ironic elevation of the latter to divine status precisely when historically they were poised on the slope of social decline.

At the same time, Sitwell makes of the country park and the garden not only a contrast but a kind of cultural continuity loosely similar, though in a reduced scope, to that of Spenser in *The Faerie Queene*. Sitwell's poem has the farm lying

within the country park, and within it lies the garden: the pastoral world of cre-
ation and cultivation lies at the heart of the established, civilized world inhabited
by divine and human creatures. Inherent in this relationship is her rationale for
her elaborate style. It recalls the highly formal, exquisitely mannered and fash-
ioned society that surrounds and overlays her essentially simple vision of the par-
adigm of human existence. The transformative persistence of images of the di-
vine in human societies is, for her, archetypal rather than historical, and this, she
argues, is what the studies of Venus's historians reveals. Both style and theme
tease out the implications of "dead fashion" until both are perceived as inher-
ently elegiac.

The disappearance of gods and nymphs of the classical world is reflected in
the actual present's changed perception of the natural world. Where the eigh-
teenth-century figures imitate their view of the classical deities and life, now even
their play-acting and elaborate simulations of an even more distant past are lost
to the narrative's voice. The apprehending of the classical past is achieved only
by seeing also the eighteenth-century imitations and reflections. By seeing through
the eighteenth-century styles of brightly colored petticoats, deep-brimmed round
straw hats, green mohair gowns, and high kid boots, one recognizes them to be
an exquisite but outmoded fashion.

This insight allows the narrative voice to see their artifice as artifice and to
see what it considers to be the actual reality of the classical world, namely, its
gods and nymphs. In place of the obvious artifice of the eighteenth-century sim-
ulators of the classical life stands a far more primitive sight. This occurs when
"roughest and uncouthest shapes did live" (198) and when mankind's mother is
nature in the form of a wolf enacting a universalized version of the Romulus
and Remus myth. Yet even this purging of one fashion of perception does not
yield essential reality, as the image of the wolf implicitly suggests. Its primi-
tivistic style suggests the ancient world is now being seen not in the fashion of
eighteenth-century high society but rather in the late nineteenth's combination
of a gentleman's command of Greek and Latin and a scholar's evolutionary
perspective.

In looking at the past, Sitwell suggests, one unconsciously develops a habit of
discreetly shifting one fashion for another in accord with the needs and tastes of
the present. This is the rationale for the elegizing of dead fashion. Any fashion is
but the form in which the divine and human, immortality and mortality, elevated
and lowly, leisure and work are cast by the succession of historical periods and
human cultures. Each fashion is but its civilization's encoding of its values and
attitudes regarding these concepts. Each is both trivialized and celebrated by the

very passage of time and the backward glance of human consciousness. A fashion while alive and flourishing is adulated and celebrated, even as are deities. And after its time has passed and it has died solely into memory, it is recalled at the most fondly and at the worst deprecatingly. In either case, however, the memory carries an elegiac sense of mingled regret and puzzlement that anyone or any age or culture should have actually valued and esteemed such creations. The reason for stressing the past as a matter of fashion is to see it as a subject for amusement at its ultimate triviality. At the same time, it entails the recognition that all human pursuits such as history and the scholar's preservation of knowledge have both their own triviality and value because they record the differences in cultures conferred by the passing of time.

The main difference between her version of modernism's attitude toward the past and that of the classical modernists is that she does not ostensibly—here at any rate—evaluatively differentiate between past and present. Past fashions are valuable because they represent beautiful, elaborate human accomplishments despite their artificiality, extravagance, and apparent irrelevance to present styles of dress, thought, and belief. They are seen as curiosities almost of an anthropological order rather than preferred orders of existence and value and reality. Sitwell is, in effect, fighting both a rearguard action on behalf of vanished and vanishing ways of life, on behalf of cultural history if you will, and advancing the cause of the new. Unlike Eliot and Pound, she does not eschew or disavow the immediate poetic past so much as she views it as a historical phenomenon deserving of respect even though, or perhaps because of, its being outmoded. For her, this view applies as much to the immediate past of the nineteenth- and eighteenth-centuries as to the classical past so remote in time as to be beyond the reach of living memory though not of historical, scholarly speculation.

It is precisely the extreme distance between the narrative, twentieth-century present and the earliest of human pasts that she confronts. And with it, she grasps the irretrievability of that past in any other than a context of imaginative speculation. In the process of underscoring this distance, she identifies multiple forms of loss visited upon the present: loss of rest, nurture, innocence, the unity of natural and moral law, and of awareness of the archetypal basic forms of existence. Out of this, she invokes a kind of Wordsworthian Platonic view of the origins of life reaching beyond mortal ken but still ingrained in the human soul. It now stands as a "forgotten tomb" (199) that still retains glimpses of "the light / Of vaster suns [that] gave wisdom to our sight" (198).

With this, Sitwell ushers in an implicit contrast between historical knowledge as assembled by "Venus' old historians" (192) and immortal wisdom deriving from an archetypal vision of origins. Sadly rather than vituperatively, she contemplates the loss or at least the profound diminishment of such wisdom in the present. In contrast to Pound, particularly the early one of the London years, she, however, avoids sharp trenchant ironies and satiric comments about the present. Her *métier* is that of regretfulness for the passage of fashions of recent memory and intense sorrow mixed with spiritual pain for the dimness of the memory of the original serene condition of mankind:

> Now, days like wild beasts desecrate each part
> Of that forgotten tomb that was our heart;
> There are more awful ruins hanging there
> Than those which hang and nod at empty air.

> Yet still our souls keep memories of that time
> In sylvan wildernesses, our soul's prime
> Of wisdom, forests that were gods' abode,
> And Saturn marching in the Dorian mode. (199)

Central to the poem is Sitwell's classical adaptation of the Christian paradox of death and life beyond death. She suggests that although "all the nymphs are dead" (199), a phrase repeated three times in six successive stanzas, nevertheless they continue to exist "deep in the dark secret of the rose" (200). By conjoining the divine and the natural life cycles, the nymphs and the rose, she is able to problematize the elegiac response to death.

If the individual human heart is closed, then the natural emblem of continuing imaginative or spiritual life—the rose—too is dead. But if it is still open or receptive, then it is still capable of being aware of modern or contemporary manifestations of ancient gods and goddesses even though the present natural elements, the fruits and flowers, are isolated and alone:

> But Janet, the old wood-god Janus' daughter,
> All January-thin and blond as water,
> Runs through the gardens, sees Europa ride
> Down to the great Swiss mountains of the tide,

> Though in the deep woods, budding violets
> And strawberries as round as triolets
> Beneath their swanskin leaves feel all alone . . .
> The golden feet that crushed them now are gone. (200–201)

These modern manifestations of divine creatures (Janet, Nettie, and Alexandrine) also simulate eighteenth-century fashions in their clothes in order to summon up memories of yet earlier and more splendid times that capture "the glamour of some huger eves" (201). In so doing, they point up the human rationale for the search for origins: it is a compulsion to regain a spiritual Golden Age. The acknowledgment of the passing of time and the loss of archetypal awareness of immortality is beset by the recognition that all is not of necessity lost.

Toward the end of the poem, the narrative voice, the poetic "I," links itself with this dual awareness. It sees loss as a reduction in imaginative scope and a diminishment of spiritual power. But it also construes memory as a recollection of that which can still exist. It does so by stressing its association with Fortune:

> And there, with Fortune, I, too, sit apart,
> Feeling the jewel turn flower, the flower turn heart,
> Knowing not goddess's from beggar's bones,
> Nor all death's gulf between those semitones. (201)

Fortune is a compound of destiny and chance in whose company the individual senses the transition of mineral to vegetable to human form. They have a common identity through being subject to change, destruction, and transmutation. The isolation imposed by death is transcended by the acceptance of the unity of existent things. But this acceptance carries with it a profound dislocation of perspective:

> We who were proud and various as the wave—
> What strange companions the unreasoning grave
> Will give us . . . wintry Prudence's empty skull
> May lie near that of Venus the dead trull! (201)

Human esteem for individuality and diversity of temper, interests, and attitudes among the living is undercut by death and the grave. There the difference between chastity and promiscuity, between differing responses to Venus, appears far less significant than in life. To the dead, this striking change in fashion constitutes manners of valuing radically different styles of living. It testifies to the gradual expansion of the ways and the extent to which death and fashion are intertwined and worthy of being elegized.

To the living narrative voice, however, the unity of existence remains problematic. It is both something to be sought after and to be doubted as attainable:

There are great diamonds hidden in the mud
Waiting Prometheus' fire and Time's vast flood;
Wild glistening flowers that spring from these could know
The secret of how hell and heaven grow.

But at a wayside station near the rock
Where vast Prometheus lies, another bock
Is bought by Ganymede . . . why dream the Flood
Would save those diamonds hidden in the mud? (201)

The growth or evolution of the concepts of heaven and hell is potentially know-
able to those who accept the unity of existent things. But both classical and Chris-
tian myths are unsustained beliefs devoid of rationale or purpose because of the
presence of Fortune as chance or luck. In effect, what is questioned here is the
likelihood of time's being subject to human desire and so of actually preserving
the ground of life's renewal.

What the changing course of fashions in men and gods reveals ultimately is
exactly a polarity between past creatures and prospects for the future. A farmer
bent on simple sustenance stands over against aristocratic ladies seeking idle plea-
sure and amusement. In the same way, elegant pastoral simulations of ancient
wood nymphs counterpoint mythic monsters associated with the underworld and
death. This polarity focuses on youth opposed to age and spring to winter in or-
der to suggest the inevitability of a period of closure, disintegration, and cessa-
tion for the human soul. Even Fortune or chance is subject to time as destroyer:
"'Her face is winter, wrinkled, peaceless, mired, / Black as the cave where Cer-
berus was sired'" (202).

The immediate present of the narrative voice affords a starker perspective on
history and its dead fashions of event and attitude. Thus, history began in the hu-
man soul with a gay, adventurous dance of Venus "with divine, deathless
Chance" (202) only to decline into a vision of her as bitterly subject to time and
fortune. The goddess of youthful love, desire, and beauty—the very epitome of
living rather than dead fashion—comes to have "known the anguished cold, /
The crumbling years, the fear of growing old!" (202). The dance that begins as
a kind of play or game, thoughtless and endless, concludes as also subject to
change, which transforms, threatens, and chills the soul into a broken, inanimate
statue. From her position in the present, the narrative voice sees human history
as a record of shifting, changing fashions that survive but briefly though beauti-
fully. In doing so, it identifies the ultimate darkness of life with the heart's forget-

fulness of the ultimate paradigm of that life, which is man's slow emergence as ruler of the world:

> Here in this theater of redistributions,
> This old arena built for retributions,
> We rose, imperial, from primeval slime
> Through architecture of our bones by Time;
>
> Now Night like lava flows without a chart
> From unremembering craters of the heart,
> Anguished with their dead fires. (202–203)

Thus, time is both the creator or ground of existence and the destructive diminisher of mankind. As the former, it structures through changes of an evolutionary order the very nature of mankind. As the latter, it leads even Venus, the embodiment of desire, passion, and generation, to disintegrate into a mere shattered statue aware of the eternal cold of death and fearful of aging. For the narrative voice or poetic "I," the present carries the articulated prophecy of the Sibyl. It, together with the lovers's kiss, exactly embodies Venus's power and ostensibly portends their immortality. In the kiss, however, is finally discovered the symbol of death as a function of time and change, the Worm that slowly and relentlessly decomposes the unity of being.

With this recognition in the present, the dead Venus over the next fourteen stanzas takes on the lineaments of her eighteenth-century simulation, though not with their past gaiety and sense of accomplishment. Now her role as a great lady of wealth, privilege, and position is subtly eroded by her residences being identi-fied as fanciful "castles of the air" (203) and her gardens as mournful. Similarly, her servants' names (Miss Ellen and Miss Harriet) underscore the existence of a historical and geographical gulf between them and her. They are of nineteenth-century England, she of eighteenth-century France; neither is but an isolated past recollection and therefore a species of dead fashion. Coupled with their laughter being "melancholy" (204), these facts underline their diminution. They know that compared to their Olympian status of ancient classical times, they have lost their divinity and become mere human beings no matter how privileged their position.

The same awareness of loss and diminution—of status, of kind of position, of prophetic power—affects the poetic "I," the voice of the immediate present moment. Through her sedulous probing of history and the stories of classical myth, she comes to the very brink of chaos. Sadly, she realizes that the whole panorama of gods and men is but a puppet show staged by time, death, and chance. Myth and history, events and lives, tales and stories are but random performances played by death and time ("the apish shuddering dust" [204]) to appeal to unfettered human desire for immediate profit and pleasure.

They are all forms of death for and to the spirit even though this is not known by the figures of the past. These representatives of dead fashion we historically remember essentially in order to despise or criticize them for their myriad forms of failure to triumph over time, death, and chance:

> The gods, Time-crumbled into marionettes.
> Death frays their ageless bodies, hunger frets
> Them, till at last, like us, they dance
> Upon the old dull string pulled now by Chance.
>
> This is the game the apish shuddering dust
> Plays for the market and the house of lust;
> There are a thousand deaths the spirit dies
> Unknown to the sad Dead that we despise. (204)

The fragility and uniqueness of the human spirit consists of its being destined to lose, to diminish, to make mistakes, to exercise faulty judgment, to be—quite simply—human. Yet it is what subsists beneath all the tides of fashion and despite the immediate strength of its diverse currents.

The concluding element in this elegiac view of fashion writ large is the fact that it still continues even in the present. Ladies of fashion still continue to perform their rituals and elegant simulations of other cultures. The narrative voice pities them in that these apparent embodiments of life—fashion as the highest, most intense, liveliest expression of culture and civilization—are actually their tombs as individuals:

> Rich as a tomb each dress! oh, pity these!
> I think the rich died young, and no one sees
> The young loved face show for a fading while
> Through that death-mask, the sad and cynic smile. (205)

There is an inevitable irony inherent in all their futile efforts to express the full, playful, aesthetic freedom of choice for their limited historical time. Yet the narrative voice recognizes, too, a further redeeming sort of irony. No one perceives their self-awareness of the cruel joke in which they are participating. To be fully aware of and to participate in fashion and its history is to recognize its transitory, ephemeral, and yet inevitable nature.

The last six stanzas constitute a kind of retrospective coda to the poem. Myth and history are narrative records of death and the dead—all their participants are in fact dead—and yet because of their being remembered and elegized however fleetingly, they, though dead, are not yet wholly dead. Sitwell implicitly suggests it is only when the dead become anonymous, totally forgotten, obliterated from human memory, that they are completely and truly dead. For her, to be forgotten, and so unmourned and unmournable, is to attain the apparent ultimate death and to pass beyond the elegiac temper of any age.

And yet even this prospect is queried as to being the consummate and ironic conclusion to the saga of human fashion and its ceaseless changes seen as one phase of the mind's recurring effort to imagine more than in fact actually exists. For the narrative voice continues its speculations by wondering whether those so dead have their own backward glance at those still living in the present. Do, in short, they have their own kind of elegy for those residing in a world necessarily populated by a multitude of dead fashion? May it not be that those still alive continue to face the prospect of complete isolation in their own consciousness? May not death be simply that of individual consciousness with which they are so intimately familiar and which they prize so profoundly:

> Do these Dead, shivering in their raggedness
> Of outworn flesh, know us more dead, and guess
> How day rolls down, that vast eternal stone,
> Shuts each in his accustomed grave, alone? (205)

Compared to the isolation conferred by the nature of consciousness, that imposed by death is but the denial of awareness and with it of the elegiac temper. To accept this isolation as the final truth of the human condition is to simulate a death-like state. To accept it as ultimate reality rather than as a secular ideology, a momentary fashion of thinking, is to deny the imaginative, spiritual conviction of the existence of the eternal human spirit rooted in the divine:

> Upon this rock-bound march that all we made
> To the eternal empire of the shade—
> To the small sound of Time's drum in the heart.
> The sound they wait for dies, the steps depart.

> Come not, O solemn and revengeful Dead—
> Most loving Dead, from your eternal bed
> To meet this living ghost, lest you should keep
> Some memory of what I was, and weep! (205)

This death-in-life condition calls up not so much an explicitly religious context. Rather, it conveys the conditions that will generate the elegiac temper for the narrative voice and all other living creatures subsisting in this condition.

Sitwell, as we have seen, ranges from the present to the classical past in her effort to explore the ambiguities in the impulse to elegize select segments of past cultures. In contrast, Allen Tate focuses down on a single historical event—the American Civil War—and the complexities surrounding the culture's concern with mourning and celebrating its occurrence. His "Ode to the Confederate Dead" is, however, like Sitwell's poem, as much an interrogation of the elegiac impulse, of its justification, worth, and inevitability in the human economy, as it is a full-blown elegiac tribute to his region's heroically hapless ancestors. This last would entail an acceptance of their defeat, whereas to mount a heartfelt praise of their courage, nobility, and honor is to incline the sentiments more to those of the ode as a literary form:

> You know the unimportant shrift of death
> And praise the vision
> And praise the arrogant circumstance
> Of those who fall. (21)

It is as if Tate is trying to find a way of mourning the Confederate dead that more nearly fits the historical circumstances in which he finds himself than the stereotypical language of heroic dedication, denial of defeat, and threat of renewal embedded in the slogan "The South shall rise again." How to separate the stereotypical sentiments of its present supporters from the initial sacrifice of the dead and how to honor the latter while not saluting the simplicities and inadequacies of the former is the challenge Tate engages in the poem. And yet by merging the mourning sorrow for the dead of the elegy with the elevated, philosophical sentiments of the ode, he enables an honorable salute to the past to disengage itself from the conventional cul-de-sac of contemporary verbal resistance to the facts of history.[2] His goal is to shape a viable contemporary response to his region's past that allows for the emergence of an attitude that neither forgets its history nor commits it to repeating it.

For this reason, he begins with a simple recording of multiple deaths wrought by the war and memorialized by the forces of nature:

> Row after row with strict impunity
> The headstones yield their names to the element,
> The wind whirrs without recollection;
> In the riven troughs the splayed leaves
> Pile up, of nature the casual sacrament
> To the seasonal eternity of death;
> Then driven by the fierce scrutiny
> Of heaven to their election in the vast breath,
> They sough the rumour of mortality. (20)

The headstones, the wind, and the leaves, all are natural facts of the universe. However much they summon up the permanence of death, they also suggest the uncertainty of mortality. The poem's speaker is drawn by this ambiguous uncertainty to postulate a continued existence for so many dead buried "in the plot / Of a thousand acres" (20). The very number buried begets at the same time an incipiently puzzled or contradictory or ambiguous set of memories. They are elegiac because of past persons and seasons that are over and yet not done with. And yet they are fraught with introspective uncertainties brought on by the passage of time. The November wind stains the dissolving gravestones, threatening them and their inhabitants with disappearance from memory and history.

Here, the speaker implicitly identifies the elegiac with memory and convention and so with the stereotypical. For Tate, this is the dominant southern attitude to the war. Because he entertains his own uncertainties about such an attitude, he is paralyzed and left floundering in a state of confusion, indecision, and irrational blindness as to a viable alternative:

> Turns you, like them, to stone,
> Transforms the heaving air
> Till plunged to a heavier world below
> You shift your sea-space blindly
> Heaving, turning like the blind crab. (20)

To attempt a separating of present and past, a reformulation of the conventional southern cultural resistance to its opponents, and an abandonment of the stock emotional denial of defeat is for Tate profoundly disconcerting and dismaying: "Dazed by the wind, only the wind / The leaves flying, plunge" (20).

As a result, he immediately turns to a reiterative summing up of what it is that he has known and experienced before encountering the trauma of the past's persistence into the present. This list ranges from the sensory "certainty of an animal" (21) through the rationalities of pre-Socratic philosophers, to current personal dilemmas constituted by the complex interactions of personal desires with fatalities following from them. This review provides no resolution but only a renewed awareness of the Confederate dead as the pivotal point from which his problem emerges:

> You know the unimportant shrift of death
> And praise the vision
> And praise the arrogant circumstance
> Of those who fall
> Rank upon rank, hurried beyond decision—
> Here by the sagging gate, stopped by the wall. (21)

His lack of intellectual movement toward a solution is mirrored in the past interruption of the Confederate advance: both are "stopped by the wall."

It is his identification with his region's military dead that impels him to a closer examination of their fate and destiny and what they presage for his own life. Just as they have become shadowy "demons out of the earth" who "will not last" (21) and lost victims of historic battlefields of the war, so he "will curse the setting sun" (21) if he and the South remain committed to their futile view of their present place in history:

> You hear the shout, the crazy hemlocks point
> With troubled fingers to the silence which
> Smothers you, a mummy, in time. (21)

Merged as the Confederate dead are now seen to be with the universal sterility of the past as past, the narrative voice faces directly and for the first time the empirical, given reality of their existence:

> What shall we say of the bones, unclean,
> Whose verdurous anonymity will grow?
> The ragged arms, the ragged heads and eyes
> Lost in these acres of the insane green? (22)

Whatever cultural honorifics of praise, remembrance, and honor are bestowed on them, they still are dead. In being so, they are cut off before their time, reduced to skeletal remains, bereft of their personal identity and individuality, lost to and for their culture except as memories of futile courage and nobility of commitment:

> The singular screech-owl's tight
> Invisible lyric seeds the mind
> With the furious murmur of their chivalry. (22)

It is the legitimacy of their sacrificial loss of life that alone remains worthy of the present culture's memory. For the rest—the knee-jerk insistence on blind defiance of the ensuing socio-political realities—"we shall say only the leaves / Flying, plunge and expire" (22).

All that a culture committed to pursuing a solipsistic ideal vision of itself can do ultimately is recognize that both its past and future are shrouded in the natural darkness of unforeseen consequences and unpredictable consequences. It cannot change its past or anticipatorily condition its future. Quite simply, it cannot unequivocally know either but can only wait with "mute speculation" (22), cursing the past and peremptorily trying to impose its own vision of itself on the future, and thereby engaging in self-victimization. Only those capable of facing this need for separating past and present by stern interrogation of their deepest values and clear-eyed acceptance of the consequences can avoid the inevitable losses inherent in living solely in the culture's past:

> What shall we say who have knowledge
> Carried to the heart? Shall we take the act
> To the grave? Shall we, more hopeful, set up the grave
> In the house? The ravenous grave? (22)

Essentially what Tate draws out most sharply in these rhetorical questions is the bitter historical and cultural choice facing his native region. It can submit to repeating blindly the act of the Confederacy's heroic acceptance of unequal struggle and subsequent defeat. Or it can retain the memory of that sacrificial act as part of its culture in order to bring about its own renascence into a viable life in the present. It is time, he tells the South, to abandon the "shut gate and the decomposing wall" (23) of stereotypical intransigency and indifference to the relentless passage of time that has dominated its culture since the Civil War. Concealed by both gate and wall lies the symbol of the interfacing of the natural and the divine, the serpent and mulberry bush, the cyclical disintegration and the restoration of life imaginatively contained within the linearity of death as the ultimate fact of all persons and cultures.

The differences between Tate's poem and Robert Lowell's "For the Union Dead" point up in a variety of ways the historical, regional, racial, and literary features that distinguish them as ironic laments and celebrations for the manner in which the present has come to memorialize the past.[3] The thirty-odd-year difference in the poems' composition figures in the difference almost as much as their authors' embodiment of the two sides in the war. Tate takes a philosophic, largely generalizing perspective compounded of seeing his troops as anonymous corpses and probing the possible relations between individual self and communal attitudes. Lowell, on the other hand, focuses on an actual existing piece of sculpture memorializing Colonel Robert Gould Shaw and his troops. Thereby, each poet works in the shadow of the dominant cultural attitude of his geographical region: Tate reflects the idealizing thrust of the South, especially with regard to the war, while Lowell captures the gritty empirical particularity of the urban North. Similarly, Tate's southern perspective leads him to completely ignore the controversial place of blacks in his celebration of his region's military dead. In contrast, Lowell sets himself apart from his community by ironically indicting it for its ingrained covert response to the statuary honoring the sacrifice of black Northern soldiers: "Their monument sticks like a fishbone / in the city's throat" (71). And finally, Tate encourages the South to think analytically about its present stance toward both history and the present and so is content to raise challenging questions for it. Lowell, already feeling alienated and deracinated from his regional culture, challenges it directly. He poises the idealistic racial equality of the North's past against its present racial polarization and its juxtaposition of squalid urban mechanical modernization against small town maintenance of "sparse, sincere rebellion" (71) and dedication to the values of the North's past. Lowell's harsher, more savage critical attitude reflects the literary world's shift from urbane, sophisticated, civilized irony as the medium of communication to the direct, impatient, incipiently ideological declarations that dominated American culture in the 1960s.

Lowell's opprobrium for the present and its attitudes is counterpointed against his personal regret at the disintegration of "the old South Boston Aquarium" (70) and his public sorrow at the gulf separating the statue of Colonel Shaw from the present world:

> He is out of bounds now. He rejoices in man's lovely
> peculiar power to choose life and die—
> when he leads his black soldiers to death,
> he cannot bend his back. (71)

The enormity of the racially unified regiment's sacrifice is remembered only officially in the memorial sculpture and personally in the poet's bitter reflections on historical change and the cultural disintegration of his community into "a savage servility" that "slides by on grease" (72). His indictment of the present does not, like Tate's adjurations to his culture, assume the tutorial, reflective tone of one calmly and almost surgically suggesting an alternative to its current attitudes. Rather, it savagely criticizes what the society has made of its critical opportunity to better itself out of its past "power to choose life and die" (71): its intensification of vulgar, mechanized ugliness, its repudiation of and indifference to other forms of life, its refusal to memorialize the sacrifices generated by subsequent wars, and its advertising trivialization of profound secular and spiritual events alike.

For both poets, however, the elegiac temper is almost covert, and only in a very loosely philosophical manner does it extend to embracing the individual regional cultures of both past and present. Tate's fierce commitment to the South as a family home stops short of or at least falters in its single-minded intensity when it becomes the new urban South of the present that is subjected to the elegiac temper. For it, there is little to celebrate, little to honor, and nothing to feel as an irremediable loss. Only in the Confederate troops who unquestioningly sacrificed their lives is there an emblem of nobility of conduct and attitude worthy of elegiac celebration. Lowell's sharpest focus is on the North's descent into mindless commercial and technical opportunism in the twentieth century. To it, he brings a primary attitude that shares more with a savage Juvenalian satiric attack than with the plangencies of loss engendered by the conventional or traditional elegiac approach.

The one poet retains the elegiac sense of pity for his ancestors and their communal fate, the other memorializes not so much them as their statuary, symbolic as it is of an ignored or dismissed past rather than of present communal honoring. For Tate, the separation of past and present attitudes toward the elegiac subject is essential for the well-being and survival of the regional culture. For Lowell, it is the fact of this very separation's having already been so firmly instituted that occasions a profound regret for the loss of a once firmly held socio-intellectual position that made both public and private elegiac expressions appropriate.

Their joint hesitation to embrace fully the elegiac temper toward their respective regional cultures testifies both to their inheritance of the multiple ironies of modernism and to the growing skeptical attitude of their joint American inheritance concerning its present nature and its historical past. By comparison with postmodern poets such as the British Geoffrey Hill and the American Robert Duncan, both Tate and Lowell hesitate to invoke the traditional or conventional elegiac voice or to stretch it into new tonalities and inflections. Instead, they merge it with ancillary poetic modes such as the ode and the satire in order to deflect attention from their elegiac concerns. At the same time, they still retain an awareness of the very deep losses sustained by their ancestors and regional cultures as a result of the war which embedded the very idea of fissure and division into their common American culture.

The strategies of Hill and Duncan are more direct: both write elegies that directly engage the concept of culture, though with radically different emphases. Hill's concern is with the analytic recollection and reconsideration of history—English and European, Renaissance and modern—while Duncan is preoccupied with envisaging images of an alien culture—African—as emblems for what he regards as his true home, namely, the imagination. In doing so, each distances himself from his native culture: Hill attitudinally and Duncan geographically.

Hill, in his "Requiem for the Plantagenet Kings," uses the sonnet form to condense his view of that royal family's three-hundred-year reign into a summary stressing its essential and ambiguous consequences for itself and others of the historical period:[4]

> At home, under caved chantries, set in trust,
> With well-dressed alabaster and proved spurs
> They lie; they lie; secure in the decay
> Of blood, blood-marks, crowns hacked and coveted. (18)

Despite their being historically remembered and honored, this does not divorce them from their basic fatal mortality and decay, emphasized as it is by their almost ceaseless spilling of blood in repeated violent conflicts. Though their intentions and military struggles may have been good and just, the result has been "ruinous arms" (18). Both they and their successors, including historians, however, were not deceived by this ironic juxtaposition of cause and effect, good and bad, for "men, in their eloquent fashion, understood" (18).

Nor is this the end of Hill's straight-faced irony generated by his objectively stated scrutiny of history, as the terms "eloquent" and "understood" suggest.[5] Both words, for Hill, convey their customary direct positive meanings. Simultaneously, however, they carry skeptical, ironic doubts about their implications.[6] They also possess the sense of taciturnity or, conversely, of public bombast as well as of a congenital failure to understand why mankind should persistently pursue good intentions and yet achieve only destruction, disaster, and death.

The second and third quatrains develop in greater detail this contemplative paradox. It, as the poem's title indicates, is composed of religion's deliberate and dispassionate assessment of human history and mankind. On one level, the Plantagenets' public historical role and appraisal is set over against the actualities of their individual fates. At home, they lie memorialized and in state, "well-dressed" (18) and exhibiting the conventional justification of their noble warrior position as if these tokens are sufficient to establish it permanently and completely. In fact, however, the kings rest secure only "in the decay / Of blood, blood-marks, crowns hacked and coveted" (18). The resolution of this paradox of the public and the personal, the historical as role- playing and as ultimate actuality, is provided by powers neither human nor secular. It is not the elegist himself who is capable of compelling a secular recognition of the absolute finality of death and of establishing the inescapable centrality of the loss suffered by the living. Rather, it comes when "the scouring fires of trial-day / Alight on men" (18), when religious judgment becomes the end-point for the elegiac temper. Only when the dead have been divinely judged are they able physically to resurrect themselves. Only then are they able to rise from their place of destruction and disintegration, which is "the possessed sea" with which the poem began.

Once again Hill pursues his elegiac paradox by extending the significance of "possessed" to encompass two poles of meaning so as to unite rather than separate the religious and historical perspectives. The sea is "possessed" by the arms of at least two countries (historically England and France) and enwrapped in a state of almost demonic possession. The former sense captures the historical, secular context, while the latter conveys the spiritual consequence of the lengthy Plantagenet reign. By subjecting themselves and their countrymen to war, emotional turmoil based on irrational frenzy and pride, and the ignoring of their mortality— "the dropping-back of dust" (18)—and its significance, the kings have historically linked themselves with the demonic. Only when they and their descendants experience the divine Judgment Day will the sea become populated with the risen dead, men's knowledge freed of the ruination associated with political power, their temper or spirit ridded of "being fired" (18), and their souls restored.

With this, the secularization of history will blend with the religious vision into a single tranformative elegiac remembrance of mankind and his past. What Hill's version of postmodern skepticism does is to extend his dispassionate, analytic perspective to the skeptical attitude itself, to probe relentlessly the legitimacy of the persistent disclaiming interrogative and its reductiveness to no final judgment. He does this by proposing the supplementing of the secular historical perspective by the finality of the religious judgment. He does so, however, not so much by privileging the latter, as was the custom of earlier modern thinkers, as by implying that the wedding of the religious and the historical in the modern world produces a more inclusive vision of the range of human possibilities.[7] This vision questions the rhetorical extravagances of conventional elegiac language and perspective at the same time as it asserts awareness of the sadness and loss inherent in human history.[8]

For him, simple verbal chronicling is sufficient to underscore the almost unbearable weight of acceptance and regret that this history imposes. By dedicating his "Two Formal Elegies" to "the Jews in Europe," he singles out the Holocaust as the principal reminder and interrogation of the nature of human history:

> Knowing the dead, and how some are disposed:
> Subdued under rubble, water, in sand graves,
> In clenched cinders not yielding their abused
> Bodies and bonds to those whom war's chance saves
> Without the law: we grasp, roughly, the song. (19)

Once again, he sees knowledge of the past and its inhabitants as approximate, apprehended only in its larger contours, and even then conditioned by the presumptiveness of certitude and conviction that makes possible the elegiac song which is the record of human history. In comprehending the song "roughly," man, Hill suggests, is doing two things. He is testifying to his approximation to its truth and reality. And second, he is seizing it in a crudely vigorous fashion that is an inherent part of the human condition, rooted in its death and destruction and yet generating its persistence and continuance.

It is with the last quatrain and the final two lines that Hill departs from the modernist inclination to set human history within a cyclical perspective, either one that focuses on restoration and revivification or one that stresses the endless rise and fall of human fortunes. The former derives from anthropological and comparative religion patterns of dying and reviving gods, while the latter stems from philosophical perspectives that stress concepts of destiny, fate, and repetition.

Instead, for him, history is an ironic chronicle of a dizzying movement from divine creation to an apocalyptic moment. Its enormity lies beyond human speech in the passionate silence of stunned, shocked awareness of an event literally beyond human comprehension and thus of rhetorical elegizing:

> . . . Still beneath
> Live skin stone breathes, about which fires but play,
> Fierce heart that is the iced brain's to command
> To judgment—studied reflex, contained breath—
> Their best of worlds since, on the ordained day,
> This world went spinning from Jehovah's hand. (19)

Hill's position concerning the Holocaust, then, is that its historical actuality is so enormous, so deep in its profundity, that it lies beyond explanation or linguistic lament, beyond rationalization or transcendence.[9] In effect, it is the determined consequence of the concept of a divine creation of a world populated by human beings. To postulate a being who can envisage the great *I Am* is to commit to the certitude of an event that can simply proclaim *It Is* without explanation, justification, or commiseration. As such, Hill's notion of the elegiac temper is one that lies beyond speech and language. It consists of the muteness of the incomprehensible but actual event that lies both within and beyond history. As such, it is a kind of demonic version of the religious or spiritual act.

The second of Hill's "Two Formal Elegies" shifts away from the fact of the Holocaust and the effort to explain it. Instead, it concentrates on Europe's concern with remembering it and the questions to which this gives rise. Unlike many other commentators, Hill is not so much concerned with the culture's likelihood or possibility of forgetting the event and its protracted process for "we have enough / Witnesses (our world being witness-proof)" (20). He points rather to its steady, almost imperceptible, absorption into the ordinary life of ordinary people concerned with their immediate world and its actualities, expectancies, and gratifications:

> Here, yearly, the pushing midlanders stand
> To warm themselves; men brawny with life,
> Women who expect life. They relieve
> Their thickening bodies, settle on scraped sand. (20)

The threat to the cultural elegiac memory is, then, not deliberate forgetfulness. Rather, it is the constant and subtle pressure to live one's own life with others beset, as people are, by the destructive power and force of nature and time: "The sea flickers, roars, in its wide hearth" (20).

It is in the final quatrain and couplet that Hill most tellingly probes the nature and significance of the cultural memorial to the Holocaust. Here he sets declarative syntax over against interrogative grammatical symbols so as to call up a meaning or significance that lies beyond that postulated by the statements themselves:

> It is good to remind them, on a brief screen,
> Of what they have witnessed and not seen?
> (Deaths of the city that persistently dies . . . ?)
> To put up stones ensures some sacrifice.
> Sufficient men confer, carry their weight.
> (At whose door does the sacrifice stand or start?) (20)

The first couplet provides a declarative statement which counters the octave's proclamation that there are already enough witnesses in public designed to call to mind the Holocaust. It ostensibly suggests there is an ongoing value to reminding each generation of its horrors, even through its brief presentation in media such as movies and television. This testimonial squares with the culture's current practice only subtly to question its veracity in the very process. The repetitiveness of the public reminders do make the populace witnesses, visual spectators apprised of the ghastly nature of the events comprising the Holocaust. Hill, however, suggests the likelihood that the society as a whole merely catalogues them as having occurred without fully or truly perceiving their profoundest significance.[10] Here, he raises the issue of the difference between memory as record and memory as meaning. Hill then questions even the worth of the most passing and public of memorials by asking his audience to interrogate whether such reminders confer any good at all.[11] The parenthetic phrase immediately following uses its interrogative end symbol to broaden the historical context and significance of the event: "(Deaths of the city that persistently dies . . . ?)" (20). The incomprehensibility of death deliberately inflicted on six million Jews is subsumed in the endlessly recurring deaths of people in the urban symbol of civilized life. The effect is to demystify or to qualify the uniqueness of the size of that slaughter inflicted in the middle years of the twentieth century. When set over against all human beings from all cultures (so many as to be beyond counting, as the reiterated punctuation underlines) who have historically died, the issue of the number of Jews killed in the Holocaust ceases to be the crucial issue. Death is the companion of everyone; what matters most is whether its rationale is natural or inflicted arbitrarily.

It is to this moral significance inherent in the Holocaust that Hill devotes the last lines of his second sonnet. Having pointed out the universality of death, he finds himself bound to remember yet a further historical and cultural fact. Mankind, nevertheless, insists on memorializing at least some if not all of death's victims: "To put up stones ensures some sacrifice. / Sufficient men confer, carry their weight" (20). It is a social, communal ritual gesture embodying thought, discussion, decisions, and assumption of responsibility. It can be performed taking but minimal account of its full significance on some, perhaps many, occasions.

This, however, does not alter the fact that it is just such public memorials that trigger the profound moral question for the individual with which the poem concludes: "(At whose door does the sacrifice stand or start?)" (20). Just as on the historical plane, Hill expands the context in which the Holocaust can be placed, so he does the same thing on the philosophical or ethical level. He raises both the conventional issue of individual personal responsibility and a more searing question of the measure of responsibility invested in the victims themselves. The first verb ("stand") raises the historical, moral, psychological issues to be faced by the German people guilty of participating in the Holocaust. It is the second verb ("start") that embraces both them and their silent, dutifully compliant, helpless victims, the Jews, a culture different from that of the nations of the so-called Christian West.

While Hill's elegies essentially articulate a postmodern version of the austere, tough-minded, religious perspective of modernists such as Eliot, Robert Duncan's "An African Elegy" betrays affinities with loosely Romantic second-generation modernists such as Dylan Thomas and postwar groups such as the British New Apocalypse poets. Hill scrupulously reduces conventional judgments and attitudes about his culture to a moral and empirical ground. This reveals the culture's illusions (and its fundamental nature), each of which begets and results in an ultimately interrogative perspective. Duncan, on the other hand, eschews any direct treatment of American culture in favor of a geographically visionary world that is the product of his own mind and imagination. Africa, for him, is a realm of "the marvelous," death, darkness, and the unfamiliar:

> In the groves of Africa from their natural wonder
> the wildebeest, zebra, the okapi, the elephant,
> have entered the marvelous. No greater marvelous
> know I than the mind's natural jungle. (33)

This imaginative Africa is the world of death felt not so much as extraordinary and a threat to life. Rather, it is the constituent of "ordinary occasions" and a gentle forgetfulness of "all our tortures absolved in the fog" (33). Death for the speaker, as for Virginia Woolf and Ophelia, both of whom are cited, occasions not a raging against it in an unwilling final gesture but a graceful and quiet accepting of the peacefulness and tranquility of the solitude it offers. Both women, ostensibly embodiments of insanity, accept the call of death as "a last / pastoral gesture of love toward the world" (33). In so doing, they, in effect, reverse the traditional elegiac role of nature and the pastoral. They see the pastoral not as a contrast to but as an identification with death. It is not something mourning the individual's passing. Instead, it is that which welcomes him or her to a relief and release from the multiple tortures of living and consciousness.

This basically quietistic vision of death as something sought and easily accepted is countered in the second half of the poem. There the focus is on the speaker's envisaging of the mythic descent into the world of death as akin to Conrad's journey into the heart of darkness, which is equated with "this / dark continent of my breast" (34). For Duncan, it is marijuana that affords him the magical talismanic entry into this culture of the imagination. In doing so, it enables him to bear the fall downward into the mental jungle populated by princely Negroes, Desdemona, and Othello where he endures the tortures inflicted by the mind upon the mind. Here is the antithesis of tranquility and peacefulness. Physical tortures, desertion, and warnings against selfhood as well as lamentations of its loss make up this culture of death entered by the imagination's exploration of itself.

Self and other, black and white, African and (presumably) American, imaginary character and real individual, tranquility and tortured anxiety, all are polarized in the speaker's consciousness until he, assuming his role as the mythic poet, Orpheus, cries "Hear! / Hear in the coild and secretive ear / the drums that I hear beat" (34–35). It is the poet's consciousness alone that simultaneously apprehends both the attractions and the terrors of death for a culture and individual. By linking himself imaginatively with it, he is able to encompass both aspects of his vision—the quietistic acceptance of self and the terrifying descent to the underworld of the other—and to grasp the fact that "There is no end. And how sad then / is even the Congo" (35). Both aspects, when apprehended singly and individually, generate illusions. The former thinks death is "a hound of great purity / disturbing the shadow and flesh of the jungle" (35) of consciousness. The latter sees it as the product of "the empty" that culminates only with the "silent, seeing nowhere / the final sleep" (35).

Only when jointly perceived, as by the Orphic poet, does the duality of tranquility and tension that exists in life and the human consciousness achieve its elegiac reality:

> There is no end. And how sad then
> is even the Congo. How the tired sirens
> come up from the water, not to be toucht
> but to lie on the rocks in the thunder.
> How sad then is even the marvelous! (35)

Metaphysical duality, epistemological polarity, and psychological juxtaposition are, Duncan finds, the constituents of human existence and consciousness. And it is the marvelous desire to conceive otherwise coupled with the recognition of its ultimate impossibility that creates the romantic elegiac temper for him and his imaginatively envisaged culture. This is the culture of otherness and elsewhereness toward which Duncan persistently aspired in contradistinction to mourning the losses inherent in any and all geographical and historical cultures.

7

The Philosophical Elegy and Time

*W*hen one considers even casually the history of the elegy in English, it is apparent that the bulk of it is dedicated to lamenting and coping with the loss of persons—close friends, colleagues, relatives, contemporary celebrities, historical personages, and the like. At the same time, most of the major traditional elegies such as *Lycidas, Adonais,* and *In Memoriam* focus also on how these figures partake of or generate broader social or philosophical considerations. Reflections on time, mortality, self, the mass destruction of war, religion or spiritual faith, and the supportive consolations they may afford are inextricably intertwined with the lamentations for the death of the central subject.

With the twentieth century, however, it is possible to distinguish what amounts to a subspecies of the elegy that makes such societal and philosophical contemplations the central subject of the poet's reflections. This group of texts moves away from the individual expression of grief for a person's death to a consideration of the various universal implications linked with such *topoi*. In doing so, they contribute to the modern tendency to broaden the elegy's focus from death itself as a starkly unique and personal phenomenon to the almost infinite range of losses sufferable in life. What they bring to the elegiac temper is the recognition of the inherent inescapability of loss, and with it the necessity of developing an attitude toward existence that mutes the shock, surprise, and grief customarily associated with death. The function of this attitude is to bring to the losses a psychological response of an incorporative order, one that sees them as part of the probabilities of living. In effect, they celebrate not so much the crisis provided by death; nor do they grieve over losses as temporary as that of love or as permanent as that of cultural disintegration. Rather, they reflect on such commonplaces in order to develop either a fuller recognition of the intricacies of their dimensions or a means of shaping what can be called an elegiac metaphysic.

A modest but significant instance of this sort of elegiac attitude is found in Wilfred Owen's "Elegy in April and September."[1] Its date of composition—during

World War I—and its draft title—"Ode to a Poet reported Missing: later re-ported Killed"—as well as its probably unfinished status, all testify to its antici-pating in a somewhat uncertain fashion such a metaphysic. More than the bulk of Owen's war poems, the "Elegy" works within a poetic mode formed out of a combination of Rupert Brooke's penchant for celebrating his native land and the Georgians' pastoralism as well as his reading of Andrew Lang's translations of classical elegists.[2] In many ways, its obvious concern with poetic techniques—al-literation, internal rhyme, strict variation in line length, and stanzaic progression from one distinct natural image to another—tends to conceal or obscure its theme of the futility of searching for that which is lost.[3]

The techniques suggest the poet's focus is on the manipulation of words while the theme raises the issue of time's passing always being rendered through chang-ing spatial configurations. The starkness or bleakness of the theme, with its sense of hopelessness or futility, is belied by the rhythmic control so rigidly exercised throughout. In point of fact, this duality, effectively though subterraneously, re-flects the soldier-poet's own struggle to maintain personal, psychological control of his immediate military world. Inherent in his present situation is a dichotomy between the peacetime past and the wartime present. In the past, there would have been the opportunity for a conventionally full elegiac acknowledgment of the loss of the other. But in the present, this loss is touched on only with the use of the third person singular pronoun. Instead, it is the speaker's regret for the in-evitability of time's movement and a broad, almost infinite range of human losses that dominates the poem. The tenuousness of his effort to exercise such control is captured in compressed fashion by the juxtaposition of the patterned rigidity of the stanzas and the anarchic suggestion of the language of the subtitle or epi-graph: "jabbered among the trees" (142).

Owen's focus on the passing of time and its significance is captured initially in the title with its insistence on the presence of the elegiac at both the beginning and the ending of the year.[4] Similarly, the stanzas' invocatory and exclamatory movement through "thrush," "daffodil," "brook," and "daisy" suggests a quasi-emblematic rendering of time's essential act of moving into the past through the several seasons. Too, the alternating of present and past verb tenses underlines the sense of continual change being at the very heart of Owen's concept of time. In the past, he has heard the sounds of another human being approaching. In the present, however, he can ask the thrush only to be silent while he strains to hear again that which each stanza in differing ways and degrees reiterates is past. By the second stanza, the speaker recognizes that the bright promise of nature embodied in the daffodil is deceptive. Actually, it discourages the prospect of success in recovering the past togetherness of self and other, the community or commonality of others. In wartime, there is only the isolation of the individual (the speaker) and the imminence of death and loss.

The first half of the poem, the opening two stanzas, stresses the struggle to have nature do the speaker's bidding. In contrast, the last half accepts nature's behavior and encouragingly enjoins both brook and daisy to continue to perceive, to look for that which they will never see—he who has been apprehended by the sense of hearing rather than sight in the past. Here the result of the passing of time begets the recall of the past in the present and with it the acceptance of the profound difference existing therein. The movement of the running brook is one of futile pursuit of the past. Nevertheless, it steadfastly persists in its and the speaker's effort to recover the object of its search, another human being: "Yet search till grey sea heaves, / And I will stray among these fields for him" (184).

The heroism of this effort is not, however, allowed to remain the final attitude taken to the changes wrought by the passage of time.[5] Neither Victorian duty nor Romantic exaltation of the desperately heroic are allowed to embody the incipiently modern recognition of the actuality of time's role:

> Gaze, daisy!
> Stare up through haze and glare,
> And mark the hazardous stars all dawns and eves,
> For my eye withers, and his star wanes dim. (184)

Time as seen in wartime renders only partially obscured and distorted perspectives. These, nevertheless, cannot hide the dangers and threats inherent in the steady passage of the succession of days and nights. In so marking time's incessant lapsing into an ever-receding past, the unrelenting persistence of this succession makes it increasingly difficult to recapture and its occupants to remember or recall.

For Owen, the passing of time leads to the stark fact of the insurmountable and irretrievable loss both of the human object and the subject or speaker. Both physical vigor and memory are in the process of declining ever more steadily; they are the fears of the young elevated to identification with the inevitable consequences of time.

Almost the exactly opposite perspective on time's movement is captured in Herbert Read's "The Gold Disc: An Elegy." Its speaker is an old man assessing the arc of his entire life. Included is its evasion of all its "wintry storms" (239); its balancing of mind and body "In equal pace, two fettled mares / Yoked to a featherweight car" (240); its perception of love as an ageless aspiration for "The never defin'd, the always unrealiz'd pattern of our delight" (240); and its acceptance of the inherent limits of human knowledge. His tone toward the passing of time is not one of railing against it, lamenting the losses it inflicts, or even of regretting the transformations both physical and mental it imposes. Rather, it is one of quiescent acceptance of time's changes:

> . . . I feel no remorse
> No sense of a mission that fail'd
> As I savour the smoke of the burning leaves, and the acid decay. (241)

With this acceptance, there is, however, not simply a quietistic relapse into a passive waiting for the elegiac end of life. Instead, there is the articulation of a fully explored wisdom derived from the very movement of time. This wisdom consists of both meta-belief or assertion and tranquil apprehension of doubt as a constituent of the most that man can know or apprehend:

> I believe in my unbelief—would not force
> One fibre of my being to bend in the wind
> Of determinate doctrine. In doubt there is stillness
> The stillness that elsewhere we may find
> In the sky above us where the fix'd stars
> Mete out infinity and space folds
> To contain the secret substance of life
> Which time in its tragic furnace moulds
> To the forms of grief and glory, of vice and holiness. (242)

What the passing of time brings for Read is the quiet realization that there is more to life than the temporal creature, man, can ever know or perceive. The polarities "of grief and glory" are folded into a paradoxical harmony consisting of "a music fraught with silence" and "a solitude full of sound" in which he finds "the peace beyond violence" (242). His final contemplation of "the gold disc that blurs all hard distinctions" (242) is his elegiac celebration not of losses of valuable experiences, achievements, persons, or insights but of the loss of illusions of knowledge, certainty, ego, and progress. By his transformation of the elegy from lament for loss of values to celebration of the loss of the valueless or erroneous or transitory, Read is able to authenticate his initial refusal to accept the traditional elegiac perspective and its verbal techniques:

I will not tread the old familiar path
Through watery meads and melancholy woods:
My autumn air is cool, the stubble crisp
And edged with frills of crystal frost: my moods
Are for endurance stript. (239)

In short, what Read suggests about the elegy is that saying farewell or goodbye is not always or necessarily an expression entailing lamentation. As such, his poem embodies an expansion in the elegy's role: from expressing grief and sorrow for a loss occasioned by time's movement and change to accepting the limitations inherent in the human condition and with them celebrating the disavowal of "all hard distinctions" (242).

While Owen and Read seek in diverse ways to tease out the implications of time's passing, they are still sufficiently traditional in poetic manner to include a human being as the focal point.[6] Archibald MacLeish's "You, Andrew Marvell," on the other hand, turns its attention to rendering the metaphysical nature of time's passing as a deliberate, unimpedible, impersonal process of transformation fraught with mystery, romance, and apprehension. The only person involved is the poem's speaker, who functions solely as a rapt, almost awe-struck spectator of the Mediterranean world's steady transition from day to night. This he records in a single, breathless sentence that constitutes the entire poem. The poem's allusive title, its insistent syntactic progression, and its ultimate dissolution of its four-line stanza form, all testify to MacLeish's modernist heritage in contrast to the premodern techniques of Owen and Read.

Like Read, MacLeish manifests no regret or sorrow for the passing of time, though he does not see it bifocally as chronicling both past and present. For him, the movement of time occurs exclusively in the present of a single day's duration which is implicitly characterized as recurring endlessly:

And here face down beneath the sun
And here upon earth's noonward height
To feel the always coming on
The always rising of the night: (150)

What time brings in its move from day to night are implicit harbingers of death: "the earthy chill of dusk," "the vast / And ever climbing shadow," "the flooding dark," and "the gate / Dark empty" (150). None of them, however, are elevated to symbols; they remain simply associative allusions suggestive of the affinities between the diurnal and the annual. In so doing, they maintain MacLeish's persistent articulation of an empirical metaphysic of the elegiac. For it is by a simple sequential rendering of the physical details of time's movement from dawn to the onset of complete darkness coupled with a Marlovian intoning of strange, foreign place names—Ecbatan, Persia, Kermanshah, Baghdad, Arabia, Palmyria—that he creates the sense of the vastness, strangeness, and mysteriousness of the geographical universe, of the world as the basic context for mankind.[7]

Owen's perspective is the soldier's lyric acceptance of the inevitability of time's entailing loss. Read's somewhat broader view is the survivor's narrative recording of time's also containing psychological and moral gains. Distinct from both is MacLeish's attitude. His is the civilian's philosophic subsumption of personal mortality as felt rather than stated into the perception of time's daily movement from light to dark. MacLeish does not articulate any explicit attitude toward this sense of the contrast between human loss and geographical/diurnal perpetuation. Instead, he is content to formulate a simple awareness of a muted recognition of the elegiac temper.

Here, it is created by the sensory conviction of two perceptions. The first is that the human loss is inevitable and natural and so necessarily grounds for a feeling of profound sadness. The second is that the perpetuation, perhaps eternal, of the world simultaneously intensifies the sorrow for the loss and modifies its severity. It does so by authenticating the continuing existence of the universe despite the perpetual temporal changes wrought in the human realm. For MacLeish, eternity as a physical, geographical condition envelops and contains mortality as a metaphysical awareness of the consequences of time's passing in but a single direction. The twofold reality makes his expression of the elegiac temper both proto-modernist and a declination to choose between lamentation and celebration. This is caught in the poem's final lines:

> . . . no more
> The low pale light across that land
>
> Nor now the long light on the sea:
>
> And here face downward in the sun
> To feel how swift how secretly
> The shadow of the night comes on . . . (151)

8

The Philosophical Elegy and Mortality

*T*hose modern writers engrossed with time and its passage tend, as can be seen from instances such as MacLeish or Woolf in *To the Lighthouse*, to focus down to a natural landscape populated sparsely, if at all, by human beings. What they are struck by is the perdurability of the physical, natural world and the transitoriness of human life. A related but nevertheless distinctive philosophical *topos* is that of human mortality and its implications for man's life and attitudes. Poems by the likes of Vernon Watkins, Ronald Bottrall, Thom Gunn, Wallace Stevens, and James Wright explore this motif assiduously. In so doing, they generate a subtle sense of how they are expanding the scope of the elegiac temper while departing significantly from the form and focus of the traditional elegy.

Two poems by Watkins—"Griefs of the Sea" and "Cwmrhydyceirw Elegiacs"— enable us to see both of these traits in tension. They capture the strength both of the hold maintained by poetic convention and of the modern insistence on acknowledging the inescapability and the irreducibility of mortality. Thus, the first of these poems begins with lines that appear to mimic the traditional elegiac mode:

> It is fitting to mourn dead sailors,
> To crown the sea with some wild wreath of foam
> On some steep promontory, some cornercliff of Wales
> Though the deaf wave hear nothing.
>
> It is fitting to fling off clothing,
> To enter the sea with plunge of seawreaths white
> Broken by limbs that love the waters, fear the stars. (7)

Lamentation and the other rituals of mourning the dead are here acknowledged as appropriate human gestures neither to be ignored nor discounted. Such efforts at remembrance, however, almost inevitably produce inflated images, turning "dead sailors" into "magnificent types of godhead" (7). Yet this, too, is psychologically legitimate in that it is a powerful response to the awesome threat of the sea. To the blind and greedy wave, the horrible sound of the hateful wind, the hissing caves at the seashore, and the prickly thistle on the cliffside enacting their cacophony of destruction and disintegration, man's only answer can be the courageous anger that imaginatively seeks to counter the reality of death with the image of something greater than mankind, something that is not subject to it.

To conclude here would be for Watkins simply to articulate the traditional resolution of the elegies of the past. Where he moves in a new direction is in the immediately following lines. These declare unequivocally that "in that gesture of anger we must admit / We were quarreling with a phantom unawares" (8). This admission essentially closes off the possibility of resolution by religious faith, whether Christian or pagan. In doing so, Watkins forces his audience to recognize more than the unreality of divine human beings. He also insists that the source of their postulation lies in the all-too-human mind, which is capable of concealing its inventions or fictions even from itself. In this last, he approaches territory more fully and sophisticatedly explored by Wallace Stevens.

What the mind is not able to conceal from the poet's lament for dead sailors is the ultimate awareness of even the sea's indifference to its power to elicit mortality from the human condition. Sea, sand, and weed, all turn away from participation in human death with a mute refusal to recognize any significance in their actions beyond their naturalness to their own intrinsic condition:

> For the sea turns whose every drop is counted
> And the sand turns whose every gain a holy hour-glass holds
> And the weeds turn beneath the sea, the sifted life slips free,
> And the wave turns surrendering from its folds
> All things that are not sea, and thrown off is the spirit
> By the sea, the riderless horse which they once mounted. (8)

In separating the human from the natural, the dead bodies from the water, Watkins accentuates nature's indifference to human calamity while underlining the inescapability of the brute fact of mortality. The surrender of the bodies back to mankind prevents their being transformed by the human mind into yet other imaginative fictions designed to conceal or obscure the fact of their no longer being alive or subject to any material transformation whatsoever. The sailors are representative of mankind. As such, they confront mortality both as finality and as the summation of life. These are conceived of as the courageous struggle to face and to surmount the inevitability of life's defeat by its limitations, enshrouded as they are in the passage of time and change.

The forging of an attitude toward the fundamental character of mortality—its brute inescapability and untransformability—is essayed more completely in Watkins's second poem, "Cwmrhydyceirw Elegiacs." In doing so, it initially advances a philosophical attitude combining the stoical and phlegmatic in equal measure. This attitude is compounded of the acknowledgment of the death of an individual and the dying of the year and how both embody "dumb secrets . . . hard as the elm-roots in winter" (380). Language, memory, and the emotion of loss combine to shape the conventional human response to death into an honest acknowledgment of mortality and the inevitable limitations inherent in that response:

> We who are left here confront words of inscrutable calm.
> Life cuts into stone this that on earth is remembered,
> How for the needs of the dead loving provision was made. (380)

The difference between Watkins's elegiac temper and that of the traditional elegy emerges from the refocusing of the nature of sorrow at the loss of the individual and the rationale for the effort to memorialize. The commemorative words are seen not as efforts to seek an explanation for the death or to protest or bemoan it, not as desperate lamentation but as conducive of "inscrutable calm" extended to the survivors. This calm is linked to the perception that memorializing is directed to "the needs of the dead." This recognition balances the roles of the dead and the living into a total response to the phenomenon of mortality.

That someone lived and now is dead, that this fact is recorded and so remembered, that this provides solace to the living and strength to the dead, all three combine to shape an elegiac temper fully cognizant of the fact of mortality: "Strong words remain true, under the hammer of Babel: / Sleeps in the heart of the rock all that a god would restore" (381). What the dead need is not the security of transcendence of their state but rather the confidence of being remembered by their peers for so long as it is possible to record. This reduction in the elegiac aspiration follows from the philosophic acceptance of mortality as the human end point. It does not lead, however, to a capitulation to the limitations of the human condition. It produces rather a stoical recognition of exactly what the elegiac possibilities are and what implications they hold for the interplay of lamentation, memory, and time: "One grief is enough, one tongue, to transfigure the ages: / Let our tears for the dead earn the forgiveness of the dust" (381).

*   *   *

While Watkins acknowledges the role of the elegiac tradition even as he redefines
its scope, Ronald Bottrall focuses even more sharply on the physical details that
figure in the mortality of the living. In so doing, he largely expunges the histori-
cal convention of explicit lamentation. Thus, his "On a Grave of the Drowned"
sketches the casualness, the violence, the physical strain, and the suddenness with
which mortality visits itself on the living, whether human or nonhuman. Here,
all attention is concentrated on the dramatic moment at which mortality becomes
the only reality for the individual:

> . . . ; on thole-pins spent
> The dizzy creak of racked sinews and
> Stalled with a thew-thrust, whipcord taut,
> Jarring alarms of singing drowsiness.
> Then glaucous eyes crammed full. (57)

Only with the last four lines of the poem does Bottrall permit his sharply
muted version of the elegiac to emerge:

> Above that mounded tale of many,
> Disintegrated one, a beacon autumn tree
> Irradiated from within swirls
> Outward in eddies of russet light. (57)

Like Watkins, he allows the one corpse to stand for many, indeed, for all. In this
way, he intensifies the significance conferred on the natural symbol of somber ac-
knowledgment of human mortality, the autumnal tree looking down on the grave.
It is not any human ritual of interment or lamentation or recollection that cele-
brates the death. Instead, it is the natural image positioned by accident rather
than intent that mutely testifies to the final effect of mortality, namely, disinte-
gration. After the violence, frenzied action, and final convulsive gesture issuing in
the presence of mortality, there is but the silent testimonial to the profundity of
difference it holds to life. In effect, Bottrall creates almost the archetype of the
Stoic elegy, the elegy as mute acknowledgment of the inherent futility of spoken
lamentation, architectural memorial, and temporal denial.

In a way, Bottrall's final image—the lone tree beside the grave mound look-
ing out over the sea—functions like that of MacLeish's in "You, Andrew Mar-
vell." Both create a picture of stark finality fused with a tacit acknowledgment
that reality for human beings is not subject to change or modification by any
words that can be uttered either by participant or poet. They focus on the single

image that embodies both the reality of and the human response to mortality. In so doing, they surrender the habit of speech or language to the visual impression. Its totality of implication and actuality makes words both unnecessary and an inevitable reduction in felt significance.

A more reflective, indeed contemplative, consideration of mortality emerges in two poems by James Wright. His treatment internalizes the elegiac sentiment by focusing on its enactment in nonhuman forms. In so doing, he emphasizes the poet's role as philosophical spectator. The first of these, "Three Sentences for a Dead Swan," by its very title endorses the modern philosophical withdrawal from the traditional resolutions of the elegy. The flat claim to be making declarative statements rather than explicit laments principally conveys two things. One is the self-control of the poet, while the other is the futility of essaying more than the chronicling of mortality as it impacts the traditional natural symbol of eternal life.

The first of the titular sentences occupies the opening section of the poem. In so doing, it captures two things: the impending nature of the inevitability of the swan's mortality and the futility of bemoaning that fact:

> . . . I heard them beginning to starve
> Between two cold white shadows,
> But I dreamed they would rise
> Together. (156)

The mortal state is a natural one common enough to all living creatures at least as a real possibility (starvation) even as its conventional transcendence is seen to be but a fiction easily and naturally created (a dream).

The starkness of this vision of mortality and its apprehension by the poet is intensified in the second section, where metaphor takes over from literal description. The bird becomes a "lonesome dragon" (156), the adjacent apple orchard an object of violent machine-gun fire, and the poet's life is faced with its own mortality. Such a metaphoric rain of death and destruction brings mortality fully into the poet's imagination. This entails the recognition of both the prior awareness and the indifference of nature to the fact. The poet, then, faces the reality of the bird's loss:

> In the autumn of my blood where the apples
> Purse their wild lips and smirk knowingly
> That my love is dead. (156)

The third section completes the abandonment of the traditional elegiac formula of lamentation and resolution. It both apes the solemn movement of the ritual act of entombment and ironically shatters the idea of its nobility and tranquility:

> Here, carry his splintered bones
> Slowly, slowly
> Back into the tar and chemical strangled tomb. (156)

Here death by water for Wright is no longer the profound elegiac symbol of Eliot's *The Waste Land* but rather a polluted ordinary twentieth-century American river in which neither resurrection nor elegiac lament is possible:

> The strange water, the
> Ohio river, that is no tomb to
> Rise from the dead
> From. (156)

In the almost strangulated awkwardness of the repetition of "from," Wright captures both the fact of and his response to the no longer accessible traditional elegiac resolution to the sorrow inherent in the mortality of a living creature.

"Elegy in a Firelit Room," as its title suggests, essays to indicate the form and tone in which the modern elegy can be wrought. Even so, by casting the poem in a conventional verse form (four-line iambic pentameter stanzas with *abab* rhyme), Wright implies that the historical shift in elegiac form is not so much a radical poetic revolution as a transition conditioned by deep-seated cultural changes in attitude and philosophy. Once again, both the elegiac subject—willow tree, sparrow, and a child's face—and its observer respond with indirection to the incipient sorrow haunting the scene:

> Beyond, the willow would not cry for cold,
> The sparrow hovered long enough to stare;
> The face between me and the wintered world
> Began to disappear. (16)

The fact that mortality haunts not only human but vegetative and animal entities does not mean they must immediately, if ever, yield to or even contemplate it. Nor does it mean the observer must generalize with elegiac sentiments explicitly lamenting the fact.

Instead, he chronicles the varied ways in which the entities approach their mortality and their implications for his own philosophic awareness. The image of the child's face inscribed on the cold window pane by his breath is seen to disappear slowly under the impress of his fingers touching the glass while the room warms from the fireplace stirred to life. The sparrow's dancing indifference to winter found in the first stanza yields in the last to its stark submission to its mortality as it "lay down among the dead / Weeds" (17). Only the vegetation denies its inevitable succumbing, for "the willow strode upon the wind / And would not bow its head" (17). Evasion, death, and denial form three philosophical responses to a reflective contemplation of the fact of mortality.

The recognition of the deadness of the bird focuses on the material change in its being. The nakedness of the pasture, the frozen condition of the bird itself, and the deadness of the weeds all stress the starkness of the transformation from life to death. At the same time, the observer's empirical, factual chronicling of it testifies obliquely to its finality and untransformability. Over against this unalterable nature of the mortal condition stands the denial to accede to it embodied in the willow's refusal to bow its head. It enshrines, in effect, life's courageous refusal to yield to its own mortality by invoking the uncertainty inherent in time as a continuum of possibility. What the observer senses here is the core of consciousness's awareness of the living response to mortality: yes, you are inevitable, but that need not mean just yet for me, whatever sort of entity I may be.

Only with the third of these philosophical responses—that of evasion of the actuality of death—does the issue of mortality as a contemplated prospect develop a reflective ambiguity toward the other two as the entirety of a metaphysical response. The image of the child is seen as both an illusory or temporary image on the window pane and as an actuality, "a child among the frozen bushes lost" (16). As the room warms and the frost image previously conjured up by the child at the window gradually disappears, the deferability of mortality is raised.

At the same time, the observer's perception that "the face among the forest fell to air" (17) raises the prospect that mortality has already actually engulfed the child and that it is for this event that the grief-suppressed, verbal remembrance of it is enacted in the poem itself. The very fact that the observer records only the disappearance of the image articulates evasively the limits of language in expressing the elegiac emotion of loss and insisting on the inevitability of simply enduring the fact of mortality:

> The glass began to weep instead of eyes,
> A slow gray feather floated down the sky.
> Delicate bone, finger and bush, and eyes
> Yearned to the kissing fire and fell away. (17)

The image (the fiction of the child's temporal reality) and the actuality fuse in the action of the dissolution of the frost on the window. It emulates the disappearance of the child when confronted by its own mortality. What Wright does here is to convey obliquely and restrainedly (and the more powerfully) the mortality inherent not only in the human condition but also in the duration of its elegiac mourning. In the face of time and mortality even the lamentation of the conventional elegiac response is restricted necessarily in length and character.

A rather different technique is practiced by Thom Gunn in his "Elegy on the Dust." There, he scrupulously details in narrative couplets the inexorability of dust's slow, remorseless documentation of the mortality of human life, nature, and the physical world. It silently is able to "cow the brain," to engage in "quiet encroachment on the wood" (144), and to reduce "material things . . . to one form and one size" (145).

For Gunn, mortality is not so much an event that terminates the individual as a process continuing endlessly and absorbing all entities:

> They have all come who sought distinction hard
> To this universal knacker's yard,
> Blood dried, flesh shrivelled, and bone decimated:
> Motion of life is thus repeated,
> A process ultimately without pain
> As they are broken down again. (145)

This process results in the de-individualization of existence and with that the cessation of complex organisms, of consciousness, and of self. The grains of dust, which are all that remain, escape thereby the normal forms of human behavior. Startlingly enough, they manage to achieve the very commonality of effort and goal that has perpetually evaded mankind:

> Too light to act, too small to harm, too fine
> To simper or betray or whine.
>
> Each colourless hard grain is now distinct,
> In no way to its neighbor linked,
> Yet from wind's unpremeditated labours
> It drifts in concord with its neighbors,
> Perfect community in its behavior. (145)

This simultaneous reduction and mastery of response provided by the extended contemplation of mortality evokes for Gunn less the philosophic acceptance of the Stoic than the ironic perspective of the Epicurean.[1] In his final lines, he provides a judgment of the ultimate effect of both the loss and gain resulting from mortality:

> It yields to what it sought, a saviour:
> Scattered and gathered, irregularly blown,
> Now sheltered by a ridge or stone,
> Now lifted on strong upper winds, and hurled
> In endless hurry round the world. (145–146)

The spiritual savior promising eternal life and the purposive transcendence of the mortal condition historically sought by mankind do not emerge. Instead, the dust is the recipient of only the random actions of a natural force committed to endless, purposeless motion and change. In getting what it started out desiring, namely, a release from its mortal condition, the dust is finally revealed to be the recipient of an almost Strudlbrugian fate. Instead of his perennial longing for eternal life being bestowed, mankind is consigned, ironically enough, to an endless existence devoid of individuality, consciousness, and purpose. Here the modern elegiac temper assumes a metaphysically ironic note that extends beyond even the classical injunction to be wary of what one desires lest one receive it.

Gunn's perspective focuses on the empirically observable details and what they imply existentially. On the other hand, Wallace Stevens—at least in "The Owl in the Sarcophagus"—teases out the philosophical consequences that the mind's operations and the limits of language hold for the concept of mortality.[2] In doing so, he implicitly questions Gunn's conclusions by a gentle but relentless skepticism. His questioning concentrates on the epistemological implications emerging from his ruminations on death, mortality, and the ways in which they have been construed and responded to historically. Indeed, the bulk of the poem deals in a detachedly reflective way with the images or "forms of thought" (432) that the mind has traditionally associated with the dead and the fact of mortality. Only with the last canto—VI—does Stevens explicitly judge their nature, truth, and ground of being as inadequate. They are found to be not fundamentally or absolutely true or accurate, but rather all that the human imagination can articulate. In so doing, he transforms his elliptical and condensed history of the metaphysics of the elegiac into a new, philosophically reflective elegy for the very notion of the elegy.

The figures traditionally associated with human mortality—sleep, peace, and a female figure later identified as a kind of cosmic mother but initially linked with farewell or separation or memory—are probed with a careful scrupulosity in canto I. It sketches both their nature and origin in a fashion that redefines them as products of the mind and the nature of language:

> These forms are visible to the eye that needs,
> Needs out of the whole necessity of sight.
> The third form speaks, because the ear repeats,
>
> Without a voice, inventions of farewell.
> These forms are not abortive figures, rocks,
> Impenetrable symbols, motionless. They move
>
> About the night. (432)

Their existence is not so much absolute as occasioned by the groping aspirations of the mind to explain by the use of images and concepts. They take the form they do because of the logical relationship of bodily organs to their existential role: they are visible precisely because the eye's function is to see. At the same time, their forms are the product of the mind that creates or summons them up in response to its felt need to do so. Memory in order to exercise its function of remembering must generate not so much reality as "*inventions* of farewell" (432; my italics). This fictive quality, however, is not so much to be contrasted with reality as to be differentiated from it:

> . . . They live without our light,
> In an element not the heaviness of time,
> In which reality is prodigy. (432)

The empirical world's existence is not simply a philosophical given but a marvelous product of the a-temporal ability of the mind to conceive of it apart from human consciousness:

> . . . Only the thought of those dark three
> is dark, thought of the forms of dark desire. (432)

Why and how human beings should be able to conceive of concepts such as sleep, peace, and remembrance in association with mortality, which itself is empirically observable, lies beyond the bounds of mankind to articulate. Instead, the way in which they are apprehended is via dimly sensed longings or desires. Within the limits of the actuality they possess, sleep, peace, and remembrance are envisage-able by the human consciousness. It is only how they can be, their very functional origin, that is obscure and, presumably, metaphysically impenetrable. The consequence of this philosophical analysis by a nonphilosopher who is a poet is a general reduction in the nature of mortality and what can be said about it. Its being linked to the mind as its originating explanatory entity results in its having to be construed not as a metaphysical absolute but as a construable concept. So seen, the attributes of peace, sleep, and memorability become provisional and limited in character.

Exactly how they do so and the implications of their newly conceived-of natures form the remainder of the poem except, as noted above, for the last canto. Canto II concentrates not on the poet but his friend, Henry Church. His death impels Stevens to assess his significance for the poet's own philosophical exploration of life and death.[3] By so doing, Stevens is able to maintain his characteristic stance of reflective observer and commentator. In continuing his philosophical detachment, he implicitly imitates the professional thinker's consideration of the thought of his predecessors. He assesses both its strengths and weaknesses in relation to his own emerging philosophical viewpoint.

Church's ability to move "living among the forms of thought / To see their lustre truly as it is" (432) is seen as a kind of philosophical advance, which is also illusory. The forms of thought exist apart from individual human consciousness and so occupy a position analogous to the Kantian *ding-an-sich*. Similarly, Church's own sense of his intellectual "passage" as occurring in a temporal mode that is "perennial" (432) or absolute results in perceptions founded on a shifting conceptual ground. These perceptions produce feelings of excitement, ecstasy, and visionary states that are sensory occurrences as such, though questionable as rational philosophical propositions.

Stevens's choice of words here, such as "twanged," "abysmal," and "dazzle" (433), indicate both his sympathy with and his gentle skepticism concerning Church's philosophical voyage and its ultimate destination. He feels powerfully the impulse for the thinking individual to arrive at absolute insights and conclusions about the nature of reality and, with it, of mortality. Yet simultaneously he senses their illusory character, stemming as they do from the persistent movements of the mind and its existence in a temporal order the opposite of one that "stood still" (432). Thought, conceived of by an inherently changing entity such as the mind that itself exists in a world endlessly subject to change, is problematic as a series of absolute propositions capable of being identified as perennially true.

And yet the mind's traditional association of death and mortality with peace, sleep, and remembrance is not absolutely false either. How they can have a relevance, a reality, for the questioning mind entails an exploration of the mind itself and the way it functions linguistically. Therefore, it follows for Stevens that his interpretive analysis of Church's probings of death and its associations requires him to adjust or adapt his language to the given conditions he faces. In cantos III, IV, and V he casts what he thinks Church perceived in terms that are not precise, clear, or absolute but rather imprecise, uncertain, and metaphoric rather than literal. As a poet, he uses the language of metaphor and imagery to capture the mind's exploration of the borders between the conscious and the unconscious, the light and the dark, from which concepts and ideas emanate. Both mind and metaphor operate by an endless suggestiveness.

Sleep's multiplicity of characteristics and variability of significance are captured by Stevens's invoking of terms such as "foldings," "vanishing-vanished," and the "water of an afternoon in the wind / After the wind has passed" (433). Each of these images captures an aspect of sleep as an association fit for mortality. They render the only articulation possible in an empirical world of objects subject to time and change. Historically and philosophically, they are continually presenting themselves and being apprehended by minds similarly subject.

It is not language itself that is inadequate, Stevens implies, so much as its, too, being subject to time, change, and mortality, which makes it unable to function as a conceptual absolute. Its resultant fluidity is what prevents a single statement or perception from sufficing to capture reality. By identifying sleep with "the whiteness that is the ultimate intellect" and "a diamond jubilance beyond the fire" (433), Stevens is able to convey not only the significance of its association with death and mortality but the reason for that association:

> Then he breathed deeply the deep atmosphere
> Of sleep, the accomplished, the fulfilling air. (433)

When mortality is seen as a kind of sleep, one recognizes that it is not only the end of life but the goal intended by life for itself. Mortality perceived philosophically is the culminatory conclusion, not the peremptory interruption, of life. And as such, its elegiac acknowledgment requires neither lamentation, consolation, nor requital.

The fulfillment found by the mind in the linking of sleep with mortality is a product of two things: their joint motionlessness or inactivity and their stasis-like state of accomplishment. Peace, however, is more ambiguous in its characterization, perhaps because it means so many different things to so many different people. Canto IV, therefore, opens sounding cautionary and teasing notes followed in the second stanza by acknowledgments of the positive traits associated with peace:

> There peace, the godolphin and fellow, estranged, estranged,
> Hewn in their middle as the beam of leaves,
> The prince of shither-shade and tinsel lights,
>
> Stood flourishing the world. The brilliant height
> And hollow of him by its brilliance calmed.
> Its brightness burned the way good solace seethe. (434)

Peace's estrangement, its forced creation, and its illusory, transitional effect are Stevens's way of insisting that we recognize two facts. The first is that in life talk is easier than accomplishment, and second that in death peace is a concept of doubtful relevance and meaning.[4]

Here Stevens is questioning the traditional elegiac view that death brings peace. At the same time, he almost immediately sketches the legitimacy and actuality of the human desires that make the image of peace a compulsively sought-after attribute for death. To make such an attribution is understandable, Stevens feels. That, however, doesn't make it true for the philosophical mind that, much like the insurance executive, requires verification of claims. Thus, he identifies the figure of peace as "an immaculate personage in nothingness / With the whole spirit sparkling in its cloth" (434).

And yet it is the august eminence and attractiveness of peace "adorned with cryptic stones and sliding shines" (434) that testifies to the mind's historically persistent fascination with the concept. Here Stevens suggests it functions almost teleologically for "generations of the imagination" in functioning as "an alphabet / By which to spell out holy doom and end" (434). It extends, he claims, from human beginnings collectively and individually, where it is "damasked in the originals of green" (434), to their end, which extends imaginatively even beyond death. The figure of peace, then, is composed by the mind's positive impulse for structure, coherence, continuance, and resolution:

> This is that figure stationed at our end,
> Always, in brilliance, fatal, final, formed
> Out of our lives to keep us in our death,
>
> To watch us in the summer of Cyclops
> Underground, a king as candle by our beds
> In a robe that is our glory as he guards. (434–435)

Existentially questionable as the figure may be, nevertheless, it is for Stevens clearly psychologically, because historically, certain. It may be a fiction of the mind, but it is one necessary to the mind's very operation, and so in some curious sense a participant in epistemological, if not metaphysical, reality.

The next canto—V—poses the most compelling, because the most personal, challenge to Stevens's philosophical integrity. It considers the action of loss and farewell under the image of the mother. She embodies the source of life itself, the survivor of life who mourns the mortality inherent in it, and the Muse who engenders the poet's own creativity. As such, she compels him to confront the philosophic question of how his creative spirit interacts with the facts of death and mortality. Can it remember in any truly meaningful way the past, what is lost through mortality? In short, is poetry itself in some sense mortal or can it indeed survive eternally?

His answer is the most elliptical and enigmatic of the three analyses of the traditional associations provided mortality. As a result, his ambiguity of response here is less polarized and so subtle as to move into an obscurity that is not so much rhetorical as philosophical. It is a determinedly honest effort to articulate shades of perception, feeling, and conviction so mysterious in their evanescence as to be at the very edge of the mind's capacities to grasp. Thus, the originating power of life in its acknowledgment of mortality's presence and actuality, its "losing in self / The sense of self" (435), manages to retain its essential individuality so that it "stood tall in self not symbol" (435). The difference is one of consciousness or awareness as distinct from the entity itself: "the sense of" self versus simply "self." The epistemological limiting condition of the former bespeaks the role of mortality and is set over against the metaphysical reality of the entity, which is the nature of life. Similarly, the characterization of the female figure as "rosed out of prestiges / Of rose" (435) captures exactly her unawareness of or indifference to her traditional associations with beauty, attractiveness, and value. It is as the entity or force or power inherent in life itself that she stands "quick / And potent, an influence felt instead of seen" (435).

A living force such as this, Stevens suggests, is more intuitive than rational knowledge. Consequently, it is characterizable only at the very limits of language, which hint at perceptions beyond human capabilities to apprehend directly:

> She held men closely with discovery,

> Almost as speed discovers, in the way
> Invisible change discovers what is changed,
> In the way what was has ceased to be what is. (435)

The inspiration to use language at its full reaches, the Muse if you will, enables the mind to sense qualities of change and existence—motion, time, and reality in interaction—that lie almost beyond the scope of sensory faculties.

The wisdom of the Muse, the perception of a direct reality "beyond artifice" (435), is sustained by a conviction whose power both initiates and maintains it. In being "impassioned by the knowledge she had, / There on the edge of oblivion" (435), she is both like Descartes in possessing that which is undoubtable, the self, and unlike him in her possession being intuitive rather than cogitative. Both, however, are arrived at by a process of philosophical deliberation and reflection. What she possesses, however, is not the "knowledge of" but the "knowledge that." She has not knowledge of language's (or poetry's) mortality or eternality but knowledge that as an existent phenomenon it exerts a felt influence on life and the living:

> O exhalation, O fling without a sleeve
> And motion outward, reddened and resolved
> From sight, in the silence that follows her last word— (435)

No poet, much less a philosophically minded one like Stevens, can offer predictions on temporal events (including poetry) since they necessarily entail mortality, the cessation of being. Language's nature, then, is simply to be indifferent to or removed from materiality, and therefore capable of the paradoxical and problematic facing of the unanswerable. For Stevens, language and poetry exist in the present; whether they can or will in the future is a question without an answer and so beyond the bounds or scope of philosophy.[5]

In the final canto—VI—Stevens presents his self-assessment of his extended probing of the nature of man's thought about death and mortality. His use of declarative syntax suggests initially a negative judgment of the truth of associating sleep, peace, and memory with mortality. Thus, he asserts apparently unequivocally, "This is the mythology of modern death / And these, in their mufflings, monsters of elegy" (435). Balancing this inclination of the judging mind, how-ever, are the subsequent lines that declare, "These are death's own supremest images, / The pure perfections of parental space" (436). Myth or narrative in-vention versus unmediated reality, monsters versus perfect figures, celebratory farewells versus organic initiators of life are all subjected to Stevens's persistent and recurring philosophical meditations (Cantos I—V). This, however, results not in the conventional manner of judging as a matter of acceptance and rejec-tion of a variety of apparently contradictory or divergent postulates.

He arrives rather at a more sophisticated manner and attitude. It teases out the subtlest ways in which the very language itself accepts the totality of the mind's ruminations, including all as elements of and in reality. The implicit con-trasts summoned up by "mythology," "modern," "mufflings," and "monsters," and with them the judgment of their inadequacy as true renderings of the na-ture of mortality, are but part of reality. They are almost immediately balanced by the poet's wonder and recognition that they are the products of individual lives responding to the recurrent fact of mortality and what it brings to the human imagination. First, there is the awesome confrontation with the profound differ-ence between death and life made apparent by mortality; and second, the in-evitable and inescapable regret for the loss of life:

> Of their own marvel made, of pity made,
>
> Compounded and compounded, life by life,
> These are death's own supremest images. (435–436)

In this way, Stevens confronts the justification for tradition, history, and the elegy itself. He does not root his justification in the external world and meta-physical propositions about it. Instead, he focuses on its epistemological qualities as they are accreted historically in response to the psychological needs of mankind. Even here he maintains the barest hint of ambiguity concerning the appropriate judgment to be made of these *ur*-like images of mortality and its hu-man implications.

Thus, the phrase "death's own supremest images" can be read in two differ-ent ways. One takes the phrase as referring to those images summoned up by death itself as a postmortem assessment of mortality. The other sees it as ren-dering the ultimate characterizations of death itself entertainable by the mind. The one grounds the images in a metaphysical condition of reality and the world. The other finds its warrant in the fact that all things thought are the product or consequence of a being capable of thought, in other words, of a mind. How these two apparent polarities are reconciled is made clear by the poem's final lines:

> The children of a desire that is the will,
> Even of death, the beings of the mind
> In the light-bound space of the mind, the floreate flare . . .
>
> It is a child that sings itself to sleep,
> The mind, among the creatures it makes,
> The people, those by which it lives and dies. (436)

The images of sleep, peace, and recollection linked with mortality are creations of the mind, reside in it, and suffer the same end as the mind, namely, mortality. As a result, to elegize in the traditional manner—to lament, to seek transcendency of mortality, and so to sustain the imagination—is to misconstrue the relationship between the mind, reality, and mortality. All are created by a limited or not fully developed entity ("a child") whose nature it is to sleep and ultimately to die.[6] Thus, in underscoring mortality as a limiting condition for the defining of the mind and the human being and his world, Stevens is attesting to its being part of the rock of reality. It is this that the owl conveys in the sarcophagus.[7] The embodiment of knowing through questioning is the very act of interrogating not only the final repository but also the essential condition of life as becoming.

Notes

Chapter 1. Friends and Relatives

1. For succinct summary statements of the views of contemporary anthropologists, psychologists, and historians, see Homans, 1–20; Stannard, viii–xv; Aries in Stannard, 134–158; Choron, *Modern Man and Mortality*, 7–9, 37, 178–183; Toynbee, 145–152; Marcuse in Feifel, 64–76; Freud, 289–317.

2. Ross (1869–1918) was the youngest son of a socially and politically prominent Canadian family. He became an art expert with a gift for making friends in the art and literary worlds of London society. At age seventeen, he seduced Oscar Wilde and ultimately became one of his most loyal friends and finally his literary executor. Sassoon often visited his London home, and Ross, together with Dr. W. H. R. Rivers, were the only two people allowed to visit Sassoon while he was recovering from the head wound that ended his military career. Ross's unexpected death occurred just before he was about to leave on a trip to Australia to view the National Gallery there. See Wilson, 202–205, passim; Fryer, 18–19, 21–22, 42, 176–177, 192–193, for a rather extended treatment of their relationship. Despite the large number of Sassoon's poems devoted to war and death, it is remarkable that this is the only one in his *Collected Poems* that carries the title "Elegy." Quinn, 176–177, notes that one other poem, unpublished during Sassoon's lifetime, dealing with the death of a fellow officer is labeled an elegy. For a reprinting of it, see Campbell, 209. Others, of course, carry related titles associated with the elegiac, such as "memorial service," "monody," and "eulogy."

3. On the varieties of consolation—from encouragement of the suppression of grief through compassionate moderation to direct expression of sorrow to religious faith in heaven and regeneration—found in the Renaissance elegy, see Pigman, 3–5, passim.

4. Fussell, 90, points out the extent to which Sassoon relies on such polarities and dichotomies in both his poetry and his prose. See also Lane, 107–108, for Sassoon's ironic contrasting of prewar civilized life and military mechanized savagery.

5. Ross died only two days after last seeing Sassoon. The poet's shock was shared by most of Ross's friends, including Wilde's son and Edmund Gosse. See Fryer, 258.

6. These traits are summed up in Edmund Gosse's letter to Ross's brother. See Fryer, 259.

7. Quinn, 245, speculates that this poem's being one of two omitted from the *Collected Poems* may arise from Sassoon's concern that he did not do justice to Ross in it. See Quinn, 244, for its being part of a series dealing with self-discovery in *The Heart's Journey* (1928).

8. See Moeyes, 55, 100, 101, 123–125, 215, 259–261; Wilson, 1–3, 63, 139, 151–152, 196, 200, 202–205, passim. Hoagwood, 13, briefly reviews the legal status of homosexuality: sodomy was punishable by death from 1533 to 1861; in 1885, all homosexual acts became punishable by law. Hynes,

187, speculates that W. H. R. Rivers may have helped Sassoon comprehend his sexual identity so that in 1917 he was able to reveal his homosexuality to Ottoline Morrell in confidence. Campbell, 32, 34, suggests that her candor and vigorous unconventionality helped make her the only woman friend to surmount Sassoon's inveterate misogyny.

9. See Fryer, 249.

10. No imputation of a sexual relationship between Sassoon and Ross is intended here, for there is no evidence of such. See Fryer, 243. It is Sassoon's awareness of the public and legal attacks on Ross's own character and reputation for his own indiscretions as well as Ross's vigorous and outspoken defense of Wilde that are at issue here. See Fryer, 249. Hynes, *A War Imagined*, 16–17, points out that Ross's 1914 legal suit against Lord Alfred Douglas for defamatory libel had again brought Wilde and homosexuality into the foreground of public discussion and criticism. Hynes, 225, also draws attention to a 1916 court-martial that involved Ross's nephew and a 1918 libel case, 226–229, 232, involving private performances of Wilde's *Salomé* and charges of homosexuality and lesbianism as illustrative of the era's attitudes and of Sassoon's sensitive awareness of them. See J. H. Johnston, 92–93, for Ross's encouragement of Sassoon's early satiric period, which again suggests Ross's willingness to support candor and outspokenness. Quinn, 178, remarks of the same period that Ross assisted Sassoon in finding a publisher for his initial collection of war poems.

11. On this aspect of the Renaissance elegy, see Kay, 92, 98, passim. The poem suggests Sassoon's covert and somewhat envious admiration for Ross's candor over his sexual nature, a candor he was never able to emulate wholeheartedly in his own life. See Campbell, 168–169.

12. On the traditional relation of elegy and panegyric, see Schenck, *Mourning*, 56, 92, and, in greater historical detail, Hardison, 24–42.

13. Fussell, 272–309, and more specifically Martin, 48–51, 80–97, 101–104. For a tartly caustic dismissal of Martin's reading of Hopkins, see Lawler, 49–91. My concern here is simply with the existence of the cultural phenomenon rather than with the extent of its applicability to Hopkins.

14. See Quinn, 214–219, 226–228, for Sassoon's continuing postwar struggles with this problem. These suggest both the severity of his ambivalent attitude and his need for its concealment, as does his marriage in 1933.

15. Fussell, 90; cf. J. H. Johnston, 81, 88 n. 9, the latter of which cites Robert Graves's comment recognizing Sassoon's dual nature. Lane, 96, cites an instance of his military exploits that earned Sassoon this sobriquet.

16. Mellown, 110; I use "vision" here in connection with the elegy as Potts, 38–40, does; Knight, 124, finds the poem to be more an example of a domestic lyric than of an elegy, while Mellown, 115, though cognizant of its calm reflective tone, sees it as more resembling a conventional elegy.

17. On some of the roles of paradox in the elegy, see Shaw, 2–4, 170, 218.

18. Potts, 38.

19. See Fryer, 249.

20. See Fryer, 249.

21. Mellown, 114.

22. One would have thought that the intensity and meaningfulness of Muir's friendship with John Holms, coupled with the latter's premature death prior to his having realized the enormous potential

his friends attributed to him, would have led Muir to a more personal tribute. See McCulloch, 35, and Huberman, 107; also Tschumi, 99.

23. As Fitzgibbon, 16, and Ferris, 86–87, point out, the poem's subject is Thomas's maternal aunt, Ann Jones. On Thomas's awareness of the role of self in the poem and its gestation, see Hardy, 7, for a citation to a letter by Thomas to Ted Hughes.

24. The differences between the two versions of the poem—this one and an earlier one begun the day after her death—testify not so much to a lack of authenticity in Thomas's emotions about her as to variability of focus dictated perhaps largely by poetic considerations. See Ferris, 86, and Fitzgibbon, 32; also Hardy, 8–9.

25. Emery, 51–52, invokes *Lycidas* as both comparison and contrast to Thomas's poem: similar in his reliance on satirical comments on religious practices only loosely connected to Ann's fate and in its occasional character, and different in its registering a deep personal loss.

26. See Hardy, 11–15, on Thomas's affinities with Welsh prosody and Celtic traditions and his detailed reliance on alliteration, assonance, half-rhymes and the like to shape subtly the shifting tones and attitudes of the poem.

27. Korg, 83, finds the poem to focus rather on the fusing of actual memory and public celebration and so to invoke the qualities of the traditional elegy. Cf. Hardy, 9, 117. His admission, however, that "life may end in modesty, resignation, and silence" (83) pulls against aligning the poem with elegiac conventions.

28. Korg, 83, points out Thomas's reliance on specific details of Ann's life in developing his tribute to her and how the poem is a reconciliation of realistic and cosmic imaginations.

29. On Thomas's diversified reliance on dialectic, see Moynihan, 50–54, 158–160.

30. Kidder, 148–154, sees Thomas's elegiac resolution to lie in its final acceptance of a Christian Johannine reliance on love. I find him more nearly approximating what Kidder, 149, calls a pagan approach. Actually, Thomas's attitude accords more fully with the Reformation protest against the conventions of the Church, which, to his mind, warp, confuse, and denigrate the individual's spiritual impulses and feelings.

31. Korg, 83, calls attention to Thomas's matching of his style in this verse sentence to his claiming the title of bard.

32. Kidder, 151, identifies them as either doves or, following Ackerman, 80, the four winged beasts of Revelation. I see nothing in the poem itself to warrant either attribution. Kidder himself admits the poem "contains no referential or allusive images" (148).

33. Cf. Potts, 440.

34. Miller, 211, sees this transformation as Thomas's effort to make life of death through the exercise of the imagination.

35. Kidder, 167, rightly polarizes formalized religion against love and sees the latter as the ending-point of the poem. Miller, 211, sees such resistance to death as futile. Both miss the elegiac function of sustaining survivors only until they in turn confront their own actual mortality. Thus, both critics are right to a point: Kidder in the poem's consolatory role and Miller in the ultimate inadequacy of its argument.

36. See Hart, 22, and in Robinson, 17; also Sherry, *The Uncommon Tongue*, 47. This is one of three

poems on this fictitious family. See Sacks, 307–309, on Hill's dual relation to the elegiac tradition in this poem.

37. Cf. Sherry, *The Uncommon Tongue*, 47–48.

38. On Hill's avoidance of punctuation elsewhere, see Ricks's essay in Robinson, 75–78.

39. On the difference between these original lines and the 1967 revision of the poem, see Sherry, *The Uncommon Tongue*, 48–49.

40. See, for instance, Frye in Patrides, 200–211, and Adams in Patrides, 120–125.

41. Lucas, 158, identifies this poem along with several others by Olson as providing an unrelenting view of the hopelessness of existence. As I suggest, this strikes me as an unduly harsh assessment of what is a deliberately chastening experience of imaginatively envisaging one's own death actually occurring and, in so doing, discovering the limits or the end-point of philosophical interrogation.

42. Other poems that fall into this general category include Geoffrey Hill's "Cycle," Donald Hall's "Elegy for Wesley Wells," Seamus Heaney's "A Postcard from North Antrim" and "Casualty," C. Day-Lewis's "Elegiac Sonnet," and Thom Gunn's "Lament" and "The Reassurance."

43. The subject of the poem was John Cooper Fitch, a wealthy young American, whom Barker first met in 1939 on board a ship bound for New York when headed for a teaching position in Japan. Later, Fitch and Barker became lovers while Barker was still married to Jessica Woodward and heavily involved with Elizabeth Smart. With the beginning of World War II, Fitch joined the Air Force and became one of the first Americans to shoot down a German jet fighter. After four years of combat duty, and just two months before the end of the war, he was himself shot down and became a POW. It was Fitch's being reported missing in action that led Barker to write this poem. See Fraser, 123–124, 171, 176–177, 228. Fitch subsequently had an extraordinary life—to which Fraser does not allude—during which he was a blue-water sailor, a test pilot, a professional race car driver, a prolific inventor, a highway safety expert, an auto-maker, and an entrepreneur. The contrast between Barker's poetic rendering of him as one of the heroic victims of the Battle for Britain and Fitch's actual long and highly successful life is both striking and ironic.

44. The poem's opening couplet captures the suddenness and swiftness not only by the uninterrupted speed of its lines but by the roughness of its images, such as "fury" and "broke through my wall." The anguish is generated by terms such as "fury," "Friday," and "death certificate," which create a context compounded of classical, Christian, and contemporary associations. In terms of stanza length, the couplet is part of stanza one; its separation from the stanza proper is Barker's way of simultaneously presenting the shock that occasions the poem and of maintaining the narrative and formal coherence necessary to face that shock.

45. The differences between Sassoon's elegy to Robert Ross and Barker's remembrance of John Cooper Fitch, his poetically anonymous beloved, provide an index of the historical changes between the two wars in how homoerotic friendships can be celebrated. Sassoon's strangulated, almost inarticulate murmurs contrast with Barker's flamboyant and elaborate rhetoric—"his body on my tongue," "joystick hand," and "sensual satisfaction"—which appears deliberately to flaunt the nature of the relationship. In addition, temperamental differences between the two poets—the withdrawn isolate country gentleman versus the outspoken bohemian—should also be figured into the equation as well as the differing sexual identities—the essentially homosexual who marries to produce a child

versus the often-married progenitor of numerous children who also engaged in homosexual relationships. On this last, however, see Fraser, 83, who notes both Barker's early declaration that he preferred men as sexual partners and its function as a way of discouraging an older American woman with whom he'd made love.

46. Myers, 139, may somewhat exaggerate by calling it one of the greatest elegies of the century, though certainly the tenderness of its feelings give it an extraordinarily powerful appeal.

47. To these there probably should be added the rather complex rhyme pattern of abcdeedcba. Dougherty, 12, suggests John Crowe Ransom was an influence on the rhyme scheme, though on nothing else, in the poem.

48. Myers, 139, argues the poem employs traditional elegiac themes, such as the contrast of age and youth and the injustice of death. While this may be true in a rather limited sense, I don't feel it sufficient to alter the thrust of my remarks.

49. Dougherty points out that the first two friends "are the kind for whom elegies have always been made" (29). Thus, Wright's eschewing of explicit lamentation would appear to be a conscious choice designed to reconfigure the elegy.

50. See Elkins, 18.

51. Structurally, Wright's poem bears comparison with R. P. Blackmur's "An Elegy for Five," though their contexts are quite different. Blackmur, while ill, addresses a serial visit from five friends in ten stanzas that first describe the visitor's demeanor and then offer the poet's essentially dispassionate but precise judgment of the visitor's anticipated response to death. Both poems dislocate conventional elegiac sentiments by infusions of the specific detail and insight.

52. See Clark, 181.

53. Other works in this general group might include Mark Strand's "Elegy for my Father," Stephen Spender's "The Ambitious Son," C. Day-Lewis's fifth section of "Overtures to Death," Donald Hall's volume *Without* for his dead wife, and Sandra Gilbert's *Ghost Volcano*. Gelpi, 208–214, points out the importance of elegy and the theme of death to Day-Lewis.

54. Parents, siblings, in-laws, and more or less close relatives obviously constitute a large group to be elegiacally remembered. Some poems commemorating individuals from it include, among others, Seamus Heaney's "The Strand at Lough Beg," Stephen Spender's "Elegy for Margaret," Wendell Berry's "Elegy" and "Three Elegiac Poems," Sherod Santos's "Elegy for My Sister," and Amy Clampett's "Procession at Candlemas."

55. MacLeish's use of the sand image contrasts with Thom Gunn's similar image in his "Elegy on the Dust." The former follows the modernist impulse to stress the regenerative nature of the earth, whereas the latter hews to the bleaker postmodernist conviction that denies or seriously questions such a capacity.

56. Cf. Kidder, 187–188, on Thomas's recognition here that death is no longer a metaphor or distant event but an unmediated reality.

57. A more detailed consideration of this subtype of elegy would require a sustained comparative study of these poems of MacLeish and Thomas as well as of Stevens's "To an Old Philosopher in Rome."

58. Holbrook, 196–197, treats the poem as an effort to transcend the traditional elegiac mood, but does not address its perforce being an anticipation of the elegy.

59. The traits Thomas ascribes to his father reflect his respect for him and do not encompass all of his father's qualities. See Fitzgibbon, 13–15, 337; Read, 22. Nevertheless, the public and poetic contrasts between the two warrant the one I draw here.

60. See Moynihan, 186.

61. See Moynihan, 188.

62. Another poem on a similar subject is X. J. Kennedy's "On a Child Who Lived One Minute." See Prunty's, 84–87, sensitive analysis of it.

Chapter 2. Historical Presences

1. Given Pound's varied interest in the interactions of history and literature, it is worth noting that his use of de Born may indicate his awareness of the sixteenth-century outpouring of lamentation, societal as well as poetic, for another, later Prince Henry. By creating his version of de Born's poem, he may be recalling a rather brief but important English poetic tradition from the vantage point of another culture. In so doing, he is anticipating one of the central strategies of the *Cantos*. Thus, de Born may serve as an oblique and tangential reminder of a vital English elegiac tradition and a signal historical occasion, namely, Henry's death on November 6, 1612, as well as a reiteration of the Provençal troubadour tradition. For Pound, the occasion would have been important because, as Kay, 124, has pointed out, "never before had so many elegies been written on a single occasion." How many of these Pound was aware of is quite uncertain, but it is worth keeping in mind Kay's point that "the only major writers who did not join in were Jonson, Daniel, Drayton, and Shakespeare" (124). Certainly one would not be surprised to find Pound familiar with Donne's "Elegie on Prince Henry." An earlier critical treatment of the elegiac tradition surrounding Prince Henry is Wallerstein, 59–95. Factors mentioned by Kay, 125–131, emerging from this elegiac outpouring likely to have intrigued Pound include: the lack of an agreed-upon poetic form to satisfy the subject's demands and the consequent improvisational character of the form; the intrusion of political and religious considerations; the prince's well-known sternness and anti-Catholic sentiments; the prince's interest in learning of all sorts and his extensive patronage of literature and the arts; his role in heightening the nostalgia for Elizabeth's court and its values; and his contemporary reputation as a compendium of excellence.

2. See Witemeyer, 72, who regards it as simply a translation. Monk in Grover, 67, sees it as a translation that refuses to limit itself to being a translation.

3. Witemeyer, 81, suggests the dramatic monologue form assists in the development of verisimilitude.

4. See Witemeyer, 83; Monk, 67, 68, 73–74; Schneidau, 110–114; Tiffany, 67, 129.

5. Monk in Grover suggests that the irretrievable loss of historical context makes the "history itself ambiguous" (68) so that de Born's original intent in writing the poem cannot be determined. Pound's own reasons for bringing it into English culture are perhaps enigmatic but at least arguable.

6. What sounds to the modern ear like overly fulsome praise and grief for the figure's death has to be offset against the encomiastic element in the late medieval and early Renaissance elegy. See Hardison, 114–115, 117, 122. For Pound, such an element was an index to the earlier period's awareness of the centrality of such cultural figures and forces. By invoking it in his own text, he endeavors

to provide a comparative historical perspective from which to assess both his own age and that of de Born.

7. Here de Born's Prince Henry Plantagenet historically anticipates one of the major features of the sixteenth-century English Prince of Wales. See Kay, 134–135.

8. Cf. Monk in Grover, 68, on the formality and courtliness inherent in the poem.

9. Cf. Schneidau in Bell, 114.

10. Monk in Grover, 68, argues that it is de Born's poetic and personal imperfections that attract Pound as mirroring de Born's age and capturing the modern world's limited knowledge of it. This may well be so, but my point is that even so when compelled to compare and judge the two ages, Pound almost inevitably is led to prefer the older one if for no other reason than that it is less immediate and less well known to him. In short, modern life in London at that time was his problem in a way that de Born's world was not.

11. In point of fact, it would appear from the *Collected Poems* (1966) that it first appeared in his *Moon's Farm and Poems Mostly Elegiac* (1955). As such, its poetic form would obviously be a deliberate choice to depart from modernist lines.

12. For the centrality of Kropotkin to Read's form of anarchism, see Tschumi, 165–166.

13. Cf. Dupree, 75.

14. Nelson, 215, points out that Tate and Robert Penn Warren are part of a larger American historiographic shift from a pastoral elegiac approach to what he calls, following Bruffee, a Romantic elegiac one. This entails an elaborate interplay of irony, inversion, and interrogation of the southern past aimed at celebrating it through calling attention to its absence from the present.

15. Shaw, 208, links Tate with both Whitman and Lowell in their Civil War elegies. He finds they all employ an antiphonal style, to which I draw attention here, in an endeavor to unite the contestants.

16. Cf. Nelson, 9, on the Romantic elegy's inversion of the earlier pastoral elegy's celebration of the dead hero.

17. Cf. Tate's observation in his biography of Davis, cited by Dupree, 114, about the South's being "permanently old-fashioned, backward-looking" and its intellectual alignment being with Europe rather than America.

18. See Nelson, 213, on Tate's contrasting historical assessments of Stonewall Jackson's and Davis's heroic natures as entailing both alienation and attachment.

19. Nelson, 209, 216, 232, suggests Tate himself suffered a defeat of a similar order to that of Davis when he moved from political activism to Catholic contemplation in his 1950 conversion, which was concomitant with his ceasing to write poetry.

20. On the limitations of the historical imagination and its entailing failure to generate a viable model for the present, see Dupree, 108–130. The elegiac sense of being haunted by a past loss is thus endemic to Tate's perspective.

21. Brown, 184–185, rightly qualifies this philosophical dimension when he suggests the poem "must be read not as doctrine but as aged experience." The experience, however, is that of Stevens fully as much as of Santayana, as Ramazani, 131, points out.

22. Cf. Doggett, 36–37.

23. Brown, 185–186.

24. Bloom in Mack, 361, accurately calls the poem a "pre-elegy," a term that links it implicitly with Dylan Thomas's piece on his father's impending death. Ramazani, 131, characterizes it as "a self-elegy cast as a premortem elegy."

25. Bloom in Mack, 361.

26. Doggett, 124, suggests "the celestial possible" is for Stevens "only metaphorical." This disregards the poet's willingness to entertain, though on radically different grounds, the existence of both worlds.

27. Cf. Pack, *Wallace Stevens*, 113–114.

28. Mendelson, *Later Auden*, 85, 88, underscores the interrelation of Auden's loss of long-held personal beliefs and the impact of Freud's death on his culture. See also Ramazani, 192–197, who describes the poem as a psychoanalytic elegy in which Freud is both humanized and deified.

29. Hecht, 132, suggests Auden is querying and explaining why one person's death is so important when the world is being enveloped in suffering and death. Implicitly he is trying to confront consciously the problem faced earlier by the World War I poets.

30. Mendelson, *Early Auden*, 366, sees this as a departure from the elegy's "conventional mourning for a lost perfection" in favor of a celebration of the achievements of an imperfect great man. Teaching the living rather than encomiastically praising the dead he finds to be the core of Auden's elegy. See also Ramazani, 178, on Auden's inclination both to resist and then to submit to his elegiac human subjects.

31. See Popper, 1:158–159, and all of chapter 9.

32. Mendelson, *Later Auden*, 86–87.

33. How this overall view is worked out on a personal level is explored by Auden in his "In Memory of Ernst Toller," a companion piece to the Freud elegy. Hecht, 136, shrewdly links the three allegorical figures—Toller, other refugees, and Freud himself—as exiles.

34. Perloff, *Frank O'Hara*, 180, contrasts this poem with some of O'Hara's earlier elegies, pointing out that here he eschews all the traditional elements of the elegy.

35. She was born in 1889 and died in France in 1938. Her most famous film was *The Perils of Pauline*. Ironically enough, her life as an itinerant show business singer and actress was filled with almost as many adventures as her films—poverty and hard times, difficult and often dangerous circumstances in Cuba and South America, stratospheric success, and unhappy marriages. Thus, both life and career were invested with elegiac overtones.

36. Perloff, *Frank O'Hara*, 181–182, ingeniously argues that the details are not so much random as ostensible disconnections which prove ultimately to be connections.

37. E. E. Smith, *Louis MacNeice*, 93, points out that it is one of almost a dozen surrounding poems dealing with death or defeat. Neither he nor Moore, 93, attend to its elegiac role.

38. She was born in Australia in 1896 and died in Scotland in 1940. A runaway at sixteen, her natural talent provided her with some local success, from which she moved on to England and a career spanning both world wars. She was known as the queen of the music hall sing-along chorus. As such, most of her songs had catchy tunes and easy to sing choruses. Her final performance was in 1940 before troops in Aberdeen, Scotland, where she collapsed on stage and died.

39. On Auden's poem, see Ramazani, 197–201. Somewhat similar in focus to Auden and Crane are Robert Pinsky's *City Elegies* and Robert Hayden's "Elegies for Paradise Valley" and "Bone-Flower Elegy."

40. Other poems dealing with the death of a modern poet, other than Dylan Thomas, include Seamus Heaney's tribute to Robert Lowell titled simply "Elegy," C. Day-Lewis's to T. S. Eliot "At East Coker," George Barker's "The Death of Yeats" and "At the Grave of Vernon Watkins" as well as three of his five "Memorials for Dead Friends," David Gascoyne's "Elegiac Improvisation on the Death of Paul Eluard," Frank O'Hara's "Little Elegy for Antonio Machado," and perhaps Howard Nemerov's "Elegy for a Nature Poet" and Thom Gunn's premonitory "To Isherwood Dying."

41. Fodaski, 130, notes that the poem's later claim of Roberts's immortality coming through his inspiring Barker is part of the elegiac tradition, but she sees this opening praise as merely adulatory and forgivable bombast when it too clearly calls up one of the elegy's principal conventions. Barker's praise of Roberts also has a personal dimension of some substance. When only eighteen, see Fodaski, 15–16, he was introduced by John Middleton Murry to Roberts, who in turn directed him to David Archer's bookshop, which led to his first publications. Fraser, 38–39, points out both Roberts's iconic status with the young in the 1930s and Barker's awed response to his first meeting with him.

42. Clearly, there is a historical explanation for this that sharply qualifies the pertinence of the contrast. Sidney's death in 1586 preceded the publication of his literary works in the 1590s so that it was only later that his literary attainments were merged with his role as a national hero, a Christian soldier, and a patron. See Kay, 47. Nevertheless, the historical reduction in elegiac encomia for poets as subject has clearly increased from the Renaissance through the Romantic Age to the twentieth century.

43. For a treatment of it focusing on its adaptations of some of the conventions of the pastoral elegy, see Cowan, 318–321.

44. Cf. B. Adams, 35, on Laura Riding's "Elegy in a Spider's Web" dual response to Stein's handling and views of language.

45. On other uses of the epithet "little" in connection with the elegy, see Millay, 118, O'Hara, 226, 228, 230, 248, and Justice, 177; also Zeiger, 71, 73 n. 15, and Perloff, *Frank O'Hara,* 180 n. 18.

46. For a more sustained treatment of this last point, see my "Animal Elegies, Anti-Elegies, and Some Recent Transformations of a Genre," *Genre,* forthcoming.

47. The significance and contemporary impact of Thomas's death can be gauged from Firmage's comment, xv, that he based his selection of memorial poems for Thomas from some 150 written in the decade between 1953 and 1963. See also Shapiro in Cox, 169, concerning the extent of the adulatory postmortem for Thomas. Additional instances of such poems include C. Day-Lewis's "In Memory of Dylan Thomas," Louis MacNeice's cantos VII and XI in his *Autumn Sequel,* and Kenneth Rexroth's "Thou Shalt Not Kill." For a similar comparative examination of diverse elegies on the death of D. H. Lawrence, see J. Cowan in Salgado and Das, 311–326.

48. Quotations from Sitwell's "Elegy for Dylan Thomas" are taken from the 1957 Macmillan edition of her *Collected Poems.* All other quotations of Sitwell's poems are from *The Collected Poems of Edith Sitwell* (Vanguard, 1968).

49. Tremlett, 59–64, 146–148, takes issue with the public perception of Thomas as a lover and throws significant doubt on his sexual prowess.

50. Valerius Corvus was a Roman military figure who served variously as consul, general, and dictator during the early years of the republican period. He was associated with a legend in which a raven sat on his helmet while he was battling a very large enemy. The raven was reputed to have flown in his opponent's face, thereby distracting him during their struggle. The Irish epic referred to is the Cattle Raid of Cooley in which Queen Maeve of Connaught battled Cuchulainn, who led the defensive forces of Ulster. During the conflict, the great hero was slain fighting against overwhelming odds.

51. Fraser's delineation, 314, of the often strained at best relationship between Barker and Thomas points up their shared view of what he calls "the embattled self." His remarks serve also to suggest the generic demands of rhetoric on the poet writing an elegy.

52. Fodaski, 144–145, notes the element of joy in Barker's assessment of Thomas but not his fascination with language.

Chapter 3. Anonymous and Apocryphal Individuals

1. Clark, of course, was the scion of an extremely wealthy and prominent family in New York. He was, among other things, the namesake of the philanthropist responsible for the gift of Mendelssohn Hall to the Glee Club of that name in the very late nineteenth century. The Club is the oldest singing organization in the United States. Wallis (1855–1942), on the other hand, was a primitive painter. He was born in Devon but moved soon to St. Ives in Cornwall, where he lived and died after working as a fisherman for most of his life. He took up painting as an old man after the death of his wife in 1925. His work was discovered by Ben Nicholson, the painter, in the late 1920s, but it was really after his death during the war that he was recognized by connoisseurs. For Watkins, it was Wallis's Cornwall associations that impelled him to this elegy.

2. Lowell's tone and attitude toward the person he is recalling here are quite different from those he took toward the relatives whom he elegizes. For the latter, see Perloff, "Death by Water: The Winslow Elegies of Robert Lowell," 116–140.

3. St. Ives was both Wallis's home and chief artistic subject for much of his life.

4. See Quinn, 186–188, for the poem's relation to Sassoon's public protest against the war. J. H. Johnston, 106–107, notes its elegiac quality and contrasts it to "other consolatory and inspirational elegies" (107) by Brooke, Binyon, and Kipling.

5. Cf. Lane, 167.

6. See Silkin, 162.

7. See Silkin, 163.

8. For related though differing treatments of it, see Ramazani, 98–100; Bloom, 49–50; Longenbach, 70–71; Riddel, 78–79.

9. As such, it contrasts with the series "Lettres d'un Soldat." The latter, as Gilbert, 180–181, points out, originally employed epigraphs from Emmanuel Lermercier's letters from the front before his death in 1915. This fact she uses to stress the historical origin of the series and to link it, perhaps overly closely, with the immediacy of physical suffering found in Sassoon and Owen. Undeniably, Stevens shares with them a deep skepticism considering the traditional elegy, but in both the series and the poem I am discussing here I find his propensity to philosophical generalization and dispassionateness to be primary factors.

10. Pound's "Portrait d'Une Femme" has essentially the same social context, but its speaker is far less ambiguous, more negatively judgmental, and ultimately dismissive of the society represented.

11. MacNeice's attitude here counterpoints the fact that the poem deals with the death of his own stepmother. See McKinnon, 156, and Marsack, 118, neither of whom appear struck by the poet's preference for the theme of death rather than lamentation or personal distress.

12. Cf. E. E. Smith, *Louis MacNeice*, 172, on MacNeice's awareness of the indifference of time to personal values and how this permeates even a poem like this, which he calls a personal vignette.

13. Brown, 67, has a brief but acute assessment of MacNeice's awareness of the inevitability of time and death in this poem.

14. On Hopkins's poem as an elegy seen from and as a Catholic perspective, see Sendry, 494–499.

15. Other extended treatments of the spousal elegy include Donald Hall's volume *Without* and Sandra Gilbert's "Wrongful Death" and perhaps Kenneth Rexroth's seven poems "For Marthe, My Wife," which Hamalian, 265, describes as elegiac though also hopeful and optimistic. In Rexroth's case, it should be noted that his spouse was absent rather than deceased.

16. Other poems dealing with the death of an infant would include X. J. Kennedy's "On a Child Who Lived One Minute," Seamus Heaney's "Elegy for a Still-Born Child," and Jon Silkin's "Death of a Son." A related instance that considers an older but still young subject is David Ignatow's "Elegy for Youth."

17. On Heaney's development as an elegist, see Vendler, *Seamus Heaney*, 59–65; D. Johnston, 150–154. Ramazani, 334–360, provides what is to date the most concentrated and sustained discussion of Heaney as elegist.

18. D. Johnston, 140–141, 149–150, suggests the struggle to merge daily occurrences with a more universal mythologizing, the threat of depersonalization, and the pursuit of a vertical or psychological quest are factors in the early Heaney's poetry. Though D. Johnston does not deal with the present poem, it strikes me as embodying all of these elements.

19. See D. Johnston, 151, on Heaney's seeing the elegy as a mourning of mortality rather than a salute to the dead.

20. Cf. Bradford, 44, on the role of the title.

21. Knight in T. D. Young, 44, points out that love and death are among the few things Ransom deals with metaphorically. In so doing, Ransom effectively distances the notion of human mortality from its immediate impact of shock; see also Buffington in T. D. Young, 57. Cf. Williams in T. D. Young, 7, who feels Ransom treats death directly rather than obliquely. The latter certainly is correct when he observes that Ransom "is concerned not so much with mortality itself as he is concerned with the proper attitude toward mortality" (7), an attitude he defines as Christian stoicism.

22. See Williams in T. D. Young, 13, who correctly takes issue with Winters's dismissive attitude toward the child. Ransom is assuredly playful here, but as I endeavor to suggest, this does not preclude his also generating a note of solemnity.

23. See Rubin in T. D. Young, 156–168, for a salutary reminder of the terror and savagery underlying the urbanity, playfulness, and whimsical irony in Ransom's poetry.

24. Cf. Williams in T. D. Young, 27–28, on Ransom's subtlety in expressing "the sense of loss" (28) and the puzzlement it arouses in the witnesses to the child's death. Both the loss and the puzzlement Williams in T. D. Young, 31, finds profoundly conditioned by the poet's detached, classical irony about

the nature of life and the world. For an extended characterization of Ransom's irony, see Wasserman in T. D. Young, 143–155. Cf. Koch in T. D. Young, 118–119, however, for a cautionary view of the role of irony in Ransom's work.

25. On the "vexed" phrase and its implications for the conventional elegy, see Warren in T. D. Young, 35; also Koch in T. D. Young, 122–123.

26. I differ from Bradford, 44–45, who reads the poem, at least structurally, as essentially a "traditional elegy" by which he means one that proceeds from "occasion of grief to expression of grief and from thence to reconciliation to or transcendence of grief." Ransom's delicate subtleties of language and perception, it seems to me, move the poem toward a dislocation or interrogation of the traditional elegiac attitude.

27. See Apollodorus, 1:15. I opt for the classical source because of Pound's familiarity with both the classics and Frazer's work. To my mind, the tone and atmosphere of the poem suggest an ancient context and association rather than the modern, more personal one adduced by Ruthven, 155, and subscribed to by Kenner, *The Pound Era*, 63.

28. These poems are Pound's versions drawn from scattered lines and passages found in Propertius's *Elegies*. See Kenner, *The Poetry of Ezra Pound*, 148–149, and Ruthven, 107–108, for details. My remarks on them bypass the extended controversy over the exact relationship between the two texts— whether translation, imitation, or reflection—and treat Pound's as originals subject to detailed borrowing. Still the best in terms of thoroughness and critical sanity on this volatile issue is J. P. Sullivan's *Ezra Pound and Sextus Propertius: A Study in Creative Translation* (1964), but see also Grieve's cogent assessment of the views of some subsequent critics, 197–201.

29. Davidson, 83–84, 89, 95, stresses both Propertius and Pound as powerfully affected by their perception of being caught between a society largely indifferent to them and a wasteful, absurd war brought about by militaristic forces blind to anything but their own interests.

30. My comments on these two sections of the *Homage* obviously focus on the sections themselves rather than the whole poem. As such, they should be fleshed out by comparison with the fuller treatment provided by Davidson, 83–115. It should also be noted that Rosenthal and Gall, 195, single out "VI" (along with "VII") as presenting the dominant motifs—the elegiac and the erotic—of the entire sequence.

31. Davidson, 86, finds this passage to be Pound's summary of his interpretation of Propertius's entire outlook.

32. Cf. Davidson, 106, who suggests that Pound intensifies the intolerableness of mortality by seeing it hastened by the meaningless conflict of war.

33. Their actual history together was quite different. Jugurtha, after years of militarily humiliating the Romans, was finally captured by them through his brother-in-law's treacherous betrayal. He was led through the streets of Rome in a mock-coronation before being dispatched to prison, where he died in 105 from cold and starvation after six day's confinement.

34. The ironies inherent in the idea of custom are caught succinctly in Cynthia's remembering him as but "a lost friend" compared to the frenzied mourning of the ancient goddess.

35. Cf. Davidson, 104.

36. "VIII" viewed alone, as I am doing here, does not identify the woman. Only in the context of *Homage* as a whole does she emerge as Cynthia.

37. Davidson's observation, 107, that "VIII" follows Propertius in dealing with Cynthia's illness both lightens and intensifies Pound's tone here in ways not captured by the semi-mock solemnity of his words. I am aware that my remarks here perhaps fail to capture sufficiently this element of the poem, but my focus is not on the ironies generated by Pound's complex relation to either his own historical context of 1917 or Propertius.

38. Ruthven, 113, likely due to typographical error, identifies Zeus's wife as "Hero" rather than "Hera" in his note to ll. 19–20.

Chapter 4. The Love Elegy's Transformations

1. There was, of course, no possibility of actual divorce being entertained by Millay as a result of her affair with George Dillon, which underlay this sequence. See Epstein, 199–200, 210. What I am suggesting is that a fictive resolution to a romantic dilemma was culturally possible for Updike but significantly less so for Millay.

2. See Atkins, 203–204, 206–232; Tate in Thesing, 64; Fried in Thesing, 229–244; Wiltenburg in Thesing, 287–292.

3. See her *Collected Poems,* 69, 74, 91, 98, 103, 107, 118, 199, 240, 252, 284, 286, 293, 295, 382, 595, 599, 619, 622, 638, 701, 724.

4. For a quite different approach to Millay's elegies that stresses the Orpheus-Eurydice myth as a key or clue to her handling of the elegy, see Zeiger, 68–73.

5. This poem is about one of her younger Vassar classmates, described by Epstein as "an attractive singer" (96), who died of influenza in 1918.

6. Whether Claudius is an actual historical person or merely an imaginary creature given a common enough Latin name is a matter of no concern here. Millay is not invoking the specificity of history but that of the ordinary or customary.

7. For more detailed treatments of this sequence, see Klemans in Thesing, 204–211; Peppe in Freedman, 52–63; Atkins, 199–233.

8. "Rustic" obviously also carries associations with the pastoral tradition dating from Theocritus, but these associations carry the critical tone of a sophisticated perspective such as Sitwell's.

9. These traits are all part of her distinctive brand of modernism, which I have found it convenient to label "rococo modernism." See chapter 5.

10. Rayner and Crook, eds., *The Complete Newgate Calendar,* 2:206–208, has a far less romantic and sentimental account of Deborah Churchill's life and fate. Her first marriage ended, after several children, in her husband's alcoholic death. Then, in London she married a soldier in a sham or con wedding from which she soon escaped. Finally, only with her third liaison, this time to a young rake, did she find a fit companion. He treated her badly, but she loved him desperately. One night, he and a companion quarreled while returning from the theater with Mrs. Churchill; swords were drawn; and she distracted her lover's opponent, who received a mortal wound. Her lover escaped to Holland, but she was apprehended, charged, and convicted of the crime as an accomplice. She then claimed to be pregnant to avoid execution, necessitating a delay of six months. When her claim was proven false, her death sentence was carried out at Tyburn on December 17, 1708. To the end, however, she denied her guilt of murder (http://tarlton.law.utexas.edu/lpop/etext/newgate2/church.htm, accessed c. January 2005).

11. Glendinning, 44, points out that the failure of love was one of Sitwell's personal preoccupations from early girlhood and thus frequently appeared as a major theme in her poetry.

12. Glendinning, 97, cites this poem as inaugurating Sitwell's sense of life as disillusion, which received its ultimate expression with *Gold Coast Customs.*

13. As with her use of Deborah Churchill, Sitwell here, too, eliminates from her epigraph items in Aubrey that could blunt her predilection to give the story a romantic focus on personal loss. Such items include the brevity of the man's widowerhood, his having been in bed with his grandchild when the apparition appears, his being described as "hypochondrial," and his subsequent remarrying twice. See Aubrey, 61 (http://www.knowledgerush.com/paginated_txt/etext03/7misc10/7misc10_txtoc .html, accessed c. January 2005).

14. The only departure from the couplet form occurs at the beginning, which opens with a four-line stanza (abab) that initiates the elegiac mode.

Chapter 5. The Cultural Elegy and the Past

1. See Vickery, "Frazer and the Elegiac: The Modernist Connection," in Manganaro, 51–68.

2. Some of the more recent detailed considerations of one or more aspects of modernism are to be found in Kenner, *The Pound Era,* Perl, *The Tradition of the Return,* Meisel, Levenson, Quinones, Schwartz, Kubal, Sherry, *Ezra Pound, Wyndham Lewis, and Radical Modernism,* and Wilde.

3. Cowan, 43–57, is overly inclined to regard the latter group as constituting the entirety of modernism, though her stress on its concern with the past is apt enough.

4. Cf. Glendinning, 87.

5. This concern with sound's centrality to poetry is, of course, also found in poets such as Dylan Thomas, George Barker, and the New Apocalypse group in general, so they, too, may perhaps be cited as exemplars of this form of modernism. Cf. Glendinning, 249.

6. On Eliot's development of the themes of religious consciousness and formal religion proper, see Vickery, 3–10, 11, 59–67, for a more extended treatment.

7. Cf. Cowan, 42.

8. These two modes also dominate Eliot's early poetry. See Vickery, 59.

9. Cf. Perl, *The Tradition of the Return,* 34, on this term in relation to the concept of historical return and the problem of origins. Interestingly enough, Fussell, 235, suggests that World War I saw the ideas of "home" and "the summer of 1914" coming to be equated with a modern Golden Age.

10. See Ruthven, 206, for Pound's conflation of two separate poems by Li Po into his "The River Song." The effect is similar to his rendering of the original in *Homage to Sextus Propertius.* As with it, I concentrate on Pound's text in my comments.

Chapter 6. The Cultural Elegy on the Present and Future

1. Glendinning, 122, suggests Sitwell's reliance on such vocabularies was a deliberate technique for creating atmosphere and the sense of historical periods.

2. See Maddison, 1–3, 4, 288, 296–304, for traits of the ode which Tate both imitates and uses ironically to distance his poem from the ode's historical tradition. Her comments on Jonson and Cowley are particularly apt in relation both to Tate's intent and execution.

3. See, however, Shaw, 161–162, who brackets the two poems as both being instances of the use of disjunction, or what he calls "fracture," to recover a lost wholeness.

4. Cf. Hooker in Robinson, 22–23; also Sacks, 309.

5. Cf. Sherry, *The Uncommon Tongue,* 18.

6. On Hill's linguistic conflicts as a distinct style in this poem, see Sherry, *The Uncommon Tongue,* 63; cf. Haughton in Robinson, 145.

7. Cf. Haughton in Robinson, 29, for Hill's attraction to and hesitation concerning the religious perspective of Christianity. See also Sacks, 310, and Ramazani, 8.

8. Shaw links Hill with Hopkins as poets "who honor the dead by composing a poetry of silence" (9) that relies heavily on ellipsis and deletion to test currently received views.

9. Cf. Sherry, *The Uncommon Tongue,* 19, who stresses Hill's moral sense of the duplicity inherent in language but not the consequences, such as I suggest here, that follow from it.

10. See Sherry, *The Uncommon Tongue,* 27.

11. See Sherry, *The Uncommon Tongue,* 66–67, on Hill's persistent calling in question of his own efforts as a vatic poet addressing historical realities.

Chapter 7. The Philosophical Elegy and Time

1. Ramazani, 74, calls it a dismal failure largely because he sees it as uncritically adopting the pathetic fallacy. I regard it as evidence of the difficulty early modern poets like Owen experienced in shaping a new elegiac temper.

2. See Kerr, 282.

3. Cf. Kerr, 288.

4. Kerr, 278, points out that Owen was thinking much about elegies during this period in his life and even considered many of his war poems as elegies. Lane, 17–18, usefully differentiates Owen's poems as elegies of fact rather than of reflection, which are meditative and consolatory.

5. Kerr's many illuminating remarks on Owen's sustained grappling with the changing nature of the elegy, 282–295, fail to consider the poet's struggle to come to terms with the concept and impact of time.

6. Wendell Berry's *The Wheel* shows something of the range inherent in the philosophical elegy, as it sets the personal loss of a friend, the nature of married love, the recurrent nature of life together with its transience, and the cyclical nature of time in a metaphysical context. See Triggs, 284.

7. Shaw, 155, links this poem with Stevens's "The Auroras of Autumn" and finds both to be a lament for the passing of a world. My own sense is that MacLeish is endeavoring to capture the individual's sense of his own perishability being set over against the persistence of the physical universe and to locate his feeling in the effect of a conundrum inherent in time. If the poem is a lament, then it must be an unuttered one, for it is precisely the irrelevance of lamentation that dominates MacLeish's mind here.

Chapter 8. The Philosophical Elegy and Mortality

1. On the differentiation between Stoic and Epicurean, see Rosenmeyer, 11–12; also Long for a professional philosopher's treatment, 20–21, 108–109. Needless to say, my use of both terms, though

influenced by both these scholars, is less precise and considerably more provisional. To a certain degree, I find the terms analogous to more modern senses of rationalism and empiricism.

2. A critical context to which my remarks on this poem may be related can be found in, among others, Bloom, 281–292; Carroll, 213–237; Miller, 268–270, 280; Riddel, 240–242, 276–277; Doggett, 11; and Jarraway, 272–278. The subtleties of both the poem and its commentators together with the considerable number of differences among the latter preclude more detailed consideration of how my reading differs from them.

3. See Carroll, 213.

4. The phrase "godolphin and fellow" is a compelling instance of Steven's subtlety of mind and the challenge it poses for critics. Bloom, 288, for instance, ignores the ambiguities inherent in "fellow" and stresses the stallion's estrangement as due to its "inhumanity" rather than its separation from its birthplace and its possible dual ancestry. See, for instance, the remarks of Colonel Ironside cited in Prior, 20 (http://www.bloodlines.net/TB/Bios/GodolphinArabian.htm, accessed c. January 2005).

5. Cf. Steiner, 15, on the modern transformation of the future into something truly unknowable and so of the impossibility of hope itself. Stevens's view of the mind enables him to see speculation as endless and absolute truth as unobtainable. Steiner, 335–338, ultimately comes close to Stevens's view while still clinging to hope.

6. Cf. Bloom, 291.

7. Cf. Bloom, 282.

Works Cited

Articles cited from edited collections are listed solely under the editor's name and volume title.

Primary Works

Auden, W. H. *Collected Longer Poems*. London: Faber and Faber, 1968.

————. *Collected Shorter Poems: 1927–1957*. London: Faber and Faber, 1966.

Barker, G. *Collected Poems*. Edited by R. Fraser. London: Faber and Faber, 1987.

Bottrall, R. *Collected Poems*. London: Sidgwick and Jackson, 1961.

Brinnin, J. M. *The Selected Poems of John Malcolm Brinnin*. London: Weidenfeld and Nicolson, 1963.

Day-Lewis, C. *Collected Poems, 1954*. London: J. Cape; Hogarth Press, 1954.

Duncan, R. *The Years as Catches: First Poems, 1939–1946*. Berkeley: Oyez, 1966.

Eliot, T. S. *The Complete Poems and Plays, 1909–1950*. New York: Harcourt, Brace, and World, 1952.

Gunn, T. *Collected Poems*. New York: Farrar, Strauss, and Giroux, 1994.

Heaney, S. *Poems, 1965–1975*. New York: Farrar, Straus, and Giroux, 1980.

Hill, G. *New and Collected Poems, 1952–1992*. New York: Houghton Mifflin, 1994.

Justice, D. *Collected Poems*. New York: A. A. Knopf, 2004.

Kavanagh, P. *Collected Poems*. New York: Devin-Adair, 1964.

Lowell, R. *For the Union Dead*. New York: Farrar, Straus, and Giroux, 1964.

MacDiarmid, H. [C. M. Grieve]. *The Collected Poems of Hugh MacDiarmid*. New York: Macmillan, 1962.

MacLeish, A. *Collected Poems, 1917–1982*. Boston: Houghton Mifflin, 1985.

MacNeice, L. *Collected Poems*. Edited by E. R. Dodds. London: Faber and Faber, 1966.

Merton, T. *The Collected Poems of Thomas Merton*. New York: New Directions, 1977.

Millay, E. St. V. *Collected Poems*. Edited by N. Millay. New York: Harper and Row, 1956.

Muir, E. *The Collected Poems*. New York: Oxford Univ. Press, 1965.

O'Hara, F. *The Collected Poems*. Edited by D. Allen. Berkeley: Univ. of California Press, 1995.

Olson, C. *The Collected Poems of Charles Olson: Excluding the Maximus Poems*. Edited by G. F. Butterick. Berkeley: Univ. of California Press, 1997.

Olson, E. *Collected Poems*. Chicago: Univ. of Chicago Press, 1963.

Owen, W. *The Complete Poems and Fragments*. Edited by J. Stallworthy. London: Chatto and Windus; Hogarth Press; Oxford Univ. Press, 1983.

Pound, E. *Cantos.* New York: New Directions, 1948.

———. *Personae.* New York: New Directions, 1926.

Ransom, J. C. *Selected Poems.* New York: Knopf, 1945.

Read, H. *Collected Poems.* New York: Horizon, 1966.

Roethke, T. *Collected Poems.* New York: Doubleday, 1966.

Sassoon, S. *Collected Poems, 1908–1956.* London: Faber and Faber, 1961.

Silkin, J. *Selected Poems.* London: Routledge and Kegan Paul, 1980.

Sitwell, E. *Collected Poems.* London: Macmillan, 1957. "Elegy for Dylan Thomas" quoted from this edition.

———. *Collected Poems of Edith Sitwell.* New York: Vanguard, 1968. All of Sitwell's poems except "Elegy for Dylan Thomas" quoted from this edition.

Stevens, W. *Collected Poems.* New York: Knopf, 1964.

Tate, A. *Collected Poems, 1919–1976.* New York: Farrar, Straus, and Giroux, 1977.

Thomas, D. *Collected Poems, 1934–1952.* London: Dent, 1952.

Watkins, V. *The Collected Poems of Vernon Watkins.* Ipswich, U.K.: Golgonooza Press, 1986.

Williams, W. C. *The Collected Poems of William Carlos Williams.* Edited by A. W. Litz and C. MacGowan. 2 vols. New York: New Directions, 1986.

Winters, Y. *The Collected Poems of Yvor Winters.* Manchester, U.K.: Carcanet, 1978.

Wright, J. *Collected Poems.* Middletown, Conn.: Wesleyan Univ. Press, 1971.

Secondary Works

Adams, B. *The Enemy Self: Poetry and Criticism of Laura Riding.* Ann Arbor: UMI Research Press, 1990.

Alexander, E. *The Resonance of Dust: Essays on Holocaust Literature and Jewish Fate.* Columbus: Ohio State Univ. Press, 1979.

Apollodorus. *The Library.* Translated by Sir James Frazer. 2 vols. London: Heinemann, 1921.

Aries, P. "Death Denied." *The Hour of Our Death.* Translated by H. Weaver. New York: Vintage–Random House, 1981.

———. "The Reversal of Death: Changes in Attitudes toward Death in Western Societies." In *Death in America,* edited by D. E. Stannard. Philadelphia: Univ. of Pennsylvania Press, 1975. 134–158.

———. *Western Attitudes toward Death from the Middle Ages to the Present.* Translated by P. M. Ranum. Baltimore: Johns Hopkins Univ. Press, 1976.

Atkins, E. *Edna St. Vincent Millay and Her Times.* New York: Russell and Russell, 1964.

Aubrey, J. *Miscellanies upon Various Subjects,* 5th ed. London: Reeves and Turner, 1890.

Bell, I. A. F., ed. *Ezra Pound: Tactics for Reading.* London: Vision Press, 1982.

Bergonzi, B. *Heroes' Twilight: A Study of the Literature of the Great War.* London: Constable, 1965.

Bloom, H. *Wallace Stevens: The Poems of Our Climate.* Ithaca: Cornell Univ. Press, 1976.

Bradford, M. E. "A Modern Elegy: Ransom's 'Bells for John Whiteside's Daughter.'" *Mississippi Quarterly* 21 (1968): 43–47.

Brown, T. *Louis MacNeice: Sceptical Vision.* New York: Harper and Row, 1975.

Buffington, R. *The Equilibrist: A Study of John Crowe Ransom's Poems, 1916–1963.* Nashville: Vanderbilt Univ. Press, 1967.

Caesar, A. *Taking It Like a Man: Suffering Sexuality and the War Poets.* Manchester: Manchester Univ. Press, 1993.

Campbell, P. *Siegfried Sassoon: A Study of the War Poetry.* Jefferson: McFarland, 1999.

Cannadine, D. "War and Death, Grief and Mourning in Modern Britain." In *Mirrors of Mortality: Studies in the Social History of Death,* edited by Joachim Whaley. New York: St. Martin's Press, 1981.

Carroll, J. *Wallace Stevens's Supreme Fiction: A New Romanticism.* Baton Rouge: Louisiana State Univ. Press, 1987.

Choron, J. *Death and Western Thought.* London: Macmillan, 1963.

———. *Modern Man and Mortality.* New York: MacMillan, 1964.

Clark, T. *Charles Olson: The Allegory of a Poet's Life.* New York: Norton, 1991.

Comito, T. *In Defense of Winters: The Poetry and Prose of Yvor Winters.* Madison: Univ. of Wisconsin Press, 1986.

Corrigan, F. *Siegfried Sassoon: Poet's Pilgrimage.* London: Gollancz, 1973.

Cowan, L. "The Elegy and Modernism." *Studies in the Humanities* 19, no. 1 (1992): 43–57.

Cox, C. B., ed. *Dylan Thomas: A Collection of Critical Essays.* Englewood Cliffs: Prentice-Hall, 1966.

David, H. *Stephen Spender: A Portrait with Background.* London: Heinemann, 1992.

Davidson, P. *Ezra Pound and Roman Poetry: A Preliminary Survey.* Amsterdam-Atlanta: Rodopi, 1995.

Doggett, F. A. *Stevens's Poetry of Thought.* Baltimore: Johns Hopkins Univ. Press, 1966.

Dollimore, J. *Death, Desire and Loss in Western Culture.* London: Routledge, 1998.

Dougherty, D. C. *James Wright.* Boston: G. K. Hall, 1987.

Draper, J. *The Funeral Elegy and the Rise of Romanticism.* New York: New York Univ. Press, 1929.

Dupree, R. S. *Allen Tate and the Augustinian Imagination.* Baton Rouge: Louisiana State Univ. Press, 1983.

Elkins, A. *The Poetry of James Wright.* Tuscaloosa: Univ. of Alabama Press, 1991.

Emery, C. *The World of Dylan Thomas.* Coral Gables, Fla.: Univ. of Miami Press, 1962.

Epstein, D. M. *What Lips My Lips Have Kissed.* New York: Henry Holt, 2001.

Farrell, J. J. *Inventing the American Way of Death, 1830–1920.* Philadelphia: Temple Univ. Press, 1980.

Feifel, H., ed. *The Meaning of Death.* New York: McGraw, 1959.

Ferris, P. *Dylan Thomas: A Biography.* New York: Dial Press, 1947.

Firmage, G. J., ed. *A Garland for Dylan Thomas.* New York: Clarke and Way, 1963.

Fitzgibbon, C. *The Life of Dylan Thomas.* Boston: Little, Brown, 1965.

Fodaski, M. *George Barker.* New York, Twayne, 1969.

Fraser, R. *The Chameleon Poet: A Life of George Barker.* London: J. Cape, 2002.

Freedman, D. P., ed. *Millay at 100: A Critical Reappraisal.* Carbondale: Southern Illinois Univ. Press, 1995.

Freud, S. *Collected Papers.* Vol. 4. Translated by J. Riviere. New York: Basic Books, 1959.

Fryer, J. *Robbie Ross: Oscar Wilde's Devoted Friend.* New York: Carroll and Graf, 2000.

Fussell, P. *The Great War and Modern Memory.* London: Oxford Univ. Press, 1975.

Gelpi, A. *Living in Time: The Poetry of C. Day-Lewis.* London: Oxford Univ. Press, 1998.

Gilbert, S. "'Rats' Alley': The Great War, Modernism, and the (Anti)Pastoral Elegy." *New Literary History* 30, no. 1 (winter 1999): 179–201.

Glendinning, V. *Edith Sitwell: A Unicorn Among Lions.* London: Weidenfeld and Nicolson, 1981.

Gorer, G. *Death, Grief, and Mourning.* Garden City, N.Y.: Doubleday, 1965.

Grieve, T. F. *Ezra Pound's Early Poetry and Poetics.* Columbia: Univ. of Missouri Press, 1997.

Grover, P., ed. *Ezra Pound: The London Years, 1908–1920.* New York: AMS Press, 1978.

Hamalian, L. *A Life of Kenneth Rexroth.* New York: Norton, 1991.

Hammond, J. A. *The American Puritan Elegy: A Literary and Cultural Study.* Cambridge: Cambridge Univ. Press, 2000.

Hardison, O. B., Jr. *The Enduring Monument: A Study of the Idea of Praise in Renaissance Literary Theory and Practice.* Chapel Hill: Univ. of North Carolina Press, 1962.

Hardy, B. *Dylan Thomas: An Original Language.* Athens: Univ. of Georgia Press, 2000.

Hart, H. *The Poetry of Geoffrey Hill.* Carbondale: Southern Illinois Univ. Press, 1986.

Hecht, A. *The Hidden Law: The Poetry of W. H. Auden.* Cambridge: Harvard Univ. Press, 1993.

Hibbard, D. *Wilfred Owen: The Last Year, 1917–1918.* London: Constable, 1992.

Hoagwood, T. A. *A.E. Housman Revisited.* New York: Twayne, 1995.

Hogg, J., ed. *The Salzburg Peter Russell Seminar, 1981–82.* Salzburg: Institut fur Anglistik und Amerikanistik, 1982.

Holbrook, D. *Dylan Thomas: The Code of Night.* London: University of London, Athlone Press, 1972.

Homans, P., ed. *Symbolic Loss: The Ambiguity of Mourning and Memory at Century's End.* Charlottesville: Univ. of Virginia Press, 2000.

Huberman, E. *The Poetry of Edwin Muir: The Field of Good and Evil.* New York: Oxford Univ. Press, 1971.

Hynes, S. *A War Imagined: The First World War and English Culture.* New York: Atheneum Press, 1990.

Jackson, C. O., ed. *Passing: The Vision of Death in America.* Westport: Greenwood Press, 1977.

Jarraway, D. R., *Wallace Stevens and the Question of Belief: Metaphysician in the Dark*. Baton Rouge: Louisiana State Univ. Press, 1993.

Johnson, M. A. *Robert Duncan*. Boston: Twayne, 1988.

Johnston, D. *Irish Poetry after Joyce*. Notre Dame, Ind.: Notre Dame Univ. Press, 1985.

Johnston, J. H. *English Poetry of the First World War*. Princeton: Princeton Univ. Press, 1964.

Kay, D. *The English Funeral Elegy from Spenser to Milton*. Oxford: Oxford Univ. Press, 1990.

Kenner, H. *A Sinking Island*. London: Barrie and Jenkins, 1988.

————. *The Poetry of Ezra Pound*. London: Faber and Faber, 1951.

————. *The Pound Era*. Berkeley: Univ. of California Press, 1971.

Kerr, D. *Wilfred Owen's Voices: Language and Community*. Oxford: Clarendon Press, 1993.

Kidder, R. M. *Dylan Thomas: The Country of the Spirit*. Princeton: Princeton Univ. Press, 1973.

Knight, K. F. *The Poetry of John Crowe Ransom: A Study of Diction, Metaphor, and Symbol*. The Hague: Mouton, 1964.

Knight, R. *Edwin Muir: An Introduction to His Work*. London: Longman, 1980.

Korg, J. *Dylan Thomas,* updated ed. New York: Twayne, 1992.

Kubal, D. L. *The Consoling Intelligence: Responses to Literary Modernism*. Baton Rouge: Louisiana State Univ. Press, 1982.

Lambert, E. Z. *Placing Sorrow: A Study of the Pastoral Elegy Convention from Theocritus to Milton*. Chapel Hill: Univ. of North Carolina Press, 1976.

Lane, A. E. *An Adequate Response: The War Poetry of Wilfred Owen and Siegfried Sassoon*. Detroit: Wayne State Univ. Press, 1972.

Lawler, J. G. *Hopkins Re-Constructed*. New York: Continuum, 1998.

Levenson, M. *Modernism and the Fate of Individuality*. New York: Cambridge Univ. Press, 1991.

Lewalski Kiefer, B., ed. *Renaissance Genres: Essays on Theory, History, and Interpretation*. Cambridge: Harvard Univ. Press, 1986.

Libby, A. *Mythologies of Nothing: Mystical Death in American Poetry, 1940–70*. Urbana: Univ. of Illinois Press, 1984.

Lipking, L. *The Life of the Poet: Beginning and Ending Poetic Careers*. Chicago: Univ. of Chicago Press, 1981.

Lipstadt, D. *Denying the Holocaust: The Growing Assault on Truth and Memory*. New York: Free Press, 1993.

Long, A. A. *Hellenistic Philosophy: Stoics, Epicureans, Sceptics,* 2nd ed. London: Duckworth, 1986.

Longenbach, J. *Wallace Stevens: The Plain Sense of Things*. New York: Oxford Univ. Press, 1991.

Lucas, T. E. *Elder Olson*. New York: Twayne, 1972.

Mack, A., ed. *Death in American Experience*. New York: Schoeken, 1973.

Maddison, C. *Apollo and the Nine: The History of the Ode.* London: Routledge and K. Paul, 1960.

Magnanaro, M., ed. *Modernist Anthropology.* Princeton: Princeton Univ. Press, 1990.

Marsack, R. *The Cave of Making: The Poetry of Louis MacNeice.* Oxford: Clarendon Press, 1982.

Martin, R. B. *Gerard Manley Hopkins: A Very Private Life.* New York: G. P. Putnam's Sons, 1991.

McCulloch, M. *Edwin Muir: Poet, Critic and Novelist.* Edinburgh: Edinburgh Univ. Press, 1993.

McKinnon, W. T. *Apollo's Blended Dream: A Study of the Poetry of Louis MacNeice.* London: Oxford Univ. Press, 1971.

Meisel, P. *The Myth of the Modern.* New Haven: Yale Univ. Press, 1987.

Mellown, E. W. *Edwin Muir.* Boston: Twayne, 1979.

Mendelson, E. *Early Auden.* New York: Viking, 1981.

————. *Later Auden.* New York: Farrar, Strauss, and Giroux, 1999.

Meyers, J. "The Background of Theodore Roethke's *Elegy for Jane.*" *Resources for American Literary Study* 15, no. 2 (1985): 138–144.

Michelson, B. *Wilbur's Poetry: Music in a Scattering Time.* Amherst: Univ. of Massachusetts Press, 1991.

Miller, J. H. *Poets of Reality: Six Twentieth-Century Writers.* Cambridge: Harvard Univ. Press, 1965.

Ming Xie. "Elegy and Personae in Ezra Pound's *Cathay.*" *ELH* 60 (1993): 261–281.

Moeyes, P. *Siegfried Sassoon: Scorched Glory.* New York: St. Martin's Press, 1997.

Moore, D. B. *The Poetry of Louis MacNeice.* Leicester: Leicester Univ. Press, 1972.

Moynihan, W. T. *The Craft and Art of Dylan Thomas.* Ithaca: Cornell Univ. Press, 1966.

Nelson, C., and E. Folsom, eds. *W. S. Merwin: Essays on the Poetry.* Urbana: Univ. of Illinois Press, 1987.

Nelson, R. *Aesthetic Frontiers: The Machiavellian Tradition in the Southern Imagination.* Jackson: Univ. of Mississippi Press, 1990.

Pack, R. *Affirming Limits: Essays on Mortality, Choice, and Poetic Form.* Amherst, Univ. of Massachusetts Press, 1985.

————. *Wallace Stevens: An Approach to His Poetry and Thought.* New York: Gordian Press, 1968.

Parfitt, G. *English Poetry of the First World War.* London: Harvester, 1990.

Parker, P. *The Old Lie: The Great War and the Public School Ethos.* London: Constable, 1987.

Patrides, C. A., ed. *Milton's Lycidas: The Tradition and the Poem.* New York: Holt, Rinehart and Winston, 1961.

Penniman, T. K. *A Hundred Years of Anthropology,* 3rd ed. London: G. Duckworth and Co., 1965.

Perl, J. *Skepticism and Modern Enmity: Before and After T.S. Eliot*. Baltimore: Johns Hopkins Univ. Press, 1989.

———. *The Tradition of the Return: The Implicit History of Modern Literature*. Princeton: Princeton Univ. Press, 1984.

Perloff, M. "Death by Water: The Winslow Elegies of Robert Lowell." *ELH* 34 (1967): 116–140.

———. *Frank O'Hara: Poet Among Painters*. New York: Braziller, 1977.

———, ed. *Postmodern Genres*. Norman: Univ. of Oklahoma Press, 1988.

Pigman, G. W., III. *Grief and English Renaissance Elegy*. Cambridge: Cambridge Univ. Press, 1985.

Popper, Sir K. R. *The Open Society and Its Enemies*, 2nd ed. 2 vols. London: Routledge and Kegan Paul, 1952.

Potts, A. F. *The Elegiac Mode: Poetic Form in Wordsworth and Other Elegists*. Cornell Univ. Press, 1967.

Prior, C. M. *The History of the Racing Calendar and Stud-Book: From Their Inception in the Eighteenth Century, with Observations on Some of the Occurrences Noted Therein*. London: Sporting Life, 1926.

Prunty, W. *"Fallen from the Symboled World": Precedents for the New Formalism*. New York: Oxford Univ. Press, 1990.

Quinn, P. *The Great War and the Missing Muse*. Selingsgrove: Susquehanna Univ. Press, 1994.

Quinones, R. J. *Mapping Literary Modernism: Time and Development*. Princeton: Princeton Univ. Press, 1985.

Ramazani, J. *Poets of Mourning: The Modern Elegy from Hardy to Heaney*. Chicago: Univ. of Chicago Press, 1994.

Rayner, J. L., and G. T Crook, eds. *The Complete Newgate Calendar*. 5 vols. London: Navarre Society, 1926.

Read, B. *The Days of Dylan Thomas*. New York: 1964.

Riddel, J. *The Clairvoyant Eye*. Baton Rouge: Louisiana State Univ. Press, 1965.

Robinson, P., ed. *Geoffrey Hill: Essays on His Work*. Milton Keynes: Open University Press, 1985.

Rosenmeyer, G. *The Green Cabinet: Theocritus and the Pastoral*. Berkeley: Univ. of California Press, 1969.

Rosenthal, M. L., and S. M. Gall. *The Modern Poetic Sequence: The Genius of Modern Poetry*. New York: Oxford Univ. Press, 1983.

Ruthven, K. K. *A Guide to Ezra Pound's Personae (1926)*. Berkeley: Univ. of California Press, 1969.

Ryle, G. *The Concept of Mind*. London: Hutchinson's University Library, 1952.

Sacks, P. *The English Elegy: Readings in the Genre from Spenser to Yeats*. Baltimore: Johns Hopkins Univ. Press, 1985.

Salgado, G., and G. S. Das, eds. *The Spirit of D. H. Lawrence.* New York: MacMillan, 1988.

Schenck, C. M. "Feminism and Deconstruction: Re-Constructing the Elegy." *Tulsa Studies in Women's Literature* 5 (1986): 13–27.

————. *Mourning and Panegyric: The Poetics of Pastoral Ceremony.* University Park: Pennsylvania State Univ. Press, 1988.

————. "When the Moderns Write Elegy: Crane, Kinsella, Nemerov." *Classical and Modern Literature: A Quarterly* 6 (1986): 97–108.

Schwartz, S. *The Matrix of Modernism: Pound, Eliot, and Early Twentieth-Century Thought.* Princeton: Princeton Univ. Press, 1985.

Schweik, S. M. *American Women Poets and the Second World War.* Madison: Univ. of Wisconsin Press, 1991.

Schneidau, H. N. *Waking Giants: The Presence of the Past in Modernism.* New York: Oxford Univ. Press, 1991.

Sendry, J. "The Wreck of the Deutschland as Heroic Elegy." *Thought* 65, no. 259 (1990): 494–499.

Shaw, W. D. *Elegy and Paradox: Testing the Conventions.* Johns Hopkins Univ. Press, 1994.

Sherry, V. *Ezra Pound, Wyndham Lewis and Radical Modernism.* London: Oxford Univ. Press, 1993.

————. *The Uncommon Tongue: The Poetry and Criticism of Geoffrey Hill.* Ann Arbor: Univ. of Michigan Press, 1987.

Sickels, E. M. *The Gloomy Egoist: Gray to Keats.* New York: Columbia Univ. Press, 1932.

Silkin, J. *Out of Battle: The Poetry of the Great War.* London: Oxford Univ. Press, 1972.

Smith, D. ed. *The Pure Clear World: Essays on the Poetry of James Wright.* Urbana: Univ. of Illinois Press, 1982.

Smith, E. *By Mourning Tongues: Studies in the English Elegy.* Ipswich, U.K.: Boydell Press, 1977.

Smith, E. E. *Louis MacNeice.* New York: Twayne, 1970.

Spender, S. *The Thirties and After.* New York: Vintage Books, 1979.

Stallworthy, J. *Wilfred Owen.* London: Chatto and Windus, Oxford Univ. Press, 1974.

Stannard, D. E., ed. *Death in America.* Philadelphia: Univ. of Pennsylvania Press, 1975.

Stein, K. *The Poetry of a Grown Man: Constancy and Transition in the Work of James Wright.* Athens: Ohio Univ. Press, 1989.

Steiner, G. *Language and Silence: Essays on Language, Literature, and the Inhuman.* New York: Atheneum, 1967.

Sullivan, J. P. *Ezra Pound and Sextus Propertius: A Study in Creative Translation.* Austin: Univ. of Texas Press, 1964.

Thesing, W. B., ed. *Critical Essays on Edna St. Vincent Millay.* New York: G. K. Hall, 1993.

Thorpe, M. *Siegfried Sassoon: A Critical Study.* London: Oxford Univ. Press, 1967.

Tiffany, D. *Radio Corpse: Imagism and the Cryptaesthetic of Ezra Pound.* Cambridge: Harvard Univ. Press, 1995.

Toynbee, A., et al., eds. *Man's Concern with Death.* London: Hodder and Stoughton, 1968.

Tremlett, G. *Dylan Thomas: In the Mercy of His Means.* London: Constable, 1991.

Triggs, J. A. "Moving the Darkness to Wholeness: The Elegies of Wendell Berry." *The Literary Review, an International Journal of Contemporary Writing* 31, no. 3 (spring 1988): 279–292.

Tschumi, R. *Thought in Twentieth-Century English Poetry.* London: Routledge and Kegan Paul, 1951.

Vendler, H. *On Extended Wings: Wallace Stevens's Longer Poems.* Cambridge: Harvard Univ. Press, 1969.

———. *Seamus Heaney.* Cambridge: Harvard Univ. Press, 1998.

Vickery, John B. "T. S. Eliot's Poetry: The Quest and the Way." *Renascence* 10, nos. 1, 2 (fall–winter 1958): 3–10, 11, 59–67.

Wallerstein, R. *Studies in Seventeenth-Century Poetics.* Madison: Univ. of Wisconsin Press, 1950.

Wilde, A. *Horizons of Assent: Modernism, Postmodernism, and the Ironic Imagination.* Baltimore: Johns Hopkins Univ. Press, 1981.

Williams, M. *The Poetry of John Crowe Ransom.* New Brunswick: Rutgers Univ. Press, 1972.

Wilson, J. M. *Siegfried Sassoon: The Making of a War Poet.* New York: Routledge, 1999.

Winters, Y. *The Selected Letters of Yvor Winters.* Edited by R. L. Barth. Athens: Swallow Press; Ohio Univ. Press, 2000.

Witemeyer, H. *The Poetry of Ezra Pound: Forms and Renewal, 1908–1920.* Berkeley: Univ. of California Press, 1969.

Young, J. E. *The Texture of Memory: Holocaust Memorials and Meaning.* New Haven: Yale Univ. Press, 1993.

———. *Writing and Rewriting the Holocaust: Narrative and the Consequences of Interpretation.* Bloomington: Indiana Univ. Press, 1988.

Young, T. D., ed. *John Crowe Ransom: Critical Essays and a Bibliography.* Baton Rouge: Louisiana State Univ. Press, 1968.

Zeiger, M. F. *Beyond Consolation: Death, Sexuality, and the Changing Shapes of the Elegy.* Ithaca: Cornell Univ. Press, 1997.

Index